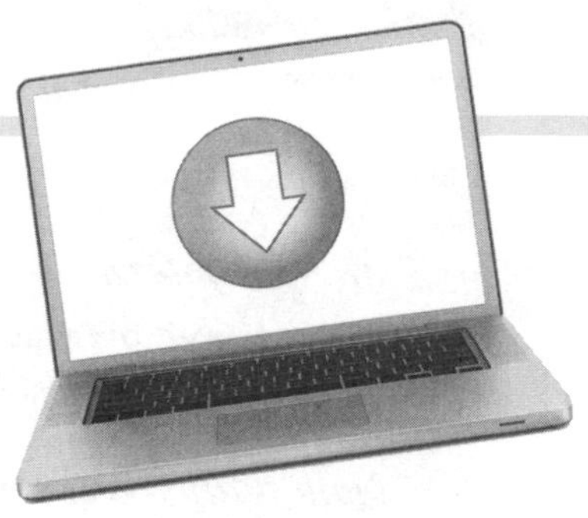

This Book Comes With Lots of
FREE Online Resources

Nolo's award-winning website has a page dedicated just to this book. Here you can:

DOWNLOAD FORMS – Access forms and worksheets from the book online

KEEP UP TO DATE – When there are important changes to the information in this book, we'll post updates

GET DISCOUNTS ON NOLO PRODUCTS – Get discounts on hundreds of books, forms, and software

READ BLOGS – Get the latest information from Nolo authors' blogs

LISTEN TO PODCASTS – Listen to authors discuss timely issues on topics that interest you

WATCH VIDEOS – Get a quick introduction to a legal topic with our short videos

And that's not all.
Nolo.com contains thousands of articles on everyday legal and business issues, plus a plain-English law dictionary, all written by Nolo experts and available for free. You'll also find more useful **books, software, online apps, downloadable forms,** plus a **lawyer directory.**

With Downloadable FORMS

Get forms and more at
www.nolo.com/back-of-book/GET.html

NOLO

The Trusted Name

(but don't take our word for it)

"In Nolo you can trust."
THE NEW YORK TIMES

"Nolo is always there in a jam as the nation's premier publisher of do-it-yourself legal books."
NEWSWEEK

"Nolo publications... guide people simply through the how, when, where and why of the law."
THE WASHINGTON POST

"[Nolo's]... material is developed by experienced attorneys who have a knack for making complicated material accessible."
LIBRARY JOURNAL

"When it comes to self-help legal stuff, nobody does a better job than Nolo..."
USA TODAY

"The most prominent U.S. publisher of self-help legal aids."
TIME MAGAZINE

"Nolo is a pioneer in both consumer and business self-help books and software."
LOS ANGELES TIMES

6th Edition

Get It Together

Organize Your Records So Your Family Won't Have To

Melanie Cullen with Shae Irving, J.D.

SIXTH EDITION OCTOBER 2014

Editor BETSY SIMMONS HANNIBAL

Cover Design SUSAN PUTNEY

Proofreading ROBERT WELLS

Index SONGBIRD INDEXING SERVICES

Printing BANG PRINTING

Cullen, Melanie, 1951- author.

Get it together : organize your records so your family won't have to / By Melanie Cullen with Shae Irving, J.D. -- Sixth edition.

p. cm.

Includes index.

ISBN 978-1-4133-2071-8 (pbk) -- ISBN 978-1-4133-2072-5 (epub ebook)

1. Estate planning--United States--Popular works. I. Irving, Shae, author. II. Title.

KF750.Z9C85 2014

332.024'016--dc23

2014011804

This book covers only United States law, unless it specifically states otherwise.

Please note

We believe accurate, plain-English legal information should help you solve many of your own legal problems. But this text is not a substitute for personalized advice from a knowledgeable lawyer. If you want the help of a trained professional—and we'll always point out situations in which we think that's a good idea—consult an attorney licensed to practice in your state.

Acknowledgments

I admit it: I've suffered an unflagging obsession with this book. Many others have suffered from it, too, enduring my insatiable curiosity about organizing their affairs, planning for death, and working through loss and grief. For the latter, if I seemed more curious than compassionate, I apologize for not simply extending my condolences.

Despite my enthusiasm, this book would not have made it to market without help from others. The book you hold in your hands is evidence of my indebtedness to several people.

Shae Irving, a talented editor and writer, brought sage judgment to bear. Her dedication to simplicity—while acknowledging complexity—fulfilled my prayers. Betsy Simmons Hannibal, editor, cheerfully brought her talents to bear on recent editions. My Nolo design team—including Susan Putney, Margaret Livingston, Ellen Bitter, André Zivkovich, and now Emily Dunn—helped make the book easy to use and a pleasure to hold.

Evelyn Crabtree, Gloria Fudim, Betty Harrison, Marilyn Moyle, Becky Tobitt, and Karen Witesman gave me thoughtful feedback on initial drafts—from practical questions to spiritual issues and emotional challenges.

I owe a debt of gratitude to the many class participants at Davis Adult School and Acalanes Adult Education. With your thoughtful and varied contributions (and unrivaled humor), *Get It Together* becomes ever more robust.

Suzanne Rotondo helped to envision this book, then responded to my seemingly endless questions and dilemmas with helpful direction.

Finally, but first of all, my mom, Bonnie Harris, and my daughters, Tanya Jones and Sasha Swanson, provided the inspiration, love, and faith that initially—and ultimately—inspired this book.

Melanie Cullen

About Melanie Cullen

With an MBA from the Graduate School of Business at Stanford University, Melanie is a management consultant with TerraSys Consulting, Inc., an avid planner, and a blue-chip organizer. She lives in Walnut Creek, California, near to loved ones who appreciate that her affairs are truly in order! For more information, to contact her, or to purchase the companion Binder & Tab Set, see www.GetItTogetherBook.com.

About Shae Irving

Shae Irving graduated from Berkeley Law at the University of California in 1993. She is the author or coauthor of many Nolo products, including *Prenuptial Agreements: How to Write a Fair & Lasting Contract*, *Living Wills & Powers of Attorney for California*, and Nolo's *Quicken WillMaker Plus* software. She has edited many of Nolo's estate planning books, among them *The Executor's Guide: Settling a Loved One's Estate or Trust* and *Plan Your Estate.*

Table of Contents

Your *Get It Together* Companion 1

About This Book 3

Who Needs to Plan Ahead? 4

How It Works 5

The Perils of Incomplete Planning 6

Completing Your Planner 9

What the Planner Contains 10

Seven Steps to Preparing Your Planner 11

1 Letter to Loved Ones 19

Tips for Writing Your Letter 20

Where to Get Help 23

In Your Planner 23

Keeping Your Letter Up to Date 24

2 Instructions 25

In Your Planner 27

Keeping Your Documents Up to Date 29

3 Biographical Information 31

Where to Get Help 32

In Your Planner 37

Keeping Your Information Up to Date 39

4 Children 41

Arranging Care for Children 42

Where to Get Help 44

In Your Planner 44

Keeping Your Information Up to Date 46

5 **Others Who Depend on Me** 47

In Your Planner 48

Keeping Your Information Up to Date 49

6 **Pets and Livestock** 51

Arranging Care for Pets 52

Where to Get Help 53

In Your Planner 53

Keeping Your Information Up to Date 55

7 **Employment** 57

In Your Planner 58

Keeping Your Information Up to Date 59

8 **Business Interests** 61

Estate Planning for Small Business Owners 62

Where to Get Help 64

In Your Planner 64

Keeping Your Information Up to Date 68

9 **Memberships and Communities** 69

Types of Memberships and Communities 70

Membership Benefits for Survivors 72

Transferring Frequent Flyer Miles 72

Where to Get Help 74

In Your Planner 74

Keeping Your Information Up to Date 75

10 **Service Providers** 77

In Your Planner 78

Keeping Your Information Up to Date 80

11 **Health Care Directives** 81

Types of Health Care Directives 82

How Health Care Directives Work 83

Choosing Your Health Care Agent 84

What You Can Cover in Your Health Care Directives 86

Duty of Medical Personnel to Honor Your Health Care Directives 89
Where to Get Help 89
In Your Planner 89
Keeping Your Documents Up to Date 91

12 Durable Power of Attorney for Finances 93
How Durable Powers of Attorney for Finances Work 95
Choosing Your Agent 97
Where to Get Help 99
In Your Planner 100
Keeping Your Documents Up to Date 101

13 Organ or Body Donation 103
Do You Want to Be a Donor? 104
Where to Get Help 106
In Your Planner 107
Keeping Your Information Up to Date 107

14 Burial or Cremation 109
Burial or Cremation? 110
Related Decisions 115
Where to Get Help 117
In Your Planner 119
Keeping Your Information Up to Date 123

15 Funeral and Memorial Services 125
Types of Memorial Services 126
Where to Get Help 130
In Your Planner 130
Keeping Your Information Up to Date 134

16 Obituary 135
What to Include in Your Obituary 136
Where to Get Help 137
In Your Planner 137
Keeping Your Obituary Up to Date 139

17 **Will and Trust** 141

Which Estate Planning Documents Do You Need? 142

An Overview of Wills and Trusts 144

Choosing Your Executor or Successor Trustee 148

Avoiding Probate 150

Where to Get Help 153

In Your Planner 154

Keeping Your Documents Up to Date 156

18 **Insurance** 157

What Kind of Insurance Do You Need? 158

Where to Get Help 168

In Your Planner 169

Keeping Your Information Up to Date 170

19 **Bank and Brokerage Accounts** 171

Making Your Accounts Accessible 172

Avoiding Probate for Bank and Brokerage Accounts 173

Where to Get Help 174

In Your Planner 174

Keeping Your Information Up to Date 175

20 **Retirement Plans and Pensions** 177

Planning for Your Retirement 178

What Happens to Retirement Accounts When You Die? 178

Where to Get Help 181

In Your Planner 182

Keeping Your Information Up to Date 183

21 **Government Benefits** 185

About Social Security 186

Where to Get Help 188

In Your Planner 189

Keeping Your Information Up to Date 191

22 **Credit Cards and Debts** 193
Evaluating and Reducing Debt 194
Where to Get Help 197
In Your Planner 198
Keeping Your Information Up to Date 200

23 **Secured Places and Passwords** 201
Who Has Access to Your Safe Deposit Box? 203
In Your Planner 204
Keeping Your Information Up to Date 207

24 **Taxes** 209
Tax Basics 210
Estate and Inheritance Taxes 211
Where to Get Help 212
In Your Planner 212
Keeping Your Information Up to Date 214

25 **Real Estate** 215
Ways to Own Property 216
Special Rules for Married Couples 218
Where to Get Help 220
In Your Planner 220
Keeping Your Information Up to Date 223

26 **Vehicles** 225
Leaving Your Vehicles to Others 226
Where to Get Help 227
In Your Planner 227
Keeping Your Information Up to Date 228

27 **Other Income and Personal Property** 229
In Your Planner 230
Keeping Your Information Up to Date 233

28 **Other Information** 235

Appendixes

A **Using the eForms** 237

Downloading the Files 238

Reviewing the Files 238

Editing RTFs 239

B **Lawyers and Other Experts** 241

What Kind of Expert Do You Need? 242

Finding an Expert 243

Working With an Expert 244

Making a Fee Agreement 244

My Planner

Cover Page and Table of Contents

1. Letter to Loved Ones
2. Instructions
3. Biographical Information
4. Children
5. Others Who Depend on Me
6. Pets and Livestock
7. Employment
8. Business Interests
9. Memberships and Communities
10. Service Providers
11. Health Care Directives
12. Durable Power of Attorney for Finances
13. Organ or Body Donation
14. Burial or Cremation
15. Funeral and Memorial Services
16. Obituary
17. Will and Trust
18. Insurance
19. Bank and Brokerage Accounts
20. Retirement Plans and Pensions
21. Government Benefits
22. Credit Cards and Debts
23. Secured Places and Passwords
24. Taxes
25. Real Estate
26. Vehicles
27. Other Income and Personal Property
28. Other Information

Index

Your *Get It Together* Companion

My mother died unexpectedly a few years ago. She had fallen and broken her leg. We knew, of course, that no one dies from a broken leg. But her mending was slow and difficult—a difficulty that, blessedly, foreshadowed her death. One blessing was that I knew I needed to spend more time with her, to share with her, to listen more closely. Another blessing was the nagging sense that I should be asking some tough questions:

Where is that burial plot you and Dad purchased years ago? Where is the paperwork?

What kind of funeral service do you want?

Who should we call for help winding up your estate—an attorney, a financial adviser, your insurance agent?

With the answers to these questions jotted down in a notepad, my siblings and I were marginally prepared for the dawn of Mom's passing. We didn't find the paperwork for the cemetery plot; it wasn't where she thought she had filed it. We were awash in a sea of decisions and telephone calls, each of which needed to be made in the first day or two. And we were in shock, moving into unfamiliar, Mom-less territory.

With this experience as a backdrop, I began to get my own affairs in order. I started the process with one goal in mind: Creating a planner to make my death far less burdensome for my daughters. I wanted to provide some direction, reducing their confusion in the first hours, days, and weeks. Yet, as the process unfolded, I found that helping my children was only the first of three benefits.

The second benefit was that, when documenting information, organizing materials, and making end-of-life arrangements, I was often thinking of my own eventual death. As sad as that made me, I soon moved on, taking with me this truth: Facing the certainty of death generates a freedom to live life more fully. I am less fearful about death and more joyful about life. I am increasingly aware of the precious moments that I have been given—and of the finite nature of that grant.

Living out my days as though each might be my last is a wake-up call, a call to be more fully aware of each day. Living each of my remaining days with attention and appreciation is an enormous challenge—and a marvelous gift.

The third benefit was a simple one: a bounty of relief and satisfaction at having my affairs in order. Despite my innate tendency to organize, I found that my portfolio—birth certificate to retirement benefits to final arrangements—was a thing of beauty. Never before had my insurance policies been gathered in one location—including even the accident policy offered with my major credit card. The process of pulling together my documents, information, and wishes has helped me to feel informed, up to date, and in control of my affairs.

I share with you this process:

- to reduce the eventual, inevitable burden on your loved ones
- to help you experience the freedom of facing your mortality, addressing unfinished business, and valuing your days, and
- to convey my hope that you will enjoy the satisfaction of organizing your affairs.

May you find direction, organization, and a certain freedom in the process of creating your planner. Ultimately, may your loved ones find direction, solace, and love in the planner that you leave behind.

About This Book

Who Needs to Plan Ahead? 4

Seniors 4

People Facing a Serious Illness 4

Family Members and Other Caretakers 4

Parents and Young Adults 5

People Planning Travel or Deployment 5

How It Works 5

The Perils of Incomplete Planning 6

Life is a great big canvas, and you should throw all the paint on it you can.

—DANNY KAYE, ENTERTAINER AND UNICEF AMBASSADOR (1913–1987)

This book will help you get organized for your own benefit and, eventually, for the benefit of your loved ones. You'll use it to complete a planner that contains everything your caretakers or survivors need to know, including critical personal, legal, and financial information.

Your planner will be a thorough and easy-to-follow guide for your family and close friends. With your planner in hand, your loved ones can more easily step in and take care of things if you become incapacitated or when you die.

Who Needs to Plan Ahead?

If you picked up this book, you're probably feeling the need to get organized. Or perhaps you want to help someone else put things in order—maybe an elderly parent or an ailing friend. Any adult can benefit from making a planner, even those without a lot of money or property, but some people might find the process particularly useful.

Seniors

As we age, most of us feel some concern about what would happen if we became ill and unable to make our own medical or financial decisions. And we wonder how our loved ones will take care of things after we die. If you're elderly, making a planner can smooth the way for your caretakers and survivors. You can gather together your health care wishes, financial plans, legal documents, and important personal information, and arrange these things in a format that will make sense to others. Those close to you will likely view your planner as a small miracle—and a wonderful gift.

People Facing a Serious Illness

If you are ill and concerned that at some point you may no longer be able to care for yourself, making a planner can help you find some peace of mind. While you're able, you can document your wishes for medical care, name someone to take care of your finances, write down what you want to have happen to your property and your body after death, and organize personal information and important paperwork for your family and friends. This book is designed to help you organize things a little bit at a time, with help if necessary; you can pick and choose the issues that are most important to you.

Family Members and Other Caretakers

If you are caring for an older or ailing person—such as a parent, grandparent, or friend—you're probably grappling with both strong emotions and lots of practical tasks. You may find it useful to help your family member or friend complete a planner. It will probably be a great relief to have personal wishes, financial information, and important legal paperwork at your fingertips.

If you have been named as an agent for health care or financial matters, executor of a will, or successor trustee of a living trust, a good planner will provide the framework that you need to carry out your eventual responsibilities in an orderly, informed way.

If you're using this book to help someone else make a planner, keep in mind that the instructions are written primarily for people who are making planners for themselves—but there's no reason you can't use the instructions to help another person through the process.

Parents and Young Adults

If you are young, you may want to use this book to get off to a good start—getting and staying organized. This book will show you how to understand and keep track of your important records, providing a solid foundation for years to come.

If you have young children, this book can help you ensure that they are provided for if something happens to you. It can alert you to the important documents you need and show you how to organize important information so your wishes for your children will be carried out if the need arises.

People Planning Travel or Deployment

When we're leaving town—especially if we're leaving family for an extended period—many of us think about what might happen if we were injured, or worse, while away from home. This book can help you get organized so that, when you leave, you will know that your affairs and records are in order and will be easily available to those who may need to step in.

How It Works

Similar to income tax or school exam materials, this book contains both instructions and companion forms. These two parts of the book are the guide and the planner:

Working With a Parent

It's easy to use this book to help your parent organize his or her information. First, if warranted, see "If Time Is Short," in Completing Your Planner, below. Then, as you work through each chapter, follow the "In Your Planner" step-by-step instructions. As your parent is able, share the steps with them, completing the planner together.

If your parent does not enter the process willingly, these tips may help.

- **Encourage collaboration.** Consider inviting an intimate, trusted sibling or friend to join the conversation. Calmly, kindly, and clearly share that you wish to help, for today's ease and tomorrow's comfort—and that to do so, you need to be informed. You and your parent have a *long-term shared objective.*
- **Promote peace of mind.** Share with your parent that your objective for them is peace of mind through organizing their documents, wishes, and business affairs—to make today easier for them. Help your parent imagine how useful the process will be if (or *when*) he or she needs your help with medical decisions, pet care, or scheduling home repairs.
- **Schedule ahead.** Set "work dates" in advance, helping your parent share control and, importantly, maintain dignity. Aging represents loss of control—which may be threatening, frightening, and just plain sad for your parent. Help your parent to feel valued as a partner in the work. Consider lightening the emotional load by scheduling social time (for example, a shared meal, an outing) following your work together.
- **Keep in touch.** Make regular contact with your parent between organizing sessions. Call or write with your thoughts, suggestions, and questions. Your contact will not only keep the effort rolling, but will help build trust and camaraderie.

- **The guide.** The first part of the book is your instruction manual. Each chapter describes a topic and shows you how to pull together the information and documents you will need.
- **The planner.** The second part of the book contains the forms where you'll actually record your information. If you prefer to use a computer to organize and store your information, you can download the pages of the planner from this book's Companion Page at: **www.nolo.com/back-of-book/GET.html**

To make your work easier, the guide and planner follow the same chapter sequence. For example, the first chapter in the guide helps you write a letter to your survivors, and that letter is also the first section of the planner.

Making Legal Documents

In the guide, you'll find lots of material to help you make the important legal documents you may need: health care directives, powers of attorney, your will, a living trust, and more. The guide also shows you how to add information about these documents to your planner. But it doesn't contain legal forms for you to fill out. Instead, you'll find basic information about each document and suggestions for how to prepare them—either on your own or with a lawyer's help.

The sequence of your planner is designed to create an easy, ready reference for your survivors. The planner begins with the materials that your loved ones will need immediately if you become incapacitated or die, and progresses to information they will need over time. But don't think you have to tackle the most daunting tasks right away. Rather than completing your planner from front to back, you can skip ahead and complete some of the simplest sections first. (You'll learn more about this in the next chapter, which contains specific suggestions and tips for completing your planner.)

You may want to take a moment now to page through the entire book, familiarizing yourself with the layout and the various topics.

The Perils of Incomplete Planning

Using this book will help you think through all the details so your family won't find themselves in a situation like this:

An organized, thoughtful woman worked diligently, pulling together information that her loved ones would need when she died. She studiously wrote out her wishes, secured burial arrangements, gathered documents, and stored all of the papers in a bank safe deposit box.

She was conscientious about reviewing and updating the information over time. She taped her spare safe deposit box key to an index card, and carefully wrote the number of the safe deposit box on the card. She showed the key and box number to her grown children and stored the index card conveniently in the top drawer of her desk.

When she died, her children met at her home. They retrieved the index card from her desk. Only then did they realize that she had neglected to tell them one small detail: the location of her safe deposit box. She had moved several times, and they didn't know where to start—which bank, at which branch or address, or even in which town.

And even if they had known where to look for the box, they would have been in for a shock. The papers that would have authorized them to look inside were locked in the box itself!

Planning ahead can make all the difference to your survivors. Read on to learn how.

Get the Planner, Updates, and More Online

You can download an eForm version of each section of this book's planner at

www.nolo.com/back-of-book/GET.html

And if there are important changes to the information in this book, we'll post updates there, too.

Completing Your Planner

What the Planner Contains 10

Seven Steps to Preparing Your Planner 11

STEP 1: Get Started 13

STEP 2: Prepare Planner Pages 13

STEP 3: Get a Planner Binder 13

STEP 4: Store Your Planner Securely 15

STEP 5: Complete Each Section 15

STEP 6: Talk to Loved Ones 17

STEP 7: Update Your Planner 17

> *Any intelligent fool can make things bigger, more complex .... It takes a touch of genius—and a lot of courage—to move in the opposite direction.*
>
> —ALBERT EINSTEIN (1879–1955)

This chapter will familiarize you with the contents of the planner and with the step-by-step process you can use to put yours together.

What the Planner Contains

The guide and planner follow the same sequence, leading you through 28 topics.

This section provides a brief introduction to each.

For many of the topics, you will find that you have related documents or other materials—birth or marriage certificates; a will, trust, or power of attorney; insurance policies; certificates of title; and so on. In each section of your planner, you can state where these materials are located. If possible, you can file them directly in your planner; it's a great place to get organized—handy for you and easy for your caretakers and survivors.

1. **Letter to Loved Ones:** A personal letter, written to those you expect will survive you. The letter is the first thing your survivors will read when they turn to your planner after your incapacity or death.
2. **Instructions:** Directions for the first few days, weeks, and months following your incapacity and death, referring your loved ones to each section of your planner as needed.
3. **Biographical Information:** Facts and vital statistics about your life and the lives of those closest to you, including your mother, father, spouse, and children—and the locations of important documents such as birth, marriage, and death certificates.
4. **Children:** A list of the children in your care, describing the guardians and property managers you have named and contact information for others who provide care—relatives, teachers, medical professionals, and so on.
5. **Others Who Depend on Me:** A list of people other than children for whom you regularly provide care, including what you do to help them and contact information for others who can help.
6. **Pets and Livestock:** Instructions and wishes for the care of your animals.
7. **Employment:** Important information about your current and former jobs, including benefits and the location of related documents.
8. **Business Interests:** A list of businesses in which you have an ownership interest, including the locations of related documents.
9. **Memberships and Communities:** A summary of your memberships and communities, including contact or login information and any accrued benefits.
10. **Service Providers:** Contact information for your current service providers, including medical, dental, personal care, property care, and others.
11. **Health Care Directives:** Information about the legal documents that set out your wishes for medical treatment and that name someone to make medical decisions if you are unable to speak for yourself.

12. **Durable Power of Attorney for Finances:** Information about the legal document that names someone you trust to handle money matters if you are incapacitated.
13. **Organ or Body Donation:** Wishes and plans for donation of your body, organs, and tissues, including the location of related documents.
14. **Burial or Cremation:** Wishes and plans for burial or cremation, including the location of any related documents.
15. **Funeral and Memorial Services:** Wishes and plans for a viewing, visitation, wake, funeral, memorial, or other service, including the locations for related documents.
16. **Obituary:** An obituary you've written for a newspaper or other publication, or details you'd like your survivors to include if they write an obituary for you.
17. **Will and Trust:** Information about your will and other estate planning documents you've made, including trusts. Here, you can also include details about any documents that affect how your property will pass after death, such as a prenuptial agreement or marital property settlement agreement.
18. **Insurance:** A description of insurance policies that you own or that cover you, including the location of the policy documents.
19. **Bank and Brokerage Accounts:** A list of your bank and brokerage accounts, including the location of related documents.
20. **Retirement Plans and Pensions:** Information about any retirement accounts you own or pension benefits to which you are entitled, including the locations of related documents.
21. **Government Benefits:** Information about Social Security or other government benefits to which you are entitled.
22. **Credit Cards and Debts:** A list of your credit cards, outstanding debts, and automatic bill-pay arrangements.
23. **Secured Places and Passwords:** All the places you keep under lock and key (or protected by password), including safe deposit boxes, property and vehicle alarms, and password-protected software devices or accounts.
24. **Taxes:** Information to help your survivors complete your final tax returns, including the locations of related documents.
25. **Real Estate:** Information about real estate that you own, lease, or rent, including the locations of related documents.
26. **Vehicles:** A list of your vehicles, including locations of related documents.
27. **Other Income and Personal Property:** Information about sources of income and important items of personal property not described elsewhere in your planner, including where the property is located and how you wish it to be handled upon your incapacity or death.
28. **Other Information:** Anything else you want to include with your planner or that you want your caretakers or survivors to know.

Couples: Make Separate Planners

If you're married or partnered, you and your mate should prepare separate planners—or one planner with separate sections for each of you. While some sections will contain shared information or documents (such as information about your home and joint bank accounts), most sections are distinctly personal. Preparing an individual planner—or individual sections within the same planner—makes it easier for loved ones to manage your unique affairs over time.

Seven Steps to Preparing Your Planner

Completing your planner need not overwhelm you. Some of the planner topics may not even apply to you; you can skip those that don't.

As to the rest, you can take them one step at a time, as described in this section.

TIP

If you skip sections. If you don't fill out some sections of the planner, don't tear them out or throw them away. It's better to keep the planner whole and make a simple note at the top of the unused section, such as "N/A." This way your loved ones will be clear that you considered the information and had nothing to include. For example, if you don't have life insurance and you note "N/A" in the life insurance section of your planner, your survivors won't have to wonder or worry whether there's a policy somewhere that you forgot to include.

CROSS REFERENCE

Learn more about using the eForms. You can find step-by-step help with the eForms in Appendix A, near the center of your book (following the guide and before the planner).

Don't expect to complete your planner in one or two sittings. It will take some time. Often you'll simply be filling in blanks with information you already have or know, but sometimes you'll have to stop and take care of a more complex task. For example, you may have to:

- track down paperwork—birth certificates, military discharge papers, account statements, pension records, insurance policies, and the like
- prepare or update estate planning documents, such as your health care directives, power of attorney for finances, will, or living trust, or
- complete an organ donor card or arrange to donate your body to a medical school.

The list of potential tasks is a long one; what you'll have to do depends on your unique circumstances. Help yourself succeed by setting aside one- or two-hour windows to work on your planner until you're done. Begin to collect important documents. Make short lists of follow-up tasks and check off each item as you finish it. Pacing yourself this way will help you make progress without becoming discouraged.

The seven steps described here will help you complete your planner with a minimum of hassle and stress.

Choosing Paper or Digital Files

Should you write on paper or use electronic files to fill out your planner? You have several options: You can use the workbook pages in the back of the book; print blank PDF pages; or type directly into the RTF files. Chose the option that feels most comfortable to you, so that you can get started on your planner with few obstacles. You can always start with paper, then later move your work to your computer.

Using the planner in the back of the book. If you wish to work with paper and don't mind tearing out pages from the book, you can remove the perforated planner pages at the back of this book, photocopy two additional sets, and then use one set for a messy draft, one for your tidy final version, and one for a future update (or additional photocopying).

Using the PDF version of the planner. If you wish to keep your book intact but still work with paper and pencil, you can download and print the book's planner in PDF. (The file is named Planner PDF.) This file contains the very same planner you'll find printed in the second half of this book, but in electronic form. You can print it as many times as you'd like, but you can't type into or edit it.

Typing onto the RTFs. If you prefer to use your computer to enter your information, you can download and use the RTF files with your word processing software. With these eForms, you can enter your information, save, print, later open and modify, print again, and so on. For more help, see Appendix A, "Using the eForms."

If Time Is Short

If it's urgent that you complete your planner quickly, there are certain topics on which you'll want to focus to provide the most benefit to your survivors. Here's a list of critical topics you should try to cover:

Section	Topic
4	Children
5	Others Who Depend on Me
11	Health Care Directives
12	Durable Power of Attorney for Finances
13	Organ or Body Donation
14	Burial or Cremation
15	Funeral and Memorial Services
17	Will and Trust
18	Insurance
19	Bank and Brokerage Accounts
23	Secured Places and Passwords

STEP 1: Get Started

Familiarize yourself with the layout of this book and with the process of preparing your planner.

- First, finish reading the two introductory chapters, About This Book and Completing Your Planner.
- Then take a few minutes to examine your book. Look at a few chapters in the guide (the first half), then review the corresponding planner sections in the back. For example, read over Chapter 6, Pets and Livestock, up front in the guide, and then review Section 6, Pets and Livestock, in the planner in the back.
- Also take a look at Appendixes A and B near the center of your book, at the end of the guide and before the planner.

STEP 2: Prepare Planner Pages

If you will use the forms printed in the back of the book to complete your planner, it's a good idea to make a full set of photocopies before you start working. Treat one set as worksheets where you can make notes—and make a mess if you need to. You'll have a clean set of pages ready when it's time to make a final draft.

If you're going to print out the forms using the eForms, you don't have to worry about making copies. You can print out as many copies of each form as you need. If you will print out blank forms and fill them out by hand or with a typewriter, go ahead and print a set. You'll then be ready for the next step.

If you plan to type directly onto the eForms using your computer, download the forms from Nolo.com (see Appendix A, Using the eForms) and save them to a logical and easy-to-remember place on your computer. If you go this route, you may want to familiarize yourself with the password-protection feature of your word processing software. After you've saved your files, and have considered password protecting them, you are ready to move onto the next step.

TIP

Use ink for your final draft. When you're satisfied with the information you've gathered for a particular topic, write everything down in ink. This will prevent others from tampering with or modifying your planner. If you use your computer to complete your forms, you should print out the planner pages—then you might want to initial and date each printed page in ink.

STEP 3: Get a Planner Binder

You can keep your planner pages intact in this book or put them in a binder, folder, or envelope, keeping in mind that the goal is to make the planner easy to use—for you, as well as for your survivors. If you want to take your organization a step further, these planner materials have been specially designed for use with a binder, with tabs and storage pockets, so that you can keep many of your important

Online Storage Services

Regularly, a new business comes along, offering online storage for your important records and information. At first blush, the proposal seems smart—especially given our increasingly digital lives. After further consideration, however, printed, physical storage (that is, a binder stored in a safe) is still your best solution.

Some of the apparent advantages of online, electronic storage include:

- Your materials are potentially available to several people—at any time, from anywhere.
- As compared to a binder in a safe, the online data bank is portable, easily accessible, "light," and "small."
- With a good structure, the online data bank seems easier to compile—type in your information and upload digital files of your documents! Viola!

At the same time, however, there are considerable disadvantages:

- There are inherent security risks with your data available electronically and across the Internet. This risk surpasses that of a home safe securely installed.
- Typically only one or two loved ones need to access your planner (not several people), and you should limit access accordingly.
- All of your documents need to be made digital (e.g., scanned) and uploaded.
- Even so, with digital documents in your data bank, the originals need to be securely stored—for best access and security, in your home safe. And you cannot include your stored credit cards, keys, or passports in an online data bank.
- Most significantly, it may be overwhelming for your loved ones—grieving, hurried, and feeling lost—to figure out how to unlock your online data and then print all of the materials for banks and attorneys. And for many documents, they will need to produce the originals as well.

Given the considerations, it's best to organize and maintain your materials physically, stored in your home safe. This storage choice will be a blessing for your loved ones.

materials right with your planner forms. If you want to set up your planner in this way, here's what you'll need:

- binder (at least 2")
- tab divider pages (labeled, one for each topic or section)
- pocket divider pages for inserting related documents or other materials
- plastic sleeves or sheet protector pages (for inserting related documents), and
- plastic binder pouches, such as those made to hold pencils and pens, for storing small, irregular items.

As you finish each topic, put the corresponding planner pages into your binder. To make it easy to find each section, create a tab divider for each topic. Following each section in the planner, include a pocket divider to hold topic-related documents. You may want to get some plastic sheet protector pages for protecting documents such as birth certificates and certificates of title, and a few zippered binder pockets for small or irregular items such as your passport, credit cards, or keys.

BINDER

As you read through the guide, you'll see binder icons like this one. These tips will provide suggestions to help you organize and file related documents and other materials in your binder.

BINDER

Ordering a ready-made binder for your planner. To make it extra easy to organize your planner, you can order the *Get It Together* Binder & Tab Set. The sturdy three-inch binder comes with tab dividers for each of the 28 sections of your planner. The set costs $26.50, including tax and shipping. For a complete description and ordering information, see the ad in the back of this book or go to www.GetItTogetherBook.com.

STEP 4: Store Your Planner Securely

Once you get started, your planner will contain significant personal details and confidential information. Now's the time to decide where you'll store it. The best place to store your planner is in a waterproof, fireproof home safe.

You may be tempted to store your planner in a safe deposit box or with a lawyer. Unfortunately, these options limit access to your planner—at least until the first business day following your incapacity or death.

Safe deposit boxes can be particularly tricky: Even if you have a co-owner on the box, or if you have previously arranged safe deposit box access for a trusted friend or relative, access to the box—and to your planner—may be delayed until well after your survivors need it. (See Section 23, Secured Places and Passwords, for more information about accessing safe deposit boxes.)

If you have concerns about the security of your planner in a home safe, or if a home safe is not available to you, you can store the materials in any location that feels safe to you. Keep in mind, however, that your survivors will most likely need the information in the first half of your planner—Sections 1 through 16—immediately upon your incapacity or death. The information contained in this first part of your planner is sensitive, but does not include information about your assets or how to access them. Make sure you keep these first sections within easy reach.

The most sensitive information in your planner is contained in the second half—Sections 17 through 28. Your survivors won't need these sections until at least the first business day after your incapacity or death. If you don't have a secure location in your home, you can think about storing these sections in a safe deposit box, with a lawyer, or with a close relative or friend who has a home safe—keeping in mind the caveats mentioned above. Also remember that you'll want relatively easy access to your planner yourself, so you can keep it up to date.

Essentially, how you store your planner depends on your own options and comfort level. Do what feels best for you.

STEP 5: Complete Each Section

Start by dispatching the simplest, most straightforward topics. These are very personal topics for which you'll have most of the information readily at hand.

Feel free to skip around from one section of your planner to another. By doing so, you'll achieve some early successes while familiarizing yourself with the whole planner and the process.

Simple Topics

As you complete the easiest sections, begin to collect your important documents for other sections and store them with your planner. This will help you do the work that comes later.

Simple Topics	
Section	**Topic**
4	Children
5	Others Who Depend on Me
6	Pets and Livestock
9	Memberships and Communities
10	Service Providers
23	Secured Places and Passwords

Essential Topics

After you've warmed up with some of the easier topics, turn to the core of your planner. These are the things that your loved ones will most need to know if you become incapacitated or die. Each of the following topics may require you to complete a small project, depending on the work you've already done. For example, if you've already made a will or if you have other estate planning documents, completing Section 17 won't be difficult at all; you should start there. If you haven't yet done any planning, take these topics one at a time, remembering that the guide provides suggestions for completing each step.

Essential Topics	
Section	**Topic**
11	Health Care Directives
12	Durable Power of Attorney for Finances
13	Organ or Body Donation
14	Burial or Cremation
15	Funeral and Memorial Services
17	Will and Trust

Complex Topics

The following topics may be a bit more difficult for you. You might have to work harder or longer to obtain the necessary information or related documents. As with the steps above, start with the topics for which you have the most information—or those you feel will be easiest for you—and then move on to the others.

Complex Topics	
Section	**Topic**
3	Biographical Information
7	Employment
8	Business Interests
16	Obituary
18	Insurance
19	Bank and Brokerage Accounts
20	Retirement Plans and Pensions
21	Government Benefits
22	Credit Cards and Debts
24	Taxes
25	Real Estate
26	Vehicles
27	Other Income and Personal Property
28	Other Information

Final Topics

You may want to leave the letter to your loved ones until last. It may be difficult, even overwhelming, to write your last letter early in the process. It will come to you more easily after you have spent time on the rest of your planner.

Similarly, it's wise to complete the Instructions section at the very end of the process. The Instructions section integrates all of your completed planner topics into a master guide or road map for your loved ones.

Final Topics	
Section	**Topic**
1	Letter to Loved Ones
2	Instructions

After you do the hard work of assembling your planner, you'll want to get the full benefit of your efforts. That means two things: telling your loved ones about your planner (it won't help them if they don't know it exists) and keeping your information up to date. Here are some suggestions to help with both of these tasks.

STEP 6: Talk to Loved Ones

No matter where or how you store your planner, it's critical that your survivors know where and how to find it. In particular, be sure to inform your agent for health care, agent for finances, executor, and successor trustee—if you've appointed these folks in legal documents. Your agents need to be familiar with:

- **How to access your home.** Make sure they know the location of your home and how to get into it, including any necessary information about keys, alarms, or gate codes.
- **Where you keep your planner.** Your agents should know the location of your planner as well as any information needed to access it, such as the location of keys to a locked desk drawer.
- **How to open your safe.** If your planner is stored in a safe, your agents should know how to get into it, including its location and information about keys or codes.

If you've stored your planner elsewhere, or if it is stored in two locations, be sure to make the locations and access instructions very clear.

Review this information with your loved ones every year or so, and be sure they know to turn to your planner first, if you are incapacitated or when you die.

STEP 7: Update Your Planner

It's a good idea to review your planner every year or so to be sure everything is current and accurate. For example, you'll want to update your planner if you:

- have a new child, or become married, divorced, or widowed
- change jobs, retire, or become a partner in a business
- purchase a new insurance policy
- open, change, or cancel a bank account
- set up new passwords or personal identification numbers (PINs), or acquire new keys or combination locks
- cancel an old credit card or get a new one
- buy, lease, rent, or sell real estate, or
- purchase a new vehicle.

You'll also want to be sure your legal documents —your health care directives, will, living trust, and so on—remain current. Throughout the guide, you'll find guidelines for reviewing these documents and updating them if necessary.

A good way to stay current is to make notes about changes as they occur—for example, as you pay bills each month. You can simply toss a scribbled note into the front of the planner so you don't forget about the change. (Post-it notes work well for this purpose.) These notes will make your annual review much easier and may also provide valuable direction to your caretakers or survivors.

CHAPTER 1

Letter to Loved Ones

Tips for Writing Your Letter 20

Where to Get Help 23

In Your Planner 23

Keeping Your Letter Up to Date 24

And I'll be waiting on the far side banks of Jordan.
I'll be waiting, drawing pictures in the sand.
And when I see you coming, I will rise up with a shout
And come running through the shallow waters reaching for your hand.

—TERRY SMITH (1944–), "FAR SIDE BANKS OF JORDAN"

The first thing your loved ones will see when they open your planner is a letter from you. This letter is an opportunity for you to say goodbye. It is a powerful way for you to offer comfort, express your love and appreciation, and set out words for which you wish to be remembered.

It is also an opportunity to give to your loved ones the gift of direction—starting on the day of your incapacity or death. In your letter, you can tell your loved ones (in particular, your agent for health care, agent for finances, executor, or successor trustee) how to use your planner to find the information they need.

SKIP AHEAD

If you've already written a final letter. If you have already prepared a last letter or something similar for your loved ones, you may want to skip right to "In Your Planner," below, for directions on including the materials in your planner. Then look at "Keeping Your Letter Up to Date" for suggestions on keeping your planner current.

TIP

Complete this section last. While your letter will be the first thing your loved ones read in your planner, it's probably not the first thing you want to prepare. As a first step, you may find it overwhelming to write a final letter to your loved ones. Instead, you might want to write the letter after you've worked through other parts of your planner—and your feelings—or when your planner is complete.

If you suspect this is the case for you, skip this chapter for now and work on other sections of your planner. When you feel ready, come back to this section. Spending time working on other parts of the planner will make writing your last letter easier.

Tips for Writing Your Letter

It's just plain hard to say goodbye. But the process doesn't need to make it harder. Write only the letter that you want to write—no longer, no more elaborate. You might write to just one important person—or two or three—but you certainly don't need to address everyone in your life.

Here are some suggestions to help focus your work and get your letter done. They cover whom to address, what to include, and some important questions to consider. These tips are designed to help you complete the preprinted letter template that comes with your planner; see Section 1. But of course you don't have to use that form. If you prefer to write a letter from scratch, by all means do so. You'll still find some tips below to help you.

Addressing Your Letter

You'll probably want to address your last letter to family and friends who will be there if you become incapacitated or when you die. Consider:

- Who do you expect will survive you?
- Who is most important to you? To whom do you wish to say goodbye, or to leave with one last word?
- Who will be in charge of handling your affairs—your agent for finances or health care, the executor of your will, the successor trustee of your living trust?

The letter that comes with your planner is designed to be written to your loved ones as a group, though there's space for special notes to individuals as well. (More about that below.) You may choose instead to write individual, more personal letters—and handwritten, not typed. Your loved ones will cherish your personal last letter.

If you're using the letter template, write the names of your loved ones in the blank lines at the top.

Alternatives to Writing a Letter

If thinking about your own death and writing a meaningful letter to those closest to you feels too overwhelming or just not right, you might want to consider an alternative. There are many ways to convey your love—and your last words. Here are just a few:

- Keep a journal, making observations and giving thanks for your loved ones.
- If you find it easier to speak than to write, make an audio or video recording.
- Purchase greeting cards that express your love and gratitude.
- Express your feelings in a poem or story.
- Transcribe a poem, quote, scripture passage, or story for each loved one.
- Buy a book and inscribe it to a loved one.
- Select and wrap special gifts for loved ones.

If you choose an alternative to the letter template that comes with the planner, use your planner to make sure your survivors find what you've left for them. See "In Your Planner," below, for instructions.

EXAMPLES:

My dearest treasures Tanya, Sasha, and Peder—the best family in the world

My best friend and loving husband, Murray

Dear friends and helpmates, JoAnn, Barbara, and Evelyn

Aubrey Swanson, agent and executor, and Alyssa Jones, alternate

Providing Instructions

The letter that comes with your planner points your survivors to the Instructions section of the planner (Section 2) to find the practical information they will need following your incapacity or death. The Instructions section is the master guide that will help your loved ones use your planner in the days, weeks, and months following your incapacity or death.

If you create your own letter, you will want to include similar directions. If you choose to write separate letters to your loved ones, be sure to direct the people in charge of handling your affairs—such as your agent under a health care or financial power of attorney, the executor of your will, or the successor trustee of your living trust—to the Instructions section of your planner.

EXAMPLE:

When you've finished this letter, turn to the Instructions section of my planner. The first pages outline most everything you need to do or know in the next 48 hours. My prayer is for a simple, courageous process for you, knowing that the emotional toll today is enough to bear.

Thoughts About Your Death

In the next section of the letter that comes with your planner, or in a letter you create on your own, you might wish to share your thoughts or visions about death. You can use this section to describe what you believe this moment will be like for you. For example, you may want to:

- Write about your vision of death—of the moment your soul or consciousness departs from your body. Write about your expectations and beliefs surrounding those moments, whether it be seeing God, becoming part of a great light, resting peacefully and free from pain, or any other statement that's appropriate to your beliefs.
- Write about reuniting with loved ones who have already passed away.
- Write about your loved ones learning to fill the spaces that your absence will create.

EXAMPLES:

I imagine seeing the face of God. I imagine Mom and Dad there to greet me, after all these years apart.

I will slip into that transforming light, the light that invites me to a warm, soft joy, free from my pain and suffering in this world.

I wish peace for each of you—and for all of you, together as a family. Know that I loved you so, cherished the time we had together, and pray for your comfort.

Messages for Your Loved Ones

In the next part of the letter template, you can write separate notes to your loved ones. (If you need more space for this, add extra pages.) Search your heart and mind for the most important messages you have for each person. As you do this, don't be surprised if you discover things you want or need to say today to the people you care about. Whether it's an expression of love, gratitude, unresolved conflict, a wish to forgive, or a longing to ask for forgiveness, you may find it satisfying to initiate conversations now. After all, you're still here to share feelings of joy, relief, or completion as you lay unfinished business to rest. The time spent together may be a great gift for both you and those closest to you.

Ideally, when the time comes, your last letter won't contain any big surprises; it will simply reinforce what your loved ones know to be true and already hold fast in their hearts.

EXAMPLES:

Tanya and Sasha, you have owned and refined my heart since the days you each were born. I have been blessed with mother-daughter relationships I could not have dreamed—much closer, much warmer, more loving than I knew was possible. Thank you both for giving me that delightful, undeserved blessing.

My dearest Murray, I know you don't care much for mushy words. Let me simply thank you, then, for being my faithful partner, my best friend, my favorite companion, and my loving husband for many, many years. You brought me great joy in this life, and I'm so grateful to have shared it with you.

My sweet Greg, we've been richly blessed by each other. I've always sought your happiness—and today is no different. Please know that if you choose to remarry, I would very much like that for you.

Your Last Words

This is the place for last thoughts and final words. What else do you want to say, while you have a chance to say it?

You may have a poem, quote, drawing, or scripture with which you want to close your letter. You might choose to encourage your loved ones to strengthen their love for one another, building new bonds that no longer include you. This is the key that unlocks the doors to healing the loss of a loved one—and to the smooth distribution of an estate.

EXAMPLES:

Whenever you see a hummingbird, remember me.

He will cover you with his feathers, and under his wings you will find refuge; his faithfulness will be your shield and rampart. For he will command his angels concerning you to guard you in all your ways.
—Psalm 91:4,11

Please work thoughtfully and lovingly to forge new relationships. It is only the love you have for others that counts for anything.

Signature

When you sign your letter, consider using your private, unique words of love and affection. Do you share special terms of affection with certain people? Are there nicknames or pet names you've used with your loved ones?

EXAMPLES:

All my love—bigger than the world, Mom

xxoo WOW

Love—John, J.T., Pop, and Bestefar

How Is an Ethical Will Different From a Letter to Loved Ones?

You may have heard about "ethical wills." This type of will is not a legal document; it's a personal letter or statement about the experiences, values, and beliefs that have shaped your life.

Your letter to loved ones is one form of an ethical will, but you are also free to include a separate ethical will in your planner. There is no set formula for an ethical will. It is a reflection of you and it can contain whatever you like. You can write and deliver an ethical will at any time, or you can leave it for your survivors at your death.

If you'd like to learn more about ethical wills, visit Celebrations of Life at www.celebrationsoflife.net or Association of Personal Historians at www.personalhistorians.org. On both websites, you will find tips, sample ethical wills, and ethical will-writing kits that you can buy. If you want to consider a form of ethical will other than a written letter, see the suggestions in "Alternatives to Writing a Letter," above. Or, for help creating a biography, see "Capture Your Stories" in Chapter 3.

Where to Get Help

If you want help crafting a letter, these books may help you:

- ***Just a Note to Say ...,*** by Florence Isaacs (Potter Style), can help you find the right words, providing clear direction and rich examples.
- ***Personal Notes: How to Write from the Heart for Any Occasion,*** by Sandra E. Lamb (St. Martin's Press), helps you tap into heartfelt feelings and write meaningful letters to family and friends.

In Your Planner

If you're using only the letter template that comes with your planner, it's easy to set up this section. Just complete the template following the instructions in "Tips for Writing Your Letter," above.

If you're not using the preprinted template, or you're expressing your last thoughts in some form other than a letter (see "Alternatives to Writing a Letter," above), how you complete Section 1 of your planner depends on the method of expression you've chosen.

Using Alternative Methods

If you're expressing your last thoughts in some form other than a letter—such as a journal, videotape, cards, or gifts—you will still want to use Section 1 of your planner to tell your loved ones what to look for—and where. To do this, you can complete the preprinted "Letter to Loved Ones" in just two steps:

1. Address the letter to your loved ones and expected survivors.
2. In "Messages for My Loved Ones," tell your survivors what you have left for them and describe the location of the items.

EXAMPLES:

As time permits, please read my journals; they're in my nightstand drawer by our bed. Stop, read, and listen for my tremendous love and appreciation for you, day by day, year after year.

I have recorded cassette tapes with messages for each of you. You can find them in a small box on the top shelf of my home safe (above this planner).

Please look in the front pocket of this planner for cards and notes I have made for several of you. There's also a large envelope for Garth Olson, my executor.

There's a plastic storage tub under my bed. It contains packages I've made for each of you.

Using Your Own Letters

If you are using your own letter or letters instead of the preprinted template, you can follow the instructions just above and use the template to direct your loved ones to the letters you've written. Or, you can replace the template with your own letters at the start of your planner. If you do this, remember to direct your loved ones to the Instructions section of your planner (Section 2), so they know how to take the next step.

BINDER

Use pocket divider pages for sealed letters, cards, or other materials. If you're making a binder to hold your planner and you want to put your letters in sealed envelopes, include other items such as cards or poems, or file an ethical will with your planner, you can add pocket divider pages or plastic sleeves to this section of the planner. If you are preparing something like a videotape, cassette, or gifts, you may want to store these items with your planner so that your survivors can easily find them.

Keeping Your Letter Up to Date

Review your letter occasionally—at least every year or two—to make sure your final words are accurate and current. You may want to create a new letter if:

- you have married, found a new life partner, or lost a spouse through divorce or death
- you have new children, stepchildren, or grandchildren
- you've named a new health care agent, agent for finances, executor, or successor trustee, or
- your thoughts about your death, messages to loved ones, or last words have changed over time.

If you make an audio or video recording, review the item periodically to make sure it still plays correctly. You'll want to be sure your survivors can listen to or watch it when they need it.

CHAPTER

2

Instructions

In Your Planner 27

Keeping Your Documents Up to Date 29

> *Amy doesn't know, for the most part, where to find all this paperwork if something happens to me. She doesn't know where all the account numbers are, or the passwords necessary to log into those accounts electronically. And I find it painful to think of her, stressed and in pain, hunting for some paper she needs quickly when she isn't even sure what it looks like or if she's even hunting in the right pile.*
>
> —JEFF D. OPDYKE, "EVERYTHING I KNOW YOU SHOULD KNOW TOO," *THE WALL STREET JOURNAL SUNDAY*, SEPTEMBER 15, 2002

The first days following your death will be especially difficult for your family and friends. Your loved ones will be absorbing the loss, whether unexpected or long anticipated. They will be experiencing a range of feelings—sadness, hope, fear, denial, anger, guilt. And they will be faced with a long list of decisions and tasks, many of which they must handle immediately.

The Instructions section of your planner is a master guide for your loved ones and other survivors. It describes what needs to be done and when, and it points your survivors to the information in your planner that will help them.

If You Become Incapacitated

If you become unable to handle your own affairs, the instructions tell your loved ones to immediately locate and review your health care directives (living will) and durable power of attorney for finances, if you have made them. These important documents are discussed in more detail in Chapters 11 and 12.

The instructions are divided into three phases to help your survivors stay organized without getting overwhelmed:

- **Days 1 and 2.** The first phase focuses on tasks that need to be handled immediately following your incapacity or death, including caring for children or pets, and contacting your employer or business. If you have passed away, these instructions focus on carrying out your final arrangements, notifying family and friends of your death, and publishing your obituary.
- **Week 2.** The second phase covers tasks that are less urgent but still time-critical. These include locating your will or trust, reviewing current bills, and contacting important agencies and individuals, such as insurance agents, banks or brokers, service providers, and the Social Security Administration.
- **Month 1 and Beyond.** The third phase covers tasks for the first month or two—for example, taking inventory of your property and gathering information to prepare any necessary tax returns.

TIP

Complete this section after you finish the rest of your planner. The instructions direct your loved ones to the appropriate section of your planner for more information about each task they must handle. Because of this, it will be easiest for you to complete this section after you've worked your way through the rest of the planner. You'll have all the information you need and the instructions will quickly fall into place for you.

In Your Planner

Turn to the Instructions section of your planner (Section 2). The following guidelines will help you complete the pages there.

CAUTION

Pay attention to checkboxes. Much of what you will do in this section of your planner is place check marks in boxes to tell your survivors whether or not certain topics apply to your situation. These checkboxes are marked "Yes" and "No." Every topic also has a checkbox in front of it—*do not mark these boxes.* They are there so that your survivors can check off each task as they complete it.

If I Am Incapacitated

Begin with the section that highlights the two tasks related to incapacity.

- **Review Health Care Directives.** Check the appropriate box (Yes/No), indicating whether you have made documents to direct your health care if you become incapacitated. If you check "Yes," the instructions refer to the Health Care Directives section of your planner (Section 11).
- **Review Durable Power of Attorney for Finances.** Check the appropriate box (Yes/No), indicating whether you have made a durable power of attorney for finances—that is, a legal document appointing someone to handle money matters for you if you become incapacitated. If you check "Yes," the instructions refer to the Durable Power of Attorney for Finances section of your planner (Section 12).

Days 1 and 2

Check the necessary boxes to indicate which steps your survivors should take in the first 48 hours following your incapacity or death. In a couple of places, you will make additional notes to help direct your loved ones to important information.

- **Care for Children.** Check the appropriate box (Yes/No), indicating whether you have children that rely on your care. If you check "Yes," the instructions refer to the Children section of your planner (Section 4).
- **Care for Others.** Check the appropriate box (Yes/No), indicating whether there are people other than children who rely on your care. If you check "Yes," the instructions refer to the Others Who Depend on Me section of your planner (Section 5).
- **Care for Animals.** Check the appropriate box (Yes/No), indicating whether you have animals that rely on your care. If you check "Yes," the instructions refer to the Pets and Livestock section of your planner (Section 6).
- **Contact Employer.** Check the appropriate box (Yes/No), indicating whether you are currently employed (including volunteer work). If you check "Yes," the instructions refer to the Employment section of your planner (Section 7).
- **Contact Business.** Check the appropriate box, indicating whether you have an active interest and personal involvement in a business. If you check "Yes," the instructions refer to the Business Interests section of your planner (Section 8).
- **Make Final Arrangements.** You don't need to provide any information here. This section tells your survivors how to prepare and order copies of your death certificate. It also directs them to the details of your wishes for body disposition and memorial services, asking them to

turn to the planner sections on Organ or Body Donation (Section 13), Burial or Cremation (Section 14), and Funeral and Memorial Services (Section 15).

- **Publish Obituary.** Check the appropriate box (Yes/No), indicating whether or not you want your survivors to publish an obituary. If you check "Yes," the instructions refer to the Obituary section of your planner (Section 16).
- **Contact Family and Friends.** Your loved ones are asked to contact family and friends who should know of your incapacity or death. To help them, provide the locations where you store contact information, such as an email or printed address book, your cell phone, or a special list that you've made for this purpose. (See the note about including related materials in your planner, below.)
- **Review Appointment Calendar.** The instructions ask your loved ones to contact anyone with whom you have an appointment. To help them, provide the location of your appointment calendar. It may be somewhere in your home, in a calendar that you carry with you, on your computer, on your cell phone, or online.
- **Additional Notes.** Include any additional comments or directions related to this first phase.

Week 2

Follow these steps to complete the information for the second phase.

- **Locate Will or Other Estate Planning Documents.** You don't need to provide any information here. If you've made a will or trust, your survivors should locate it promptly, though they don't have to review it in detail right away. This section simply directs your loved ones to the Will and Trust section of your planner (Section 17) to help them find your documents.
- **Contact Organizations and Service Providers.** In the weeks just following your incapacity or death, your loved ones will need to contact many organizations, agencies, and individuals. This section directs them to the sections of your planner that contain the information they'll need: Insurance (Section 18), Bank and Brokerage Accounts (Section 19), Retirement Plans and Pensions (Section 20), Government Benefits (Section 21), and Service Providers (Section 10). If they should contact anyone else at this time, you can add names and contact information in the "Other" spaces provided.
- **Review Current Bills and Accounts.** You don't need to provide any information here. This section directs your loved ones to the sections of your planner that will help them pay or cancel your bills: Credit Cards and Debts (Section 22) and Secured Places and Passwords (Section 23).
- **Additional Notes.** Include additional comments or direction for the first two weeks. In particular, if your loved ones live at a distance from you, suggest that they handle two additional tasks:
- File instructions with the USPO to forward your mail to your agent's address.
- If your home will be vacant for some time, arrange security—extra patrols by city police, supplemental patrols by community security, watchfulness by neighbors, or frequent visits by friends. If you can, include suggested contacts for this.

Month 1 and Beyond

You don't need to do anything to complete these final steps, though there is a place for you to add additional directions if you have any.

- **Take Inventory.** To learn about your property and how to take care of it while wrapping up your affairs, the instructions direct your loved ones to several sections of your planner: Real Estate (Section 25), Vehicles (Section 26), Other Income and Personal Property (Section 27), and Other Information (Section 28).

- **Cancel Memberships and Driver's License.** To cancel memberships or subscriptions, the instructions direct your loved ones to the Memberships section of your planner (Section 9).
- **Prepare Tax Returns.** To help prepare your final tax returns, the instructions direct your loved ones to the Taxes section of your planner (Section 24).
- **Additional Notes.** Include any additional comments or directions for the first few months.

BINDER

Including related materials in your planner. You can file any documents related to instructions—such as your contact list for family and friends—directly in your planner. Insert the materials into pocket dividers or plastic binder sleeves, or hole-punch the documents and insert them directly into your planner binder following the Instructions section.

Keeping Your Documents Up to Date

Changes in your life may call for you to update your instructions. Some changes may simply require you to check a box in the Instructions section—but you should also update the corresponding section of your planner. For example, you'll want to update this section if you:

- have a new child or stepchildren
- make new arrangements with others who depend on you
- get a new pet or acquire new livestock
- establish an active interest in a business, or
- make new legal documents, such as a health care directive or power of attorney for finances.

Also, you will want to update your instructions if you:

- retire and no longer have an employer
- change the location of your contact information for family and friends, or
- change your calendar or method for recording appointments.

CHAPTER

3

Biographical Information

Where to Get Help ... 32

Birth Certificates ... 32

Adoption Records ... 33

Baptismal Records ... 33

Marriage Certificates ... 33

Divorce, Annulment, or Legal Separation Documents ... 33

Military Records ... 34

Citizenship Documents ... 36

Social Security Cards or Records ... 36

Death Certificates ... 37

In Your Planner ... 37

Keeping Your Information Up to Date ... 39

About six months after Mom's death, I needed my [deceased] stepdad's birthdate and birthplace for preparing income taxes, I think. I rummaged around and finally found the information somewhere. I then needed the information again a year or so later and, for the life of me, I couldn't find it anywhere. I'm pretty organized, but the executor's requirements to manage the details elude even me.

—FROM AN EXECUTOR AND SUCCESSOR TRUSTEE

This section of your planner makes it easy for you to organize vital statistics and related documents—such as birth and marriage certificates, Social Security cards, military discharge papers, and the like. While this will be handy for you, your loved ones may need the information for a number of purposes, including completing your death certificate, publishing an obituary (if you want that), preparing tax returns, and distributing your estate.

Start by browsing the Biographical Information pages of the planner to get an idea of the types of information included. The long list may seem daunting, but don't feel that you need to fill in all the blanks in one sitting. Start with what you know, and take steps to acquire the most important documents if you don't already have them on file. (See "Where to Get Help" for guidance.) Then, over time, keep an eye out for other information you need. Often, you will stumble across it when you aren't directly searching for it. For example, a visit with a relative might easily net what you're looking for. Your brother Bob or your Aunt Sue might know—or may have written down somewhere—some important facts.

SKIP AHEAD

If you have your documents in hand. If you don't need to order copies of vital documents, you can turn to "In Your Planner" for directions on completing the Biographical Information section of your planner.

Where to Get Help

If you cannot locate certain documents to complete your planner, you can request copies of what you need from the issuing office or organization. This section can help you order copies of:

- birth certificates
- adoption records
- baptismal records
- marriage certificates
- divorce, annulment, or legal separation documents
- military records
- citizenship documents
- Social Security cards or records, and
- death certificates.

Birth Certificates

To request a copy of a birth certificate, you usually need the following information:

- full birth name (first, middle, and last)
- date of birth, and
- city and county of birth.

If you have it, it also helps to include the mother's and father's full names and the name of the hospital where the birth occurred.

It's easy to find online forms and instructions for ordering a birth certificate. To find out where to send your request, go to the National Center for Health Statistics (NCHS) website at www.cdc.gov/nchs/w2w.htm and select your state. Or try ordering online through www.vitalchek.com.

If you don't have online access, call the vital records office for the county where the birth occurred and ask for instructions.

Informational vs. Certified Copies

In many states, you can order copies of birth, marriage, divorce, and death certificates in two forms: informational or certified. A certified copy is stamped with an official seal, warranting that the copy is an exact replica of the original certificate. You may need a certified copy for various legal transactions, including:

- applying for a driver's license with a certified birth certificate
- applying for an updated passport with a certified marriage certificate, or
- wrapping up someone's estate with certified copies of that person's death certificate.

In most states, you can obtain a certified copy only if you can prove that you are the person named in the document or that you have a direct relationship with that person—for example, you're the spouse, child, or court-appointed executor.

An informational copy is useful for personal records, and, in most states, is available to anyone who requests it. You can't use an informational copy to obtain identification, such as a driver's license or passport.

Adoption Records

The types of adoption records you can order depend on the circumstances of the adoption and on state law. Many adoption records are confidential and difficult to obtain—but that's not always the case. For example, you can probably get the records of a stepparent adoption by calling the vital records office in the county where the adoption occurred.

To obtain other types of adoption records, you must work through a state agency. Start by accessing the National Foster Care & Adoption Directory Search at www.childwelfare.gov/nfcad. The directory will provide contact information for adoption resources in your state.

Baptismal Records

To request a copy of baptismal records, contact the church where the baptism occurred. If you do not know the specific church, or if the church no longer exists, contact a regional office for the denomination (such as the regional diocese or presbytery).

Marriage Certificates

To request a copy of a marriage certificate or a certificate of a registered domestic partnership, you usually need the following information:

- at least one spouse's full name (first, middle, and last), and
- date (or year) of marriage.

If you have it, it can also help to include:

- the other spouse's full name
- either spouse's city and county of birth, and
- county where marriage occurred.

These days, it's usually easy to find online forms and instructions for ordering a copy of a marriage certificate. Follow the instructions for ordering a birth certificate, above.

Divorce, Annulment, or Legal Separation Documents

To request a copy of a certificate of divorce, annulment, or legal separation, you usually need the following information:

- husband's full name (first, middle, and last), and
- date (or year) of divorce, annulment, or legal separation.

If you have it, it can also help to include:

- dates of marriage
- husband's city and county of birth
- wife's full former name (first, middle, and last)
- wife's city and county of birth
- county where marriage occurred, and
- county where divorce, annulment, or legal separation occurred.

You can usually obtain a copy of court documents for divorce, annulment, or legal separation by writing to the vital statistics office of the state where the event occurred. Follow the instructions for ordering a birth certificate, above.

Catholic Annulment Documents

Within the Roman Catholic Church, a couple may obtain a religious annulment after finalizing a civil divorce or annulment. To get a copy of the annulment document, contact the regional Roman Catholic diocese to find out where to send your request, as well as what information you should enclose and the amount of the fee.

Military Records

The location and accessibility of military service records depends on the veteran's date of separation from service. Recent records are often maintained by the branch of service. Older records are maintained by the National Archives & Records Administration (NARA) in St. Louis. Historical records are maintained by NARA in Washington, DC.

Access to records is limited for nonarchival records to 62 years from date of separation.

- **Archival records.** Service records are archived 62 years after the veteran's date of separation. The process is continual, such that each new year those records now 62 years old are archived. For example, in 2015, records with date of separation in 1953 (that is, 2015 less 62 years) will be archived. Archived records are available to the public without restriction.
- **Nonarchival records.** Access to nonarchival records is restricted to only the veteran or, if the veteran is deceased, to next-of kin relatives—father or mother, unremarried widow or widower, son or daughter, or sibling.

Recent Records

For someone separating from the Air Force, Marine Corps, or Navy on or after a date shown in the next table, records are maintained by the particular branch of service. For someone separating from the Army or Coast Guard on or after a date shown in the table, records are maintained by NARA in St. Louis. To request a service record, use the contact information shown in the table, below.

To request a record from NARA in St. Louis, go to www.archives.gov, click on Veterans' Service Records, and follow the instructions. If you don't have online access, you can contact NARA by telephone or mail:

The National Archives & Records Administration
National Personnel Records Center – Military Personnel Records
One Archives Drive
St. Louis, MO 63138
314-801-0800

When sending your request by mail, be sure to include the following information about the veteran with your request:

- Complete name while in service
- Service number
- Social Security number
- Branch of service
- Dates of service
- Date and place of birth

Recent Records		
Branch of Service	**Separation Date**	**Office**
Air Force	On or after 10/01/2004	Air Force Personnel Center, HQ AFPC/DPSSRP 550 C Street West, Suite 19, Randolph AFB, TX 78150-4721 www.afpc.af.mil 800-525-0102
Army	On or after 10/01/2002	Records maintained at U.S. Army Human Resources Command, while requests are serviced by NARA, St. Louis. See ordering information above.
Coast Guard	On or after 04/01/1998	Records maintained and requests serviced by NARA, St. Louis. See ordering information above.
Marine Corps	On or after 01/01/1999	Headquarters U.S. Marine Corps Personnel Management Support Branch (MMSB-10) 2008 Elliot Road, Quantico, VA 22134-5030 800-268-3710
Navy	On or after 01/01/1995	Navy Personnel Command, PERS-312E 5720 Integrity Drive, Millington, TN 38055-3120 www.public.navy.mil/bupers-npc 901-874-4885

- If known, also include place of discharge, last unit of assignment, and place of entry into the service.

Sign and date the request. If the request is submitted by next of kin of deceased veteran (for nonarchival record), also enclose a copy of the veteran's death certificate, a letter from the funeral home, or a copy of the veteran's published obituary.

Older Records

Older records are those with a date of separation between the historical dates in the table below and the recent dates shown above—for example, for Army Enlisted, between 11/01/1912 and 10/01/2002. All older records are maintained by (and requests are serviced by) NARA in St. Louis.

To request an older record (whether archived or not), follow the instructions above for submitting a request to NARA in St. Louis.

Historical Records

NARA also manages the oldest military records, but at a facility in Washington, DC. At this facility, records are maintained for those who separated prior to the dates shown below.

Historical Records	
Branch of Service	**Separation Date**
Army	Enlisted: 11/01/1912 Officers: 07/01/1917
Coast Guard (and predecessor agencies)	All: 01/01/1920
Marine Corps	Enlisted: 01/01/1905 Officers: 01/01/1896
Navy	Enlisted: 01/01/1886 Officers: 01/01/1903

To order these military service records, go online to www.archives.gov, click on Veterans' Service Records, then follow the instructions for historical, pre-WWI records. If you do not have online access, you can contact NARA in Washington, DC, as follows:

The National Archives & Records Administration
Old Military and Civil Records (NWCTB-Military)
Textual Services Division
700 Pennsylvania Avenue NW
Washington, DC 20408-0001
866-325-7208

If you submit your request by mail, include the following information about the veteran with your request:

- Complete name while in service
- State in which veteran served
- War served or dates of service
- If service in Civil War, whether serving as Union or Confederate
- Type of service, Volunteer or Regular
- If known, also include service unit, service arm (that is, infantry, cavalry, artillery, or other), rank, date and place of birth, date and place of death.

Be sure to include your contact information, then sign and date your request.

Citizenship Documents

You can apply for a replacement certificate of citizenship or naturalization if your current certificate has been lost or destroyed, or if you've legally changed your name. You must complete Form N-565, *Application for Replacement Naturalization/Citizenship Document.* You can download the form from the U.S. Department of Homeland Security, Citizenship and Immigration Services (USCIS) website at www.uscis.gov. Type "Form N-565" in the search box at upper right, press enter, then click on the first option in the list that displays. The site will provide the form for download and instructions for submitting.

You can request the citizenship or naturalization documents of a deceased relative by filing Form G-639, *Freedom of Information Act/Privacy Act Request.* You can download the form from the USCIS website at www.uscis.gov. Follow the steps for Form N-565, shown just above, but instead type "Form G-639" in the initial search box.

If you don't have online access, you can obtain forms from a local USCIS District Office Service Center. You can find the office in the government pages of your telephone book.

Social Security Cards or Records

You can replace a lost or damaged Social Security card by completing Form SS-5, *Application for a Social Security Card.* You can download the form from the Social Security Administration (SSA) website at www.ssa.gov. You can also obtain it by calling 800-772-1213 or visiting your local Social Security office. (Find your local office on the SSA website or in the government listings pages of your phone book.)

You can submit your form by mail or in person. To complete the application process, you'll need an identifying document such as a driver's license, marriage certificate, divorce decree, military record, employer or school identification card, insurance policy, or passport. If you apply by mail, you must submit an original document or a certified copy. The SSA will return your document to you when your application is complete.

If you're searching for the Social Security records of someone who has died—for example, because you're the executor and are trying to wrap up the estate—the SSA will search its archives for a fee. For more information, call the SSA at 800-772-1213 or go to ssa.gov, type "Form 711" in the search field, and press enter. Click on the Form 711 link to display the form, *Request for Deceased Individual's Social Security Record.* You can print and complete the form, enclose the appropriate fee, then mail to the SSA address provided on the form.

Death Certificates

To request a copy of a death certificate, you usually need the following information about the deceased person:

- full name (first, middle, and last)
- date of death, and
- city and county of death.

If you have it, it can help to include the deceased person's Social Security number and place of birth (city and county).

It's usually easy to find online instructions and forms for requesting copies of a death certificate. Follow the instructions for birth certificates, above.

In Your Planner

Turn to the Biographical Information section of your planner (Section 3). The following guidelines will help you complete the pages there.

Residence Information

Your survivors will use this information for a number of purposes, including preparing your death certificate.

- **Name.** Provide your current name—first, middle, and last.
- **Address.** Write the address of your current home or primary residence.
- **Telephone.** Provide the telephone number of your current home or primary residence. If you have multiple personal phone numbers—such as a cell phone or second phone line in your home—list those, too.
- **Resident of City Since (year).** Provide the year you established residence in the city where you currently live.
- **Resident of State Since (year).** Provide the year you established residence in the state where you currently live.

Self and Parents—Spouse or Partner—Children—Siblings—Others

Complete each table describing you, your close relatives, and any additional beneficiaries you have named in your will, trusts, life insurance, retirement accounts, or on individual assets (as pay- or transfer-on-death beneficiaries). If you wish to include people not already named in the tables—such as nieces or nephews, grandchildren, or close friends named as beneficiaries—you can use the final table, "Others."

- **First Name.** For the person named in the column heading, provide the legal first name. Also include any commonly used first names, if they differ from the legal name.

EXAMPLES:

Robert (R.D.)

Eunice (Bonnie)

Isaac (Ike)

- **Middle Name.** Provide the person's legal middle name. Include any commonly used middle names that differ from the legal name.
- **Last Name.** Provide the legal last name (or surname). Include any commonly used last names that differ from the legal surname.

EXAMPLES:

Plummer-Raphael (Raphael)

Kowalczykowski (Kowski)

- **Maiden Name.** Provide any maiden surname—that is, the last name used before a first marriage.

CAUTION

Use just one name to avoid confusion.

If you use different names—other than a new last name because you've married—you'll make things easier on your survivors if you make sure your name is the same on all your important legal documents and accounts, such as wills, trusts, health care directives, contracts, and bank accounts.

- **Date of Birth.** Provide the date of birth as listed on the person's birth certificate. For clarity, include the month, day, and year written in long form—for example, "March 1, 1973."
- **Birthplace (City, State, County, Country).** Provide the place of birth as listed on the birth certificate. Include the city, county, state, and country.

  EXAMPLES:

  San Jose, CA, Santa Clara County, U.S.

  Waterloo, IA, Blackhawk County, U.S.

- **Location of Birth Certificate.** Describe the location of a copy of the birth certificate. If possible, file this document in your planner.
- **Location of Adoption Documents.** Describe the location of adoption documents, if applicable. If possible, file these documents in your planner.
- **Social Security Number.** Provide the nine-digit Social Security number issued by the U.S. Social Security Administration.
- **Location of Social Security Card.** Describe the location of the Social Security card. If possible, file the card in the planner.
- **Driver's License Number and State.** Provide the driver's license number, including the state that issued the license.
- **Military Service: Country and Branch.** If the person served in the military, document the country served and the branch of military service.
- **Military Rank.** If the person served in the military, provide the highest rank attained during service.
- **Military Induction Date.** Provide the date inducted, or the date the person first joined the military.
- **Military Discharge Date.** Provide the date of discharge, or the date the person was released from the military.
- **Military Citations.** Note any citations or awards received.
- **Location of Military Documents.** Describe the location of military service documents, including citations and discharge papers. If possible, file these documents in your planner.
- **Date of First Marriage.** For the person named in the column heading, document the month, day, and year of the person's first marriage or domestic partnership.
- **First Spouse's Name.** Document the first, middle, and last name (prior to the marriage) of the person's first spouse or domestic partner.
- **Location of Marriage Certificate.** Provide the location of the marriage certificate. If possible, file the document in your planner.
- **Date of Divorce, Annulment, Legal Separation, or Death.** Provide the month, day, and year that any divorce, annulment, legal separation, or death certificate was finalized, or that the spouse passed away.
- **Location of Documents.** Document the location of any divorce, annulment, or legal separation or death certificate documents. If possible, file the documents in your planner.

The five items just above repeat, providing space for information about second and third marriages (or registered domestic partnerships) for the person named in the column heading. For each subsequent marriage or partnership, follow the guidelines provided above.

- **Date of Death.** If the named person has died, provide the date of death for the person as listed on the death certificate. Include the month, day, and year.
- **Location of Death Certificate.** Describe the location of a copy of the death certificate. If possible, file the document in your planner.

Capture Your Stories

While you're organizing materials for your survivors, you might consider preserving your life stories in an audio recording, video recording, or book. Tales about your youth, family, working life, military experience, or personal interests would be precious gifts to your loved ones.

If you like to write but aren't sure where to begin, you might enjoy a class on memoir writing at your local adult school. You can also visit your local library or a bookstore for books designed to help you document family and personal histories, including guides to memoir writing.

If you want professional help, a personal historian can assist you with all aspects of preserving your stories, from choosing and scanning photos or extracting snippets from home movies to taping interviews and selecting music. The cost for a professionally prepared video recording ranges from $500 to $10,000, depending on the project. To find a qualified professional, visit the Association of Personal Historians (APH) website at www.personalhistorians.org.

Even if you don't hire your own historian, the APH website is worth a visit. If you click "Tell Your Story," you'll find information about the process and lots of free, helpful tips on what to include in your biography.

- **Address.** Enter the person's home address.
- **Telephone(s).** Provide telephone numbers for the person. Include all numbers that may be helpful, including numbers for home, office, or mobile phones.
- **Email.** Provide email address(es) for the named person.
- **Other.** Use the Other spaces at the end of each column if you want to include additional personal data about the named person. Additional information or documents may include citizenship information, baptismal records, passports, résumé, or curriculum vitae.

Additional Notes

If you have additional information about the biographical data provided in these tables, include it here.

BINDER

Including vital records in your planner.

This section of your planner is a great place to file:

- birth certificates
- adoption documents
- baptismal certificate
- Social Security cards
- certificates of marriage or divorce
- passports
- military discharge papers
- résumés
- diplomas
- transcripts
- scholarships
- awards, and
- related records.

Pocket divider pages and plastic binder sleeves work well to organize and protect these documents.

Keeping Your Information Up to Date

When you update your planner, consider the following questions; these events will trigger additions and changes to your information.

- Have you moved?
- Have you married or divorced, or has your spouse or partner passed away?
- Have your parents or children become married, divorced, or widowed?
- Have you been discharged from the military?
- Do you have new children or stepchildren?

CHAPTER

4

Children

Arranging Care for Children 42

Naming a Personal Guardian 42

Naming a Property Manager 43

Where to Get Help 44

In Your Planner 44

Keeping Your Information Up to Date 46

In youth, the days are short and the years are long.
In old age, the years are short and the days are long.

—POPE PAUL VI (1897–1978)

If you're a parent of young children or otherwise responsible for young children, your days are probably full of activities and details about their care that only you know. You'll want to ensure that the kids in your life—be they your own, your spouse or partner's, foster children, or others—are cared for if you become unable to carry out your current responsibilities. If you include information about children in your planner, your loved ones can more easily step in to meet immediate needs and help with the transition to other care providers.

Before turning to the specifics of completing your planner, this chapter provides some basic information about choosing a guardian and property manager for your children.

SKIP AHEAD

If you've already named caretakers for your kids. If you have already formally named a personal guardian and property manager for your children, you can skip to "In Your Planner" for instructions on completing your planner. Then read "Keeping Your Information Up to Date" for tips on keeping your planner current.

Arranging Care for Children

Contemplating the possibility of early death is wrenching, especially if you have young children. Preparing a good contingency plan is important—and may even salve some of your fears. The two most important tasks are naming someone to raise your children and choosing the person who will watch over their property. Usually, the same person will take both jobs, but that's not always required.

Naming a Personal Guardian

Generally, if there are two parents willing and able to care for a child, and one dies, the other takes over physical custody and responsibility for caring for the child. But if both parents of a minor child die—or if a single parent dies—a court must appoint a personal guardian for the child. In your will, you can name the person you'd like the court to appoint as personal guardian. (See Chapter 17 for more about wills.) The person you name will be appointed by the court if:

- there is no surviving legal parent (biological or adoptive) able to properly care for the children, and
- the court agrees that your choice is in the best interests of the children.

A court will support your choice for personal guardian unless there is a compelling reason not to do so—such as a strong objection from a family member who is able to prove that your choice is not in the best interests of your child. These types of conflicts are quite rare, however.

If you and your child's other parent are both making wills, you should name the same person as guardian for each child. This will help avoid the possibility of a dispute—perhaps even a court battle—should both of you die close in time to one another. (This, too, is a very rare occurrence.)

The personal guardian you choose must be an adult. You should first consider someone with whom the child already has a close relationship—a stepparent, grandparent, aunt or uncle, older sibling, or close friend of the family. Be sure that the person is mature, good-hearted, and willing and able to assume the responsibility.

If you have more than one young child, you probably wish to keep them together, naming the same personal guardian for all children. In some families, however, the children are not particularly close to each other but have strong attachments with adults outside the immediate family. For instance, one child may spend a lot of time with a grandparent while another may be close to an aunt or uncle. Also, in a second or third marriage, a child from an earlier marriage may be close to a different adult than a child from the current marriage.

Choose the personal guardian you believe would best be able to care for each child. This may mean choosing different personal guardians for different children.

You will also want to name an alternate personal guardian for each child, in case your first choice either changes his or her mind or is unable to take over at your death. The considerations for naming an alternate are the same as those you considered in making your first choice: maturity, a good heart, familiarity with the children, and a willingness to serve.

Naming a Property Manager

Except for items of minimal value, the law does not permit minors to own property outright. Instead, a child's property must be distributed to and managed by an adult. This includes property received under a will or through a living trust, as a beneficiary on a life insurance policy or retirement account, or as a beneficiary named on an individual asset (that is, as a pay- or transfer-on-death beneficiary). It may also include property received from other sources—the lottery, a gift from a relative, or earnings from playing in a rock band.

Arranging for property management means naming a trusted adult to look after and account for the property that a young beneficiary receives, until the beneficiary turns a specific age. The property being managed for the beneficiary must be held, invested, or spent in the beneficiary's best interest. In other words, the property manager will decide if the young person's inheritance will be spent on college tuition or a new sports car.

If you are a parent, you may choose to leave your property directly to your spouse or partner, trusting him or her to use good judgment in providing for your children's needs. Even if you do this, however, you should still think about property management. To plan for the possibility that your spouse or partner dies close in time to you, you may want to name your children as alternate beneficiaries for your property and appoint a trusted adult as manager for the property they might inherit. (As with personal guardians, if both parents are making wills and leaving property to their children, they should name the same person as property manager for each child.)

CAUTION

Parents don't get the job automatically. Even if you are (and remain) married to the child's other parent, he or she probably will not be able to automatically step in and handle property you leave outright to your children. Unless you provide for some form of management, the other parent usually will have to petition the court to be appointed property manager—and handle the property under court supervision until the child turns 18. So, if you want your child's other parent to manage the property you are leaving to your child, name the other parent as property manager. If you want someone else to manage the property, name that person as property manager. With rare exceptions, your choice will be honored.

When choosing the property manager, name someone you trust who is familiar with managing the kind of assets you leave to your children, and who shares your attitudes and values about how money should be spent.

You will also want to name an alternate property manager, in case your first choice is unwilling or unable to serve at your death. Again, consider the same factors as you did when choosing your first choice for property manager.

Often, the person chosen to serve as personal guardian is also chosen as property manager. If you must name two different people, choose people who get along well; they will have to work together.

Where to Get Help

Other chapters of this book list resources that will help you name caretakers for your children. This section tells you where to find that information.

Naming a Personal Guardian

You must use a will to name a personal guardian; other estate planning documents (including living trusts) won't work for this purpose. If you don't name a personal guardian in your will, a court will have to do the job without your input. To learn more about wills, see Chapter 17.

Setting Up Property Management

There are several ways to set up management for property you leave to young children. These range from naming a property guardian in your will, to setting up a simple trust or custodianship in your will or living trust, to arranging for a more complex child's trust. (A simple trust or custodianship is often best, because it frees the property manager from court involvement.) A full discussion of these methods is beyond the scope of this book, but you can find detailed information about each option in any of the will- or trust-making resources listed in Chapter 17, or visit Nolo's website at www.nolo.com for free information on the subject.

Life Insurance

Children are often named as the beneficiaries of life insurance policies. See Chapter 18 for more information on buying life insurance for children and making sure there's someone on hand to manage the proceeds.

In Your Planner

Turn to the Children section of your planner (Section 4). The following guidelines will help you complete the pages there.

Guardians and Property Managers

Here, list each of your children, the primary caretakers you have named for them, and the documents in which you have named the caretakers.

Space has been provided to name eight children. If you need more space, copy or print out an extra page for your planner.

- **Child's Name.** Provide the full name of each child.
- **Personal Guardian.** Provide the full name of the person you have named to serve as personal guardian for each child.
- **Alternate Personal Guardian.** Provide the full name of the person you have chosen as alternate personal guardian, in case your first choice cannot serve.
- **Document.** Write in the name of the document in which you named the personal guardian and alternate. In this case, the document should be your will—the only document in which you can name a personal guardian for a child. (You may list different documents for a child's property manager, as discussed just below.)

- **Property Manager.** Provide the full name of the person you have named to serve as property manager for each child.
- **Alternate Property Manager.** Provide the full name of the person you have chosen as alternate property manager, in case your first choice cannot serve.
- **Document.** Provide the name of the document(s) in which you named the property manager and alternate. For example, you may have named property managers in your will, living trust, another trust, or a life insurance policy.

Information About Children

In this table, list and describe each child for whom you provide care.

- **Child's Name and Contact Information.** Provide the full name and contact information for each child. If you're the parent of a young child who lives only with you, your home address and telephone number will do. But think about other important contact information. For example, if your kids have their own cell phones, you'll want to include those numbers. Think about all the best ways to contact the child: address, phone numbers, and email, too.
- **Date of Birth.** Provide the birthdate (or just the year) for each child you care for.
- **Child's Relationship to Me.** Describe the child's relationship to you—for example, son, daughter, niece, or foster son.
- **Type of Care.** Briefly describe the care that you provide for each child.

EXAMPLES:

Full-time mother

Day care (M–F, 7a.m.–5p.m.)

Additional Care Providers

Here, list other care providers on whom each child relies for care and support. Include family members or other people who may be able to step in and take over your responsibilities.

- **Child's Name.** Provide the child's full name, exactly as you did above.
- **Care Provider or Family Member's Contact Information.** List everyone that your loved ones should know about when taking over care for the child. Other care providers may include family members or close friends, doctors, dentists, day care or periodic sitters, schools, or teachers. Include name, address, phone numbers, and email address.
- **Relationship to Child.** Indicate how the care provider is related to the child—for example, doctor, day care or sitter, school, father, or aunt.
- **Type of Care.** Briefly describe the ways in which the provider cares for the child.

EXAMPLES:

Neighbor, occasional sitter

Aunt and uncle

Math tutor

Additional Notes

If there is anything else your survivors should know about the children you care for, you can include it here.

BINDER

Including related materials in your planner. You can file copies of important records for children in this section in your planner. These records might include medical information, immunization records, a copy of your children's school emergency contact form, documents relating to type and location of care, the location of house keys (or copies of the keys themselves), or written arrangements with other care providers. Place the materials in a pocket divider page, plastic sleeve, or zippered binder pouch—or, for simple papers, just hole-punch them and insert them after this section of the binder.

Keeping Your Information Up to Date

This section contains a lot of contact information that could easily change. In addition, you'll want to update these tables if:

- you begin caring for a new child
- your responsibilities for a minor child come to an end or change, or
- you want to add or remove additional care providers or change information about existing providers, such as new day care arrangements, teachers, or schedules.

CHAPTER

5

Others Who Depend on Me

In Your Planner 48

Keeping Your Information Up to Date 49

Lean on me when you're not strong,
And I'll be your friend. I'll help you carry on.
For it won't be long, 'til I'm gonna need somebody to lean on.

—BILL WITHERS (1938–), "LEAN ON ME"

The previous chapter was all about the young children you provide care for. But you may provide care for others, too—perhaps your parents, other family members, friends, or neighbors. The type of care may range from living full-time with an aging parent to something as simple as walking your neighbor's dog twice a week.

In your planner, you can identify anyone for whom you provide regular care and describe what you do for each person. You can also list additional care providers—such as other family or friends, doctors, or meal programs—and provide contact information.

In Your Planner

Turn to the Others Who Depend on Me section of your planner (Section 5). Follow these guidelines to complete the pages there.

Information About People Who Depend on Me

List each person for whom you provide care and briefly describe the care that you provide.

- **Person's Name and Contact Information.** Provide the full name and contact information for each person that depends on you. Include all the best ways to contact or locate the person: address, telephone numbers, and email.
- **Date of Birth.** Provide the birthdate (or even just the year) for each person you help.
- **Person's Relationship to Me.** Describe the person's relationship to you—for example, mother, father, sister, neighbor, or friend.
- **Type of Care.** Briefly describe the care that you provide for each person.

EXAMPLES:

Check in and bring lunch, M–F, 12p.m.–3p.m.

Drive to doctor, Thursday mornings

Walk dog at noon, M–F

Additional Care Providers

List other care providers who may be able to step in and take over your responsibilities if necessary.

- **Person's Name.** Provide the full name of the person receiving care, exactly as you did in the first table.
- **Care Provider's Contact Information.** Include the care provider's name, address, phone numbers, and email address. Be sure to think through all your options when listing additional care providers here; you may want to include doctors, dentists, meal programs, hospice help, neighbors, friends, or the person's family members.
- **Relationship to Person.** Indicate how the care provider is related to the person receiving care—for example, doctor, support organization, pastor, neighbor, friend, or daughter.
- **Type of Care.** Briefly describe the ways in which the provider cares for the person.

Additional Notes

If there is anything else your survivors should know about the people for whom you provide care, you can include it here.

BINDER

Including related materials in your planner. You can file related records and other items in your planner. Such records or items might include medical information, documents relating to type and location of care, location of the person's house key, actual spare keys, or arrangements with other care providers. Place the materials in a pocket divider page, plastic sleeve, or zippered binder pouch—or, for simple papers, just hole-punch them and insert them after this section of the binder.

Keeping Your Information Up to Date

This section contains a lot of contact information that could easily change, so you should review it frequently. You may need to make changes if:

- you begin caring for someone new or stop taking care of someone you're currently helping
- you have substantially greater or fewer care responsibilities for a listed person, or
- there are new additional care providers to list, or you need to remove existing providers.

CHAPTER

6

Pets and Livestock

Arranging Care for Pets 52

Where to Get Help 53

In Your Planner 53

Keeping Your Information Up to Date 55

I like pigs. Dogs look up to us. Cats look down on us. Pigs treat us as equals.

—SIR WINSTON CHURCHILL (1874–1965)

How about your adoring pooch? Or the horse wanting a trough of alfalfa? Or the cows that need to be milked? Your incapacity or death will be a loss to your pets and may be disruptive to livestock that you own.

Use your planner to organize and store information about your animals—including your wishes for their placement if you become unable to care for them yourself. You can also add related materials to your planner, such as certificates of pedigree, medical records, or other valuable documents.

Before turning to the instructions for completing your planner, this chapter provides some basic information about arranging for others to care for your pets after you die.

SKIP AHEAD

If you've already arranged care for your pets. If you've set up a plan for others to assume care of your animals after death, you can skip right to "In Your Planner" for instructions on completing your planner. Then read "Keeping Your Information Up to Date," at the end of the chapter.

Arranging Care for Pets

You'll want to be sure that your pets go to good homes if you can no longer take care of them. You have several options, including family members, friends, sanctuaries for domestic animals, placement through the SPCA, or perhaps even a veterinary school care program.

The easiest way to arrange care for your pet is to make a plan with a friend or family member. Discuss your wishes with the prospective caretaker, making sure that your choice is willing and able to help.

Then, use your will to leave the animal to the named caretaker. You may also want to also leave some money in your will for the caretaker, to be used for your pet's care. (The law doesn't allow you to leave money or other property directly to your pet, so leave it to the person you have named to take the animal with a note stating that the money is for the animal's feeding and care.)

SEE AN EXPERT

Setting up a trust for your pet. In most states, you can establish a trust for your pet rather than simply leaving your pet to someone in your will. A pet trust is a legally independent entity, managed by a trustee you name. You define the terms of the trust—how your pet is to be cared for, including caretakers and successor caretakers—in the trust document. Pet trusts can be desirable for people who feel they'd prefer not to leave their pet outright to someone, but rather wish to have more input—such as the brand of food to be provided, exercise regimen, or frequency of vet visits. Creating a pet trust is more costly and complicated than simply leaving your pet outright. Talk with a lawyer if you're interested in this option.

If you are not able to find someone both willing and able to take care of your pet, you have some other options. Several programs help to place pets in loving homes when their owners can no longer care for them.

SPCA Programs

In many areas, the SPCA will find good homes for the pets of deceased members. The new caretakers and pets are often entitled to free lifetime veterinary care at the SPCA hospital. For more information, contact your local SPCA.

Rescue Programs

Rescue programs help to place pets in new homes. These programs are particularly popular for dogs, but there are programs for cats, birds, livestock, and more exotic animals such as reptiles and ferrets. You can use the Internet to search for appropriate programs: Go to a search engine such as Google and type "rescue program," "sanctuaries," or "pet retirement homes" and the species or breed of your pet.

Veterinary School Programs

A number of veterinary schools take in pets whose owners leave an endowment to the school. These programs typically provide a homelike atmosphere and lifetime veterinary care for the animals. Here is a list of some schools that currently offer this option:

Indiana

Peace of Mind Program
College of Veterinary Medicine
Purdue University
800-830-0104
www.vet.purdue.edu/giving/tribute-gifts.php

Kansas

Perpetual Pet Care Program
Office of Development
College of Veterinary Medicine
Kansas State University
785-532-4378
www.vet.k-state.edu/depts/development/perpet

Oklahoma

Cohn Pet Care Facility for Small Animals
Oklahoma State University
Center for Veterinary Health Sciences
405-385-5607
www.cvm.okstate.edu/development

Texas

Stevenson Companion Animal Life-Care Center
College of Veterinary Medicine
Texas A&M University
979-845-1188
http://vetmed.tamu.edu/stevenson-center

Whatever plans you make, be certain to review them with the intended recipient before you finalize your planner. This will help to ensure that your wishes will be carried out as you intend.

Where to Get Help

If you want more information about planning for your pets' care, visit the 2nd Chance 4 Pets website at www.2ndchance4pets.org. This organization provides a host of resources for planning lifetime care for your pets.

In Your Planner

Turn to the Pets and Livestock section of your planner (Section 6). The following instructions will help you complete the pages there.

Animal Care

Here, you will list your animals and provide basic details about their care.

- **Pet Name, Chip ID, Species, and Coloring.** Identify each pet or group of animals by name, microchip identification code (if any), species, and coloring or markings. Provide as much detail as others will need to recognize your animals.

  EXAMPLES:

  Flock of Araucana chickens

  Polled Hereford bull, #594

  Herd of Polled Hereford cattle

Gaggle of white domestic geese

Mollie, ID 111 222 333, DSH cat, black-white-orange

Sammy, aqua parakeet

- **Location.** Describe specifically where the pet or livestock is housed.

EXAMPLES:

Coop in backyard

SW pasture

Anderson Range (Buck Anderson: 222-222-3333); see separate grazing contract following this section of my planner.

At the willow pond behind my barn

In my house

Cage in my kitchen

- **Food and Water.** Describe what, where, when, and how often you feed the listed animal(s). If relevant, include information about where you store and purchase feed.

EXAMPLES:

Hill's Prescription Diet W/D (purchase from vet), just 1 cup daily

Cracked corn from Toby's Feed and Tack, about 4 cups, twice weekly

Suga-Lik cane molasses supplement, available from Midtown Feed

- **Other Care.** Describe any important information about caring for the listed animal(s). This may include topics such as medication, grooming, training, exercise, kennel, or boarding arrangements.

EXAMPLES:

Insulin, 6 units twice daily

Grooming at CliPPets, first Thursday of the month

Paul Stolp, farrier, 555-555-1234, maintains horses' shoes

- **Veterinarian's Contact Information.** Provide the name and contact information for each listed animal or group of animals.

Wishes for Placement

You may want your loved ones to place your animals with specific individuals or organizations, as described above. In the table, make note of your preferences in placing your animals.

- **Pet Name, Species, and Coloring.** List each pet or group of animals just as you did above.
- **Desired Placement.** Write down your preferences for the adoption or sale of animals. If you've left an animal to someone in your will or set up a pet trust, indicate that here. If you expect an animal to be put to rest, make note of that. If you have no strong preference, simply note "family choice."

EXAMPLES:

Janine Bowers has agreed to adopt Perry and Sailor. I have left some money to Janine in my will to help cover the costs of caring for them.

Frederick Kaufman has expressed interest in purchasing the goats. He can be reached at 333-444-2222.

- **Individual or Organization and Contact Information.** If a pet or group of animals will be placed with a specific individual or organization, include the name and contact information here.

BINDER

Including related materials in your planner. You can file important records for your animals in your planner. These records may include certificates of pedigree, vaccination and medical records, documents relating to any placement arrangements, or other paperwork. Use pocket divider pages or plastic sleeves, or hole-punch documents and insert them directly in your planner binder.

Additional Notes

Include any additional information about care or placement of your pets and livestock.

Keeping Your Information Up to Date

Simple changes such as the following may require updates to this section of your planner:

- You may acquire a new pet or lose an old one.
- Your investment in livestock may increase, decrease, or the type of animals you keep may change.
- Your animals' care requirements may change.
- You may change your mind about arrangements for the eventual placement of your pet.

CHAPTER

7

Employment

In Your Planner 58

Keeping Your Information Up to Date 59

I like work; it fascinates me. I can sit and look at it for hours.

—JEROME K. JEROME (1859–1927)

There are many good reasons to include employment information in your planner. While your loved ones may know where you work now, they may not know how to contact your employer or what employee benefits you're expecting. Your executor will also want information about past jobs to pursue any benefits owed to your survivors by those employers. And employment information may be useful if one of your survivors must write your obituary.

In your planner, you can provide details about current and former employment, including self-employment and volunteer work. You can also store related materials in your planner—such as a current résumé, an employment agreement, or an offer letter that guarantees certain benefits.

In Your Planner

Turn to the Employment section of your planner (Section 7). The following guidelines will help you fill in the pages there.

Current Employment

For each job you currently hold, provide the following:

- **Employer's Contact Information.** Include any information your survivors will need to contact the employer, including at least the employer's name, address, telephone number, and website. If there's a particular person your survivors should get in touch with, such as the human resources director, list that person as well. If you are self-employed, just note "self-employment" here.

EXAMPLE:
Appleton's Markets, Elway Branch
2334 Seventh Street
Elway, Indiana 22222
123-456-7890
www.appletonsmarket.com
Dorothea Parkson, Personnel Manager

- **Current Benefits and Location of Documents.** List all employment benefits to which you or your survivors are entitled, either now or in the future. These benefits may include insurance (life, medical, or disability), retirement plans, stock, or stock options. You should also describe the location of any documents related to the benefits. (See the note below for instructions on including these documents in your planner.)

EXAMPLES:

Company ESOP (see Section 20 for information and documents)

Family medical and individual life insurance (see overview and policies in Section 18)

Company stock (see Bank and Brokerage Accounts, Section 19) and Stock options (see Other Income and Personal Property, Section 27)

- **Position.** Write in some information about the position you currently hold. Include your title and whether the job is full time or part time, paid or volunteer.
- **Start Date.** List the date you began working for the employer.
- **Ownership Interest.** Indicate whether or not you have an ownership interest in the business. If you do, note the percentage.

Later, you may want to add more information about your ownership interest, in the Business Interests section of your planner. (You can use the Additional Notes section, below, to direct your survivors to that information.)

Additional Notes

Include any additional information about the topics covered above. For example, if you have a robust résumé or complete profile stored on LinkedIn or other professional network, include a note and your login information here. If you indicated that you own part of a business and you want to provide more details, you can do that here or in Section 8, Business Interests.

EXAMPLE:
See Section 8, Business Interests, for more information about my ownership interest in XYZ, Inc.

Previous Employment

The information for your past jobs is identical to that listed above, with two exceptions. First, if you held more than one position with the same company, list only your final position. Second, list both the beginning and ending employment dates with each company.

Of course, you need not list every job you ever held. List those for which any benefits are owed to you or your survivors. And you might also want to include any jobs that were particularly interesting; your loved ones might want to include the information in your obituary, or they may simply appreciate knowing this part of your life history.

Additional Notes

If you have additional information for your survivors about your previous employment, include it here.

BINDER

Including employment records in your planner. You can file materials related to your employment in this section of your planner binder. Plastic binder sleeves and pocket dividers work well for this purpose, or you may simply hole-punch documents and insert them directly into your binder.

If your employment history is documented in a résumé or curriculum vitae, include a copy in your planner immediately following this section. Supplement the résumé data by completing the outline in the Employment section of your planner.

If you want to include other employment-related documents in your planner, it's best to note the location in this section and then file the papers with the corresponding topic. For example, if your employer is a private company, papers related to stock awards would fit best right here in the Employment section. But you'll want to file documents related to publicly traded stock in Bank and Brokerage Accounts (Section 19), insurance documents in Section 18, and documents related to your retirement benefits in Section 20.

Keeping Your Information Up to Date

You'll want to update this section of your planner if your employment benefits or ownership interest change significantly, or if you:

- change jobs
- take a new position with your current employer
- relocate to a new office or a different branch with your current employer, or
- begin a volunteer job.

CHAPTER

8

Business Interests

Estate Planning for Small Business Owners 62

Where to Get Help 64

In Your Planner 64

Keeping Your Information Up to Date 68

> *My grandfather once told me that there were two kinds of people: those who do the work and those who take the credit. He told me to try to be in the first group; there was much less competition.*
>
> —INDIRA GANDHI (1917–1984)

SKIP AHEAD

If you're not a business owner. If you don't own all or part of a business, you can skip to the next chapter.

If you're a business owner, your loved ones may know the location of your business, but not much more. Your planner can help them find the answers to important questions such as:

- How much of the business do you own? If you have business partners, who are they and what are their rights and responsibilities?
- How should the business be handled if you are incapacitated and unable to run it yourself? What should happen to it after you die?
- Who should your loved ones contact to help run the business, or if your interest must be transferred or sold?
- Where are your important business records?

Your planner also lets you list any prior business interests, in case your survivors have questions about them.

Before turning to the specifics of how to complete your planner, this chapter provides a brief introduction to some of the special estate planning concerns of small business owners and some resources to help you make a small business estate plan.

RELATED TOPIC

If you own only stock or stock options. If your interest is limited to stock or stock options, you can skip this chapter and describe the assets in another section of the planner. Use Chapter 19, Bank and Brokerage Accounts, if the stock is held by a broker. If you hold the documents yourself, you can describe them in Chapter 27, Other Income and Personal Property. Finally, if your stock is part of a retirement plan, list it in Chapter 20, Retirement Plans and Pensions.

SKIP AHEAD

If your business affairs are in order. If you already have a good plan for transferring your business interests after your death, you may want to skip right to "In Your Planner" for information on completing your planner. Then read "Keeping Your Information Up to Date," at the end of the chapter.

Estate Planning for Small Business Owners

A small business (sometimes called a "closely held" business) is one that is owned by an individual or a small number of people. If you own all or part of such a business, you can save your loved ones (and any business partners) lots of headaches—and probably lots of money—by making some decisions about what should happen to the business when you can no longer participate in it.

Planning for your business should include:

- **Succession plan.** Think about what will happen to your business. Will it be sold, or are there family members or key employees who are interested in taking over when you're gone? Do you need life insurance or legal documents that will help to ensure a smooth transition? For example, if you own your business with others, you and your co-owners may need a buy-sell agreement to document your understanding about what will happen to the business when one of you passes away. Or, if you want your business to stay in the family, you may need to make estate planning documents to ensure that your business interests are distributed as you wish. To craft a solid plan, it's wise to consult an experienced financial adviser or attorney, and to talk with those you envision as future leaders of the company.
- **Business documentation.** Those who succeed you, or those who wrap up operations, will need information about the company: its owners, key employees, professional advisers, accounting records, legal and tax documents, significant assets and liabilities. You can document this information in the Business Interests section of your planner.
- **Succession training.** Finally, if you will pass your business to others, identify the characteristics you want in your successor or successors. Evaluate several candidates. Familiarize your chosen successor with the company and what it takes to run it. Expect to spend some time on this process. Choosing and grooming a successor may take a few years.

Because business owners invest so much of themselves in building a business, it's usually hard to imagine disengaging from it. But that's just what this kind of planning is about—preparing for the future and taking steps to ensure continued success for the business and for the people involved. After years of investing in your company's success, you don't want to let it slip away for lack of planning.

Basic Rules for Transferring a Business

When a business owner becomes incapacitated or dies, the options for passing the business to others depend on the form of ownership. Here are some very general rules:

- **Sole proprietorship.** The business will cease unless the assets are inherited by or sold to someone who wants to keep the business going.
- **Partnership.** A partnership can usually continue to operate if the remaining partners want to stay in business. Typically, the partnership will buy out the deceased person's interest. Your partnership agreement should set out the terms.
- **Limited liability company.** The company will dissolve when one member dies, unless the operating agreement sets out a different plan.
- **Corporation.** As an independent legal entity, a corporation is distinct from its individual owners. That means that the death of an owner has no legal effect on the business. The deceased owner's shares in the company can be transferred to heirs or purchased by the corporation. You can set out the terms in your shareholders' agreement.

While it's possible for any type of business to continue after an owner's incapacity or death, there are likely to be some practical challenges—both financial and personal. If you want your business to continue, your plan should address how others will take it forward, including who will run it and where they'll get the funds to manage the transition.

Where to Get Help

You can find extensive—and free—information for small business owners on Nolo's website, at www.nolo.com. In particular, you'll find a number of articles about planning for a business transition. There are other good sources for information, tips, and links for small business owners, including:

- **U.S. Small Business Administration:** www.sba.gov or 800-827-5722. The SBA provides assistance to small businesses, including help with succession planning, selling, transferring ownership, or liquidating your business. From the SBA home page, select "Starting & Managing a Business" and click on "Getting Out."
- **The Service Corps of Retired Executives (SCORE):** www.score.org or 800-634-0245. SCORE is an organization of retired business managers that provides free (or low cost) and confidential assistance to business owners. Face-to-face counseling is available through more than 340 regional offices, and information is available online.
- **The Business Owner's Toolkit:** www.toolkit.com. This broad resource provides practical, legal, and tax information for small business owners. Among many other topics, you can find articles on business succession and transfer.

The following books can also help you:

- ***Effective Succession Planning: Ensuring Leadership Continuity and Building Talent From Within,*** by William J. Rothwell (AMACON), is a comprehensive guide to developing, monitoring, and evaluating a succession plan.
- ***Family Business Succession: Your Roadmap to Continuity,*** by Kelly LeCouvie and Jennifer Pendergast (Family Business Publications), is a comprehensive guide to family business succession planning. It discusses the nature of family business ownership, structuring ownership bylaws, leadership transition, and retirement of the founder.

Estate planning for small business owners is a complex task that must take into account personal and family needs as well as those of business partners. It's important that you follow up with experts—an experienced small business estate planning attorney and possibly an accountant—to develop a comprehensive plan. For help finding experts, see Appendix B.

In Your Planner

Turn to the Business Interests section of your planner (Section 8). The following guidelines will help you complete the pages there.

Current Business Interests

Here, you will describe your active business interests. If you have an ownership interest in more than one business, photocopy the blank business pages or print out an additional set using the eForms so that you have enough space to list multiple businesses.

Name and Location

Use this table to provide basic information about what your business is called and where your survivors can find it.

- **Business Name and Type of Business.** Provide the full, legal name of the business and the type of business—for example, sole proprietorship, partnership, LLC, or corporation.

  EXAMPLES:

  H.H. Jones, DDS, Sole Proprietorship

  Steadman Enterprises, General Partnership

  Laboratory Services LLC, a limited liability company

  Western Vintners, Inc., S Corporation

  U.S. Services Company, Corporation

- **Main Office Address and Telephone.** Provide the address and telephone number for the main office, headquarters, or parent company.

EXAMPLES:

H.H. Jones, DDS, 123 Willow Avenue, Pacific Grove, CA 93950, 333-333-3333

333 Fourth Street, Los Angeles, CA 99999, 555-555-1234

DBA International, Inc., 40 Broadway, New York, NY 11111, 555-555-5555

- **Subsidiaries or Branch Offices.** If the business has more than one branch, list offices other than the main office here. If necessary, include additional pages to list full information about subsidiary businesses.

EXAMPLES:

Steadman Maintenance Services, 344 Fourth Street, Suite 34, Los Angeles, CA 99999, 555-555-2345; Steadman Construction, 344 Fourth Street, Building B, Los Angeles, CA 99999, 555-555-4567; Steadman Call Center Services, 978 Sixth Street, Los Angeles, CA 99998, 555-555-0123

The Laboratory, A Division of Laboratory Services LLC, 1115 Fourth Street, Rogue River, OR 88888, 555-555-4444

123 First Avenue, Ketchikan, AK 99001, 555-555-3333; 777 Willowshade Plaza, Los Angeles, CA 93333, 444-444-4444

Ownership

This section covers essential information about who owns the business—and under what terms.

- **Business Owners.** List the full name of each business owner, including yourself.
- **Contact Information.** Provide an address, telephone numbers, email addresses, or other contact information for each owner.
- **Job Title or Position.** Provide the job title or position for each business owner, including yourself.

EXAMPLES:

Director & Lead Vintner

Maintenance Services Manager

Vice President, Laboratory Operations

Owner

- **Ownership Percentage.** Provide the percentage of the business owned by each business owner. When you're done, the total for all owners should add up to 100%.
- **Ownership Documents.** Provide the titles of the governing ownership documents for the business.

EXAMPLES:

Bilow & Sellhi Investments Partnership Agreement

XYZ, Inc. Corporate Bylaws, Records, and Minute Book

Johns & Daughters Buy-Sell Agreement

- **Location of Documents.** Indicate where the ownership documents are filed, including necessary access or contact information.

EXAMPLES:

Original filed in safe in Records Room (Room 4B, SW corner of office); access information follows in Assets table. Copy of document filed at back of this section.

Minute Book stored with Ishikawa & Wright, Attorneys at Law (see contact information below).

Disposition

Here, you provide important guidance about what should happen to the business, and to your individual interest in the business, if you become incapacitated, or after your death.

- **Disposition of Entire Business.** Check the appropriate box—Continue, Transfer, Sell, or Liquidate (see below for definitions of these terms)—to indicate your plans for the business as a whole if you become incapacitated or die. If the disposition method depends on the circumstances, check two or more boxes and describe your plans in the Disposition Notes section of the table.

- **Disposition of My Interest.** Check the appropriate box—Transfer, Sell, or Liquidate—to indicate your plans for your business interest if you become incapacitated or die. Again, if the disposition depends on circumstances, check two or more boxes and describe your plans in Disposition Notes.

Business Disposition: Your Choices

There are four primary ways to handle the disposition of your business or your interest in a business:

- **Continue:** The surviving owners will continue to run the business. (Obviously, this is not an option for your individual interest in a business.)
- **Transfer:** The business will continue to operate, but ownership will be transferred (not sold) to specific others, such as your surviving business partners, family, or friends.
- **Sell:** The business will continue to operate, but it (or your interest) will be sold to new owners.
- **Liquidate:** The business or your interest will dissolve and substantially all assets will be sold.

- **Contact Information for Key Individuals.** Provide the names and contact information for those who can provide business support to your survivors if you are unavailable. Be sure to include contact information for the attorney and accountant most familiar with your business.
- **Disposition Notes.** For each business, write a brief description of your plans for the business upon your incapacity or death.

EXAMPLES:

The immediate sale and transfer of the business is outlined in the Buy-Sell Agreement; see my note below for location.

Jake and Barbara Williams (501-501-5011) are very interested in purchasing the business when we're ready to sell. Contact them when it's time.

Business has fallen off during my semiretirement, so just sell the assets. Contact the Central Mountain Taxidermist Association (email: info@centralmountain.org). They can give you direction and some leads. (See my membership information in Section 9.)

- **Title and Location of Documents.** Provide the title and location of any documents related to the disposition of the business. Include any necessary access information (such as keys or codes) or contacts (for example, if there is someone who can help with the files).

EXAMPLES:

ABC Company Buy-Sell Agreement, original in storeroom safe (combination 55-12-02, key is in pencil drawer of my desk)

Friend's Hardware, Partner Buyout Agreement and life insurance policies on all three partners. All original documents stored with our lawyer, Louise Harris (contact information above).

Key Employees

Identify key employees—those your survivors should contact for help plus anyone who has a special employment agreement with the business.

- **Employee Name.** Provide the full name of the employee.

- **Agreement.** If an agreement exists between the employee and the business—such as an employment agreement or an offer letter outlining benefits—identify the title of the document.

  EXAMPLES:

  Bilow & Sellhi Employment Agreement, dated July 1, 2014

  Offer Letter from Sally Johns, 3 pages, February 13, 2010

- **Location of Documents.** Indicate where the agreement is filed, including any necessary access or contact information.
- **Other Information.** Include any additional information related to key employees or their agreements with the business.

  EXAMPLES:

  Molly (home 555-789-1234) has been our bookkeeper since 1979. She is competent and helpful.

  He works from home (444-456-3434) two days per week (Tuesday, Thursday).

  She has been with us for years and years; please treat her very well as you sell the company.

Business Taxes

Provide the location for receipts and documents related to business tax records and returns.

- **Current-Year Records.** Give the location for the business's accounting records, including necessary access or contact information.
- **Prior-Year Records.** Indicate the location for old tax returns for the business, including necessary access or contact information.

Significant Assets and Liabilities

It will help your survivors if you provide a brief overview of the significant assets and liabilities of your businesses.

In the Assets table, describe important business assets, including bank and brokerage accounts, safe deposit boxes, inventories, insurance, judgments, real estate, fixtures and equipment, vehicles, accounts receivable, patents, copyrights, trademarks, or trade secrets.

- **Description of Asset.** Provide a brief description of the business asset.
- **Location of Asset.** Indicate where your survivors can find the asset.
- **Access Information.** Provide any directions for obtaining the asset, such as keys, codes, or combinations.
- **Contact Name and Information.** If there is someone who uses, manages, or oversees the asset, provide the person's full name and contact information.
- **Location of Documents.** Give the location of any documents related to the asset—such as account statements; inventory reports; purchase, appraisal, or title documents; or registration statements.

In the Liabilities table, provide a summary of short- and long-term liabilities of the business, including significant expenses (such as a real estate lease or equipment rental charges), loans, deferred accruals, judgments, and retiree benefits.

- **Description of Liability.** Provide a brief description of the business liability.
- **Contact Name and Information.** Provide contact information for the individual or organization that is due compensation on each business liability.
- **Location of Documents.** Provide the location of any documents related to the liability, such as purchase, judgment, or title documents.

Additional Notes

This is the place to give any other instructions that may help your survivors. For example, you might:

- identify the accounting method that you use
- give additional details about how to get into the office or building, such as keys, combinations, access codes, or security cards
- provide important vendor or customer information, including relevant documents for products, services, or maintenance
- identify benefit programs, including those for retirement, disability, and health, or
- provide an overview of any outstanding legal action in which the business has a responsibility or an interest.

Prior Business Interests

Document any business interests that have been fully resolved and terminated—just in case your survivors have questions or face a claim in the future.

Space is provided for three prior business interests. Add more pages if you need them.

- **Business Name and Type of Business.** Provide the full, legal name of the business and the type of business—for example, sole proprietorship, partnership, LLC, or corporation.
- **Main Office Address and Telephone.** Provide the address and telephone for the main office or location.
- **Ownership and Dissolution Documents.** Include the titles of the governing ownership documents and the final dissolution documents.

  EXAMPLES:

  Soldlow Investments, Inc. Corporate Bylaws, Records, and Minute Book

  Johns & Daughters Buy-Sell Agreement, Johns & Daughters Statement of Dissolution (March 1, 2005)

- **Location of Documents.** Indicate where the ownership and dissolution documents are filed, including necessary access or contact information.
- **Contact Information.** List the name and contact information for the attorney, accountant, or former co-owners who may be able to answer questions or provide information for your survivors.

Additional Notes

If you have any additional information or direction regarding your prior business interests, include it here.

BINDER

Including business-related materials in your planner. You can file key business documents or related materials in your planner. Depending on the nature of the materials, you can insert them in a pocket divider page or plastic sleeve, store them in plastic binder pouches (this works well for small items such as keys), or hole-punch documents and insert them into your planner binder immediately following the Business Interests section.

Keeping Your Information Up to Date

Review and update business information regularly, because key individuals and contact information may change. Also be sure to review and update your business information if any of the following things change:

- your ownership percentage
- your wishes for disposition, or
- major business assets or liabilities.

CHAPTER

9

Memberships and Communities

Types of Memberships and Communities 70

Professional and Civic 70

Educational 70

Fraternal and Service 71

Religious, Spiritual, and Healing 71

Social 71

Recreational 72

Charitable 72

Consumer 72

Membership Benefits for Survivors 72

Transferring Frequent Flyer Miles 72

Leave Clear Access Instructions 73

Donate Your Miles 73

Sell or Trade Your Miles 73

Where to Get Help 74

In Your Planner 74

Keeping Your Information Up to Date 75

We have lived and loved together through many changing years;
We have shared each other's gladness, and wept each other's tears.

—CHARLES JEFFERYS (1807–1865)

If someone asked you what groups or clubs you belong to, a few might spring to mind—perhaps a fraternal organization, a church, a book club. But almost all of us are members of more organizations than we commonly think of—from our local gym to frequent flyer clubs to online communities. Making a list of all the groups, clubs, organizations, and programs in which you participate can help your loved ones with many tasks, including notifying people of your death, completing your obituary, canceling memberships, and managing accounts.

Further, you may accumulate valuable assets or benefits in a membership account—such as frequent flyer miles or digital photo albums—and these may be transferred to survivors upon your death.

In your planner, you can summarize information about your memberships, including contact information, positions you have held, your membership number or other identification, and login details. You can also file related documents in your planner—for example, membership cards or certificates, certificates of honor or achievement, and recent statements for frequent flyer or frequent shopper accounts.

Before turning to the specifics of completing your planner, this chapter provides a list of membership types to help jog your mind and some basic information about transferring membership benefits to others.

Types of Memberships and Communities

This comprehensive list will help to prompt your thinking about memberships you should list in your planner.

Professional and Civic

- **Networking** (LinkedIn, Google+)
- **Business Associations** (Chamber of Commerce, Jaycees, Business and Professional Women)
- **Professional Organizations** (American Dental Association, American Farm Bureau, Association of Information Technology Professionals, Institute of Transportation Engineers)
- **Trade Unions** (AFL-CIO, International Brotherhood of Teamsters, United Auto Workers, United Farm Workers, Service Employees International Union)
- **Veterans Organizations** (American Legion, Grand Army of the Republic, Veterans of Foreign Wars)
- **Political** (First Amendment Coalition, League of Women Voters, online blog)
- **Civic Rights Groups** (American Civil Liberties Union, League of Women Voters, National Organization for Women, National Rifle Association, National Grange).

Educational

- **Honor Societies** (Sigma Xi, Phi Beta Kappa, Mensa)

- **Alumni Associations**
- **Social Groups** (fraternity, sorority, special interest clubs)
- **School Support Organizations** (PTA).

Fraternal and Service

- **All Fraternal and Service Groups** (Masonic, Kiwanis, Lions Club International, Rotary International, Odd Fellows, Moose Lodge).

Religious, Spiritual, and Healing

- **Church or Spiritual Group** (including small groups such as bible study or a meditation practice group)
- **Self-Help** (12-step, Weight Watchers).

Social

- **Ethnic or Cultural** (NAACP, Urban League, Knights of Columbus, Sons of Poland)

Online Connections After You're Gone

Practice, policy, and law are rapidly evolving for online communities and the accounts of someone who has died. You may want to research the current treatment and opportunities for the accounts that you have, and then document your wishes in Section 9 of your planner (Memberships and Communities). Here is a high-level overview of current account treatment for some popular sites:

- **Dropbox** provides transfer of account content on request from an agent or executor.
- **eHarmony** will deactivate and remove account content on request from an agent or executor.
- **Facebook** will remove pages, memorialize the account, and transfer content on request from an agent or executor.
- **Google** offers user-configured Inactive Account Manager, a module that tracks account inactivity. A user can establish a contact person who will receive notice and transfer of account data. Further, Google may transfer account content on request from an agent or executor.
- **LinkedIn** will close an account and remove the associated profile upon verified request.
- **Match** will deactivate and remove account content on request from an immediate family member or executor, and will refund to the estate any balance on an unused subscription.
- **MySpace** will delete a profile upon request by a family member or executor, who must provide the user's identification number (not user name or profile link). The company will not provide access or allow edits to content or settings.
- **Picasa** is owned by Google, so content is governed by Inactive Account Manager or special request; see Google above.
- **Shutterfly** will provide access to an account on request from an immediate family member or executor.
- **Twitter** will deactivate an account and stop "Who to Follow" upon verified request from an immediate family member or executor.
- **Yahoo!** will close an account, suspend billing, and delete account contents on request from a personal representative or executor. The company will not provide account access or transfer of content.
- **YouTube** is owned by Google, so content is governed by Inactive Account Manager or special request; see Google above.

Get details about each account's policies by searching for more information on its website.

- **Lineage** (Daughters of the American Revolution, The Mayflower Society)
- **Lifestyle** (parenting, singles, LGBT, retired)
- **Online Connections** (Facebook, Twitter, eHarmony, personal blog).

Recreational

- **Athletic** (gym, athletic teams, online fitness communities)
- **Arts and Crafts** (quilting bee, lapidary club, painters' group, writing group)
- **Special Interest** (stamp collecting, book group, bird watchers' club, gaming)
- **Youth** (Big Brothers or Sisters, Boy Scouts, Girl Scouts, Campfire USA, Future Farmers of America, 4-H).

Charitable

- **Civic Organizations** (Friends of the Library, Save Our Schools)
- **Social Support Organizations** (food banks, free clinics, hospital funds)
- **Environmental Advocacy or Conservation** (Nature Conservancy, Greenpeace, Sierra Club)
- **Support for the Arts** (foundations or funds to support artists or museums)
- **Religious or Spiritual Organizations** (faith-based charitable programs).

Consumer

- **Frequent Flyer**
- **Frequent Shopper** (grocery, major credit card with rebates feature)
- **Retail Memberships** (Costco, Sam's Club, co-op, Netflix, Pandora One, Amazon Prime)
- **Co-op Vehicle Program** (organization for sharing cars, boats, planes)
- **Other Consumer** (AAA; AMAC or AARP; subscription to online greeting cards, news, other periodicals).

Membership Benefits for Survivors

Some of your memberships may carry benefits that can be transferred to your survivors. In your planner, you will want to note any benefits or assets connected with a membership, so that your caretakers or survivors can follow up on each.

Some common membership benefits that may be transferred to survivors include:

- purchase discounts for retail products, services, or events
- newsletters, magazines, or books
- paid-up services, such as roadside assistance, and
- free products or services, such as hotel accommodations or airline tickets.

The value of free airline tickets from frequent flyer accounts can be significant. At the same time, it can be tricky to transfer these miles—and some airlines prohibit such transfers altogether. The discussion in the next section can help you ensure that your account miles are used and not lost.

TIP

Refunds of membership dues. If you pay dues or fees for your membership, your caretakers or survivors may be able to apply for a refund if you become incapacitated or die. In your planner, you can indicate possible amounts due on individual memberships.

Transferring Frequent Flyer Miles

Each frequent flyer program works a little differently, but most airlines are making it increasingly difficult to transfer miles to someone else when you die. Here are some options for using or leaving your frequent flyer miles:

Leave Clear Access Instructions

At this writing, the frequent-flyer rules for only one U.S. air carrier state that miles can be transferred upon a death. For all other carriers, program rules state that miles are nontransferrable. Yet, in practice, agents often facilitate the transfer when a beneficiary provides a copy of the death certificate and pays a fee of about $50. It's a gamble, as arbitrary as which agent will answer your call.

If you have valuable miles in a frequent flyer program, you may not wish to take that risk. As an alternative, know that you can use your miles, at any time, to book air travel for anyone you like. You can book that travel today, while you are living, or your loved ones can book that travel after your death. If this is the route you go, just ensure you leave clear access instructions in this section of your planner.

Donate Your Miles

Several organizations have set up programs that allow you to donate frequent flyer miles. If you are interested in helping others by donating your miles, here are some worthy groups to contact:

- **Hero Miles.** Miles donated to Hero Miles are made available to soldiers for round-trip leave travel from a military or Veterans Administration hospital to the soldier's home. In addition, the miles are used to fly family members to the hospital caring for the wounded soldier. To make a donation, visit Hero Miles online at www.fisherhouse.org/programs/hero-miles or call 888-294-8560.
- **The American Red Cross.** The American Red Cross responds to domestic and international emergencies, providing critical relief in the face of disasters. The organization also provides community services, produces planning and prevention publications, provides training, sponsors youth services, and much more—at no charge to those receiving aid. Frequent flyer miles donated to the Red Cross are used solely for disaster-related travel in support of Red Cross response. To arrange a donation to the American Red Cross, you must have miles with an airline that participates in the donation program. Participating airlines include Continental, Delta, United, and US Airways. Contact the airline for more information.
- **Special Olympics.** Special Olympics is an international organization "dedicated to empowering individuals with intellectual disabilities to become physically fit, productive, and respected members of society through sports training and competition." Donations of frequent flyer miles are used by Special Olympics to assist participating athletes and delegation members to reduce their costs of travel to Special Olympics events. To arrange a donation to the Special Olympics, you must have miles with United Airlines. Contact the airline for more information.
- **Make-A-Wish Foundation.** The Make-A-Wish Foundation enriches the lives of children who have life-threatening medical conditions, using more than 2.5 billion airline miles each year to grant travel wishes. Make-A-Wish has formal donation partnerships with several airlines and can generally use transferable vouchers or tickets from other carriers. Visit Make-A-Wish online at www.wish.org or by telephone at 800-722-9474.

Several airlines can arrange donations to other charitable organizations. For more information, contact the customer service center for your frequent flyer program.

Sell or Trade Your Miles

Some frequent flyer programs will let you sell or trade your miles. For example, United offers tickets to games, live theater, concerts, and other special events through auctions on their website. United also lets you purchase magazine subscriptions, brand-name merchandise, flowers or gifts, gift cards, or tickets to live performances with miles. If you want to find ways to use and enjoy your miles during your life, contact the customer service center for your frequent flyer program.

Removing, Memorializing, or Acquiring Content from a Facebook Account

An authorized representative (that is, agent or executor) may request that Facebook remove pages, memorialize the account, and even transfer content from the account of someone who has died.

- When removed, the decedent's Timeline and all content is no longer displayed.
- A memorialized account is essentially frozen. Available content can be viewed according to existing privacy settings. No friends or content may be added, changed, or removed. If privacy settings allow, friends can share memories on the Timeline (and send private messages). Friend suggestions and celebration reminders cease.
- The content of the account can be packaged and transferred to loved ones.

Facebook will not allow family or friends log-on access to the account of a person who has died.

Where to Get Help

If a membership has significant benefits associated with it, you may want to contact the group or organization now to ensure that they will be transferred without a hitch. Any arrangements or paperwork you prepare in advance will help to smooth the way for your survivors.

For more information on frequent flyer programs, visit Airfare Watchdog (www.airfarewatchdog.com), FrequentFlier.com (www.frequentflier.com), or WebFlyer (www.webflyer.com). All provide online information and advice for frequent flyer members, across all airlines. You can subscribe to free newsletters and use online forums to share information about frequent flyer programs.

In Your Planner

Turn to the Memberships and Communities section of your planner (Section 9). The following guidelines will help you fill in the pages there.

- **Organization Name and Contact Information.** List the name and contact information for any group, club, program, or organization of which you are a member. In addition to active memberships, include any important former memberships—your survivors might want to notify these organizations of your death or include your membership in your obituary. If a membership is inactive, use the Additional Notes field (described just below) to say so.
- **Account Name, Password, Membership Number, or Position Held.** Include your membership identification or account number, account name, password, and your title or position held, if applicable.
- **Additional Notes.** Include additional information about the organization, your membership, or access instructions. If you have specific directions for how an item is handled—for example, posting an update on your personal blog—include that here.

  If the membership involves any assets or benefits that should be transferred after death, such as frequent flyer miles, be sure to indicate that here—including the person who should receive the asset or benefit and the steps the beneficiary needs to take. (Keep in mind that, legally, it won't usually be enough to indicate your wishes here. You might want to make the transfer official by leaving the benefits, such as frequent flyer miles, in your will.)

Also describe whether you have paid membership dues or fees (your survivors may be able to apply for a refund), whether you received any awards from the organization, and the status of your membership—that is, whether or not you are currently active in the organization.

EXAMPLES:

Member, Elder 2011–2014

Dues paid through June 10; contact for refund ($48 per year)

Contact Twitter to deactivate and remove my account from "Who to follow."

BINDER

Including membership information in your planner. You can insert your certificates of membership or achievement, recent account statements, and related membership materials in your planner binder in pocket divider pages or plastic sleeves. Or just hole-punch the documents and add them at the end of the Memberships and Communities section.

Keeping Your Information Up to Date

You might want to skim this section once a year or so, because simply initiating a new membership or letting an old one lapse will require an update. You should also update this section if you acquire or terminate membership benefits, or change your mind about how you want to leave any transferable benefits to others.

CHAPTER

10

Service Providers

In Your Planner 78

Keeping Your Information Up to Date 80

> *Whatever you are, be a good one.*
>
> —ABRAHAM LINCOLN (1809–1865)

Service providers may include everyone from your doctor and dentist to the person who cuts your hair or mows your lawn. Listing these people or organizations in your planner will help caretakers and survivors manage expenses and provide ongoing care for you (if you are incapacitated) and your home or properties (either before or after your death).

You can also include related materials and instructions in your planner—service contracts, schedules, and important information about individual providers (such as the fact that the pool maintenance folks have a key to the back gate). In addition to helping your loved ones, keeping this type of information and material in your planner will help you stay organized.

In Your Planner

Turn to the Service Providers section of your planner (Section 10). The following guidelines will help you complete the pages there.

Health Care Providers

List those who provide your medical, dental, vision, psychiatric, or other health-related services.

- **Name and Contact Information.** Provide the name and contact information for the individual or organization. Include the address, telephone numbers, email address, and website, if any.
- **Type of Care and Location.** Describe the type of care or service. If you have a regular schedule with the service provider—such as the day and time for a regularly scheduled appointment—include that here. Also, if you see a health care provider at a location other than that listed with the contact information, note the location here.

EXAMPLES:

Primary care physician

Orthopedic surgeon

Speech therapy, 2:30 p.m. Wednesday (every two weeks)

Massage, Monday at 4:00 p.m. (June through August), at Colorado Canyon home

Other Service Providers

Identify those that provide your personal care, home, vehicle, and other services.

RELATED TOPIC

Product guides and vehicle service records. Describe the location of product guides and repair information for personal property (such as household appliances) in Section 27 of your planner (Other Income and Personal Property). Describe the location of vehicle service records in Section 26 (Vehicles).

- **Name and Contact Information.** Provide the name and contact information for the individual or organization. Include the address, telephone numbers, email address, and website, if any.
- **Type of Service and Location.** Describe the type of care or service. If the provider has a regular schedule—such as a set day and time for your housecleaner—include that here. Also note the location for the service, if it differs from the address listed with the contact information.

Common Types of Services

This list of common services may prompt your thinking about the various service providers you should list in your planner.

Medical

- Primary care
- Specialized medicine
- Chiropractic
- Physical therapy
- Massage therapy
- Acupuncture
- Holistic medicine
- Hypnotherapy
- Speech therapy
- Pharmacy

Dental

- Dentistry
- Specialized dental care

Vision

- Ophthalmology
- Optometry
- Optical products

Personal

- Beauty treatments
- Training and tutoring
- Meal preparation
- Grocery shopping
- Home care (assistance with bathing, dressing, or meals)
- Driving

Mental and Spiritual Health

- Psychiatry
- Psychology
- Spiritual direction
- Other counseling

Home and Household

- Chimney sweeping and maintenance
- House cleaning and window washing
- Water softener service
- Handywork and odd jobs
- Pool and spa maintenance
- Pond maintenance
- Firewood delivery
- Gardening
- Pest control service
- Water cooler service
- House sitting

Vehicle

- Vehicle repair and maintenance

Other

- Sports equipment maintenance
- Computer and website support
- Agricultural spraying
- Piano tuning

EXAMPLES:

Housecleaning, 1st and 3rd Wednesday each month

Pool care, every Friday (May through Sept), Lake Tahoe home

Weekly gardening services at home (345 Elm Street) and rental complexes (555 41st Street and 816 Tanglewood)

Additional Notes

Provide any other notes, instructions, or details. If you have secured access (whether physical or electronic) relating to the service provider, describe that here—including keys, codes, account names, and passwords. If you have an agreement for services—other than insurance, which you should note in Section 18—mention that here.

EXAMPLES:

Jenny (Awe Massage) has supplies stored in the study of my home. She'll want to retrieve them.

Sky Blue has keys to the side gate and the pool cover so they can service the pool each week. Service contract is filed here; pool product guides are in Warranty file (desk).

My online login information for email, Rx, and appointments is ACCT SandyShore, PW 0!23J011Y.

If you need any sprinkler or timer repairs (at home or at rentals), ask Mitch (gardener). His crew is handy—and very helpful.

BINDER

Including service provider materials in your planner. You can file any related documents—service agreements and the like—in your planner. It's probably easiest to hole-punch standard-sized paperwork and insert it in the binder immediately following the Service Providers section. If you have any small or irregularly sized items, you can include them in a plastic binder pouch, plastic sleeve, or binder pocket.

Keeping Your Information Up to Date

If you arrange for a new provider or stop working with an old one, or if you change an established schedule, you'll want to be sure your planner reflects that information. Also, you should occasionally sort through your related records, tossing out anything that is out of date (such as old contracts) and adding anything new.

CHAPTER

11

Health Care Directives

Types of Health Care Directives 82

How Health Care Directives Work 83

Who Can Make Health Care Directives 83

Who Needs to Make Health Care Directives 83

Making Your Documents Legal 83

When Your Health Care Directives Take Effect 83

When Your Health Care Directives End 84

Choosing Your Health Care Agent 84

Important Factors to Consider 84

Naming More Than One Agent 85

Naming an Alternate Agent 85

If You Do Not Name a Health Care Agent 85

What You Can Cover in Your Health Care Directives 86

Your Health Care Declaration 86

Your Durable Power of Attorney for Health Care 88

Duty of Medical Personnel to Honor Your Health Care Directives 89

Where to Get Help 89

In Your Planner 89

Keeping Your Documents Up to Date 91

> *People are like stained-glass windows. They sparkle and shine when the sun is out, but when the darkness sets in, their true beauty is revealed only if there is a light from within.*
>
> —ELISABETH KÜBLER ROSS, M.D. (1926–2004)

Health care directives are legal documents setting out your wishes for medical care in case you are ever unable to speak for yourself. If you don't do at least a little bit of planning—writing down your wishes about the kinds of treatment you do or don't want to receive and naming someone you trust to oversee your care—these important matters could wind up in the hands of family members, doctors, and sometimes even judges, who may know very little about what you would prefer.

This chapter explains in detail what health care directives are, how to make them, and how to include information about them in your planner.

SKIP AHEAD

If you've already made health care documents. If you already have valid documents directing your health care, you can skip right to "In Your Planner" for directions on including your documents in your planner. Then read "Keeping Your Documents Up to Date," at the end of the chapter.

Types of Health Care Directives

There are two basic documents that allow you to set out your wishes for medical care, both grouped under the broad label "health care directives" or "advance directives." It's wise to prepare both. First, you need a "declaration," commonly known as a "living will." This is a written statement you make directly to medical personnel that details the type of care you want (or don't want) if you become incapacitated. You can use your declaration to say as much or as little as you wish about the kind of health care you want. (For more on this, see "What You Can Cover in Your Health Care Directives," below.)

Next, you'll want what's usually called a "durable power of attorney for health care." In this document, you appoint someone you trust to be your health care agent (sometimes called an "attorney-in-fact for health care" or "health care proxy") to see that doctors and other health care providers give you the type of care you wish to receive.

In some states, both of these documents are combined into a single form.

Other Names for Health Care Directives

Depending on the state, your health care documents may be called by one of several different names, such as advance directive, medical directive, directive to physicians, declaration regarding health care, designation of health care surrogate, or patient advocate designation. A health care declaration is often called a "living will," but it bears no relation to the conventional will or living trust used to leave property at death.

How Health Care Directives Work

Here are the basics of health care directives: who can (and should) make them, how to be sure they're legally valid, and when they begin and end.

Who Can Make Health Care Directives

You must be at least 18 years old to make a valid document directing your health care. (In Alabama, you must be at least 19. In Nebraska, you must be at least 19 or married.) You must also be of sound mind—that is, able to understand what the document means, what it contains, and how it works.

Who Needs to Make Health Care Directives

Every adult can benefit from writing down health care preferences and naming someone to make medical decisions. It's especially important to plan ahead if your circumstances make it likely that family members won't understand your preferences, or if a court might be inclined to appoint someone other than your first choice to make decisions for you. For example, if you're in a committed relationship but you haven't married or registered as domestic partners, you'll probably want health care documents to ensure your partner can take responsibility for your health care decisions if you ever need help. Without the right legal documents, a court could choose another family member to make medical decisions on your behalf.

It's also crucial to prepare documents if you feel strongly about any of the details of your medical care. Only you know the particulars of your wishes—for example, that you never want to be placed on a respirator or have doctors make other heroic efforts to save your life if you are terminally ill. Writing down what you want is the best way to make your feelings known.

Even if you are married, it's wise to make health care documents. We all know that family members sometimes struggle, especially in times of stress, and it is not unheard of for family members to end up in court, fighting with a spouse about what constitutes appropriate care for a loved one. Putting your wishes in writing will provide valuable guidance for everyone—your spouse, other family members, and even a court if it ever comes down to that.

Making Your Documents Legal

Every state requires that you sign your health care documents. If you are physically unable to sign them yourself, you can direct another person to sign them for you.

You must sign your documents, or have them signed for you, in the presence of witnesses or a notary public—sometimes both, depending on your state law. The purpose of this additional formality is to ensure that there is at least one other person who can confirm that you were of sound mind and of legal age when you made the documents.

When Your Health Care Directives Take Effect

Your health care documents take effect if your doctor determines that you lack the ability, or capacity, to make your own health care decisions. The definition of incapacity varies from state to state, but lacking capacity usually means that:

- you can't understand the nature and consequences of the health care choices that are available to you, and
- you are unable to communicate your own wishes for care, either orally, in writing, or through gestures.

Practically speaking, this means that if you are so ill or injured that you cannot express your health care wishes in any way, your documents will spring immediately into effect. If, however, there is some question about your ability to understand your treatment choices and communicate clearly, your doctor (with the input of your health care agent or close relatives) will decide whether it is time for your health care documents to become operative.

In some states, it is possible to give your health care agent the authority to manage your medical care immediately. If your state allows this option, you may prefer to make an immediately effective document so that your agent can step in to act for you at any time, without the need to involve a doctor in the question of whether or not your health care document should take effect.

Making your document effective immediately will not give your agent the authority to override what you want in terms of treatment; you will always be able to dictate your own medical care if you have the ability to do so. And even when you are no longer capable of making your own decisions, your health care agent must always act in your best interests and diligently try to follow any health care wishes you've expressed in your health care declaration or otherwise.

When Your Health Care Directives End

Your written wishes for health care remain effective as long as you are alive, unless you specifically revoke your documents or a court steps in. (A health care document may remain effective after your death for very limited purposes—for instance, if you give your health care agent power to oversee your wishes for organ donation or carry out your funeral plans.)

Court involvement is very rare. A court will invalidate your health care document or revoke your agent's authority only if there is a serious problem, such as a showing that you signed your health care documents under pressure (without understanding what you were doing) or that your agent is not acting according to your wishes or in your best interests.

In some states, the authority of your health care agent may be automatically revoked if you marry or divorce. For this reason, if you get married, and your existing health care power of attorney names someone other than your new spouse as your agent, you should make a new document. Conversely, if you and your spouse part ways, you should make a new document appointing someone else as your health care agent.

Choosing Your Health Care Agent

When you make a durable power of attorney for health care, the most important decision you will face is deciding who your health care agent should be. The person you choose should be someone you trust absolutely—and someone with whom you feel confident discussing your wishes for medical care. Your agent need not agree with all of your wishes, but must completely respect your right to get the kind of treatment you want.

Important Factors to Consider

Your agent may be your spouse or partner, relative, or close friend. Keep in mind that your agent may have to fight to assert your wishes in the face of a stubborn medical establishment—and against the wishes of family members who may be driven by their own beliefs and interests, rather than yours. If you foresee the possibility of a conflict in enforcing your wishes, be sure to choose an agent who is strong willed and assertive.

While you need not name someone who lives in the same city or state as you do, proximity can be critical. If you have a long illness, your agent may be called upon to spend weeks or even months nearby, making sure medical personnel abide by your wishes for health care.

If you make a durable power of attorney for finances to name someone to manage your finances in case you become incapacitated (see Chapter 12), it's usually wise to name the same person as both your agent for health care and your agent for finances. If you feel that you must name different people, be very sure you name agents who get along well and will be able to work together. You wouldn't, for example, want your agent for finances to interfere with your health care wishes by stalling or resisting payment of medical or insurance bills, two things over which your agent for finances will most likely have control.

State Restrictions on Who Can Serve as Your Agent

Most states have rules about who can serve as your health care agent. Your doctor, other health care providers, and employees of health care facilities are commonly prohibited from serving. Some states presume that the motivations of such people may be clouded by self-interest. For example, a doctor may be motivated to provide every medical procedure available even if that goes against a patient's wishes. On the other side, treatments may sometimes be withheld because of concerns about time or cost.

Before you select an agent, be sure to learn your state's requirements and restrictions.

Naming More Than One Agent

Though you are legally permitted to name more than one person to make health care decisions for you, you should name only one agent when you make your health care directives. This is true even if you know two or more people who are suitable candidates and who agree to undertake the job together. There may be problems, brought on by passing time and human nature, with naming people to share the job. In the critical time during which they would be overseeing your wishes and directing your care, they might disagree, rendering them ineffective as lobbyists on your behalf. Feuding agents could even end up settling their dispute in court, further delaying and confusing your care.

If you fear that those close to you may feel hurt if you name someone else to represent you, take some time to talk with them to explain your choice. Or, if there are several people you'd feel comfortable naming, you might even let them decide among themselves who the agent will be. If you approve of their choice, you can accept it—and name the others as alternate agents in case your first choice can't serve.

Naming an Alternate Agent

You are permitted to name one or more alternate agents to represent you if your first choice is unable to take the job for any reason or resigns after your advance directive takes effect. Alternates serve one at a time, in the order that you specify.

It's a good idea to name at least one alternate agent, but you should be as thoughtful about naming your alternates as you are about picking your first choice: Be sure to name people who will represent you well if the need arises.

If You Do Not Name a Health Care Agent

If you don't know anyone you trust to oversee your medical care, it's not necessary to name an agent. In fact, it's better not to name anyone than to name someone who is not comfortable with the directions you leave—or who is not likely to assert your wishes strongly.

But even if you don't name an agent, you should still complete a health care declaration, stating any wishes for medical care about which you feel strongly. Even without an agent, medical personnel are required to follow your written wishes for health care—or to find someone who will care for you in the way you have directed. If you do not name a health care agent, be certain to discuss your wishes for medical care with a doctor or a hospital representative who is likely to be involved in providing that care.

What You Can Cover in Your Health Care Directives

You have many options and a great deal of flexibility when providing instructions for your medical care. Here are some issues to consider when preparing both your health care declaration and your durable power of attorney for health care.

Your Health Care Declaration

When you make your health care declaration, you'll be asked to express your wishes about many types of end-of-life care. Whether your preferences are simple or quite detailed, you should give some attention to the issues discussed here.

Life-Prolonging Treatments

Every state's health care form asks about preferences for life-prolonging treatments or procedures. A life-prolonging treatment is one that would only briefly lengthen the process of dying or sustain a condition of permanent unconsciousness. In other words, the patient would die soon—or die without regaining meaningful consciousness—whether or not the treatment was administered. Common life-prolonging treatments include a respirator, cardiopulmonary resuscitation (CPR), dialysis, surgery, and antibiotic drugs.

You can use your declaration to state that you want to receive all life-prolonging procedures or none at all. Or, you can pick and choose among procedures, naming those you'd like to receive and specifically rejecting others.

Artificially Administered Food and Water

If you are close to death from a serious illness or permanently unconscious, you may not be able to survive without the administration of food and water (often called "nutrition and hydration"). Unless you indicate that treatment should be withheld, doctors will provide you with a mix of nutrients and fluids through tubes inserted in a vein, into your stomach through your nose, or directly into your stomach through a surgical incision, depending on your condition.

Permanently unconscious patients can sometimes live for years with artificial feeding and hydration without regaining consciousness. If food and water are removed, death will occur in a relatively short time due to dehydration, rather than starvation. Such a course of action generally includes a plan of medication to keep the patient comfortable and pain free.

When you make your declaration, you can choose whether you want artificially administered food and water withheld or provided. This decision is difficult for many people. Keep in mind that as long as you are able to communicate your wishes, by whatever means, you will not be denied food and water if you want it.

Relief From Pain and Discomfort

If you want death to occur naturally—without life-prolonging intervention—it does not mean you must forgo treatment to alleviate pain or keep you comfortable. In fact, the health care documents for all states assume that you wish to receive any care that is necessary to keep you pain free, unless you specifically state otherwise.

This type of care is most often called "palliative care" or "comfort care." Rather than focusing on a cure or prolonging life, palliative care emphasizes quality of life and dignity by helping a patient remain comfortable and free from pain until life ends naturally. Palliative care may be administered at home, at a hospice facility, or in a hospital.

When you make your health care directives, you may want to take some time to learn about palliative care. In addition to stating your wishes about pain management, palliative care wishes can include other desires related to your comfort—for example, whether you would like to hear your favorite music or have others read aloud to you, whether you want a counselor or spiritual adviser to visit you, or if there are certain belongings you'd like to have nearby. You can also express any wishes you have for social engagement, such as a request that you be with and around people, even if you seem unaware of your surroundings. All of these are fine subjects for a health care directive; they are also important topics for conversations with your loved ones.

Treatment If You Have Alzheimer's Disease or Other Severe Dementia

Many states' health care forms now allow you to specify the kind of care want if you have an "advanced progressive illness," including Alzeimer's Disease or another form of severe dementia. For example, Pennsylvania's living will form covers "severe and irreversible brain disease." And Tennessee's form lets you provide directions for a state of "permanent confusion" in which you are unable to make decisions, recognize loved ones, or communicate clearly.

If your state's form doesn't include a space for your health care wishes in case of severe dementia, you can write your own instructions into the form. For an example of what you could say, see "The Dementia Provision" at www.compassionandchoices.org. Or, if this is a matter of particular concern for you, consult a qualified estate planning attorney. A good lawyer can help you draft a document that thoroughly addresses your wishes.

In an Emergency: DNR Orders and POLST Forms

Some people who do not wish to receive life-prolonging treatment when close to death—most often those who are quite elderly or already critically ill—may also want to prepare a DNR order or POLST form.

If a medical emergency occurs, a Do Not Resuscitate (DNR) form alerts emergency personnel that you do not wish to receive cardiopulmonary resuscitation (CPR). The form can be prominently posted in your home, either near the front door or next to your bed. In addition to preparing and posting this form, you can also obtain an easily identifiable Medic Alert bracelet, anklet, or necklace.

Additionally, many states use a form that is similar to a DNR order, usually called a Physician's Orders for Life Sustaining Treatment (POLST), a Clinician's Orders for Life Sustaining Treatment (COLST), or Medical Orders for Scope of Treatment (MOST). Unlike a DNR order, a POLST form includes directions about life sustaining measures—such as intubation, antibiotic use, and feeding tubes—in addition to CPR. This form helps to ensure that medical providers will understand your wishes at a glance. (But it is not a substitute for a thorough and properly prepared health care directive.) A POLST form may be used in addition to—or instead of—a DNR order.

If you think you might want to make a DNR order or POLST form, talk to your doctor or a hospital representative, or one of the staff if you live in a senior residence or long-term care facility.

Mental Health Treatment

Ordinary health care documents aren't designed to address the needs of people with serious mental illness. In fact, a typical health care power of attorney may forbid a health care agent from authorizing certain kinds of mental health treatment. If you need to address mental health issues such as hospitalization, medication, doctors, and therapists, you may want to make a separate mental health care directive, often called a "psychiatric advance directive."

A psychiatric advance directive can be used during a mental health crisis at any stage of your life, not just when you are terminally ill. Your agent for mental health care will be able to arrange any treatment you might need during this time, taking into account the preferences you include in your document.

The best source for state-by-state information on mental health care directives is the National Resource Center on Psychiatric Advance Directives at www.nrc-pad.org. You may also wish to consult a qualified lawyer to be sure your health care documents meet your needs.

Your Durable Power of Attorney for Health Care

When you make a durable power of attorney for health care, you can give your health care agent as much or as little power as feels comfortable to you. Most people give their agent comprehensive power to supervise their care. Recognizing this, the power of attorney forms for most states give the person you name the authority to make all health care decisions for you unless you specifically place limits on that authority in the document. This means that your agent will normally be permitted to:

- consent or refuse consent to any medical treatment that affects your physical or mental health (there are usually exceptions to this rule for situations such as extreme psychiatric treatments and termination of pregnancy, and your agent is not permitted to authorize any act that violates the wishes you've stated in your health care declaration)
- hire or fire medical personnel
- make decisions about the best medical facilities for you
- visit you in the hospital or other facility even when other visiting is restricted
- gain access to medical records and other personal information, and
- get court authorization if it is required to obtain or withhold medical treatment, if for any reason a hospital or doctor does not honor your health care declaration or the authority of your health care agent.

In a number of states, your agent is also permitted to direct the disposition of your body after you die. If this power is not included in the power of attorney form for your state, you may add it to your document if you wish. (You can provide extensive details about after-death ceremonies and services in your planner; see Chapter 15. But it's often wise to give your health care agent the basic power to take care of your body immediately after you die.) Think about whether you want your agent to:

- notify clergy or others for attendance and prayers, anointing, or other important rituals, and
- direct the orientation, positioning, or handling of your body.

Keep in mind that your agent steps in only if you can no longer manage on your own. If you are no longer able to communicate, your agent has a legal responsibility to make decisions for you based on what he or she knows that you want, or, if you haven't given specific directions, according to your best interests. That said, you are legally permitted to restrict your agent's authority in any way you like. For example, some people give their health care agent only the authority to carry out the health care wishes specified in their declaration, and not to make other medical decisions for them.

Think carefully, however, before you add limiting language to your power of attorney. One of the most important reasons for appointing a health care agent is so that someone will be there to respond to the needs of your situation as it develops. Your medical needs may change in ways that you cannot now foresee, and an agent who has full power can act for you no matter what the circumstances.

Duty of Medical Personnel to Honor Your Health Care Directives

After you go to the trouble of writing down your wishes for medical treatment in a health care directive, you may be concerned about what would happen if a doctor or hospital doesn't want to follow your instructions. Health care providers are generally required to comply with the wishes you set out in your health care documents—and to honor your health care agent's authority as long as the agent's directions are a reasonable interpretation of your wishes. In some situations, however, a health care provider is permitted to reject a medical decision made by you or your agent. For example, this may be true if:

- the decision goes against the conscience of the individual health care provider
- the decision goes against a policy of a health care institution that is based on reasons of conscience, or
- the decision would lead to medically ineffective health care or health care that violates generally accepted health care standards applied by the health care provider or institution.

But this doesn't mean that your health care instructions can be ignored. A health care provider who refuses to comply with your wishes or the directions of your health care agent must promptly inform you or your agent. And if you or your agent wishes, the provider must immediately take steps to transfer you to another provider or institution that will honor your directive. In some states, a health care provider who intentionally violates these rules may be legally liable for damages.

ICE: In Case of Emergency

As you plan for unexpected medical events, it's a good idea to set up one or more "ICE" entries in your cell phone. Setting up contacts as ICE—In Case of Emergency—can help paramedics or hospital staff quickly contact your loved ones in case of an emergency. Be sure to set up an ICE contact for your health care agent—for example, "ICE Esther Swanson, 1-555-555-1234."

Where to Get Help

There are a number of ways to find the proper health care documents for your state. You don't need to consult a lawyer to obtain or prepare them, though you can certainly have a lawyer draw them up if you're more comfortable that way. If you want to prepare your own forms, here are some likely sources:

- **local senior centers**
- **local hospitals** (ask to speak with the patient representative; by law, any hospital that receives federal funds must provide patients with appropriate forms for directing health care)
- **your regular physician**
- **your state's medical association**
- **Caring Connections,** a program of the National Hospice and Palliative Care Organization, provides free advance directive forms for each state (visit www.caringinfo.org or call 800-658-8898)
- ***Quicken WillMaker Plus*** (software from Nolo) contains forms for all states except Louisiana, and thorough instructions to help you complete them.

In Your Planner

Turn to the Health Care Directives section of your planner (Section 11). The following guidelines will help you complete the pages there.

Health Care Agent

Begin by providing the name of your agent for health care and any alternate agents you have named. (Remember that it's not enough to simply name these individuals here in your planner. You must name them in a valid health care power of attorney, as discussed above.)

Health Care Documents

For each document you've made, provide the following information:

- **Document Title.** As discussed above, the names for health care documents can vary widely. List the title as shown on the top of the document itself.
- **Date Prepared.** Indicate the date on which you signed the document.
- **Effective Date.** Indicate the date on which the document becomes effective.
- **Professional Help.** Include whether or not you had professional help with the document—for example, from an attorney, paralegal, or patient advocate at a hospital or other care facility.
- **Professional's Name, Title, and Contact Information.** If someone helped you prepare the document, enter enough information here to help your survivors locate that person if necessary.
- **Location of Original Document.** State where your loved ones can find the signed, original copy of the document. (You may want to include the original document in your planner; see the instructions below.)
- **Locations of Copies of This Document.** List the names of anyone who has a copy of the document, and any place where you've filed a copy. (You should keep at least a copy of each document in your planner, if possible. Again, see the instructions below.)
- **Additional Notes.** Here you can add anything you feel your loved ones should know about the document that they wouldn't be able to figure out from reviewing the document itself. For example, you may want to list any self-help resources you used to prepare your documents, or give the reasons why you selected a particular person to be your health care agent.

You may also wish to use this section to provide some details about your health, such as a list of prescription drugs that you take, your pharmacy's address and phone number, or your health history (including surgeries and allergies).

EXAMPLES:

I prepared this document myself using *Quicken WillMaker Plus* software.

This document names my daughter Suzie as my health care agent, to make medical treatment decisions for me if I am ever unable to speak for myself. I have appointed Suzie rather than one of my other children only because she lives nearby, is most familiar with my wishes, and will most easily be able to visit me and work with doctors if necessary.

Appendectomy, March 2006. Allergic to penicillin.

BINDER

Including health care documents in your planner. If you've made a health care document that takes effect immediately, you should give the original document to your agent, who will need it to act on your behalf. (But see the special instructions for DNR orders, just below.) Make a photocopy of the document and insert it in your planner behind the Health Care Directives section.

If your health care document takes effect only if you become incapacitated, you should file the original document in your planner and be sure your agent knows how to get to it if necessary. Insert the original document in a pocket divider at the end of the section.

If you have outlined your prescription drug regimen or medical history in separate documents, you should also file these records in this section, with your health care directives.

CAUTION

Don't file a DNR order in your planner. If you prepare a Do Not Resuscitate order (described above), you should not file the original document in your planner. Instead, make a photocopy of the document for your planner and keep the original in a more obvious place. Even if you are wearing identification, such as a Medic Alert bracelet, you should do all you can to be sure that medical personnel will see your form in the event of an emergency. Consider keeping it by your bedside, on the front of your refrigerator, in your wallet, or in your suitcase if you are traveling. If your DNR order is not apparent and immediately available, CPR will most likely be performed.

Keeping Your Documents Up to Date

It's a good idea to review your health care documents occasionally—at least once a year—to make sure they still accurately reflect your wishes. Advances in technology and changes in your health are two shifts in course that may prompt you to change your mind about the kind of health care you want. In addition, you should consider making new documents if:

- you move to another state
- you made and finalized a health care directive many years ago
- the agent you named to supervise your wishes becomes unable to do so, or
- you get married or divorced.

If you make a new health care document, be sure to update this section of your planner to reflect the current information.

CHAPTER

12

Durable Power of Attorney for Finances

How Durable Powers of Attorney for Finances Work 95

Who Can Make a Durable Power of Attorney for Finances 95

Specific Powers You Can Grant 95

Making Your Documents Legal 95

When Your Document Becomes Effective 96

When the Power of Attorney Ends 96

Choosing Your Agent 97

Important Factors to Consider 97

If You're Married 98

If You Make a Health Care Directive or Living Trust 98

Naming More Than One Agent 99

Naming an Alternate Agent 99

If You Can't Think of Anyone to Name 99

Where to Get Help 99

In Your Planner 100

Keeping Your Documents Up to Date 101

> *The first wave says, "You don't understand! We're all going to crash! All of us waves are going to be nothing! Isn't it terrible?" The second wave says, "No, you don't understand. You're not a wave, you're part of the ocean." I smile. Morrie closes his eyes again. "Part of the ocean," he says, "part of the ocean." I watch him breathe, in and out, in and out.*
>
> —MITCH ALBOM, *TUESDAYS WITH MORRIE: AN OLD MAN, A YOUNG MAN, AND LIFE'S GREATEST LESSON*

Making a durable power of attorney for finances ensures that someone you trust will have the legal authority to take care of financial matters if you become incapacitated and unable to handle things yourself. (The term "durable" simply means that the document remains effective if you become incapacitated. A nondurable power of attorney would automatically end if you are no longer of sound mind.) The tasks may range from paying bills to handling insurance, managing government benefits, and filing taxes.

If you become incapacitated and have not prepared a durable power of attorney for finances, your relatives or other loved ones will have to ask a judge to name a conservator to manage your finances. Conservatorship proceedings can be complicated and expensive, and they put private matters on public record—rarely a desirable outcome. On the other hand, preparing a power of attorney for finances is usually simple—and the benefits of the document far outweigh the small effort involved in making it.

There may be times when a nondurable power of attorney will meet your needs. People sometimes use this type of document if they will be unavailable for a period of time—away for work or on a long vacation, perhaps—and want someone to take care of one or more financial tasks in their absence. Even though a nondurable power of attorney automatically ends at your incapacity or death, you may want to use the document to specify a particular date when the document ends—for example, the date you expect to return home.

Because most adults need to prepare a durable power of attorney, this chapter focuses on durable documents. Here you will find an overview of durable powers of attorney for finances, basic instructions on how to prepare one, and essential information about describing the document in your planner.

RELATED TOPIC

Making a power of attorney for health care. A power of attorney for health care enables your agent to make medical decisions for you. Health care documents are discussed in detail in Chapter 11.

SKIP AHEAD

If you've already made a durable power of attorney for finances. If you've already prepared this document, you can skip right to "In Your Planner" for directions on including information in your planner. Then review "Keeping Your Documents Up to Date" for tips on keeping your document and planner current.

How Durable Powers of Attorney for Finances Work

Here are the basics of durable powers of attorney for finances, including who can make the document, what you can cover, when the document takes effect, and when the powers end.

Who Can Make a Durable Power of Attorney for Finances

You can create a valid power of attorney for finances if you are an adult, at least 18 years old, and of sound mind. (In Alabama, you must be at least 19. In Nebraska, you must be at least 19 or married.)

Specific Powers You Can Grant

When you make a durable power of attorney for finances, you give your agent as much or as little authority as you wish. Typical powers include:

- using your assets to pay your everyday expenses and those of your family (including pets)
- handling transactions (including access to safe deposit boxes) with banks and other financial institutions
- buying, selling, maintaining, paying taxes on, and mortgaging real estate and other property
- filing and paying your taxes
- managing your retirement accounts
- collecting benefits from Social Security, Medicare, other government programs, or civil or military service
- investing your money in stock, bonds, and mutual funds
- buying and selling insurance policies and annuities for you
- operating your small business
- claiming or disclaiming property you inherit
- hiring someone to represent you in court
- making gifts of your assets to organizations and individuals that you choose, and
- transferring property to a living trust you have already set up.

In this increasingly online and electronic age, you should consider granting your agent the power to access and manage your "digital assets," such as email, social network activities, images on photo-sharing websites, purchase transactions on retail websites, and online bill paying. You can also place conditions or restrictions on your agent. For example, you can give your agent authority over your real estate, but with the express restriction that your house may not be sold.

There are a few powers you cannot usually grant to an agent under your durable power of attorney for finances:

- making health care decisions on your behalf (again, see Chapter 11 for information about making health care documents)
- marrying, adopting, voting in public elections, or making a will on your behalf, or
- exercising powers you have already delegated to others, such as managing your business if a separate agreement grants sole management authority to partners.

Making Your Documents Legal

Every state requires that you sign your power of attorney documents. If you are physically unable to sign them yourself, you can direct another person to sign them for you. Depending on the laws of your state, you will also need to have your document notarized, witnessed, and/or recorded.

Notarization. In almost all states, you must sign your durable power of attorney in the presence of a notary public. But even where law doesn't require it, custom usually does. A durable power of attorney that isn't notarized may not be accepted by people with whom your attorney-in-fact tries to deal.

Witnesses. Most states don't require the durable power of attorney to be signed in front of witnesses. Nevertheless, it doesn't hurt to have a witness or two watch you sign, and sign the document themselves. Witnesses' signatures may make the power of attorney more acceptable to lawyers, banks, insurance companies and other entities the attorney-in-fact may have to deal with.

Attorney-in-fact signature. In the vast majority of states, the attorney-in-fact does not have to agree in writing to accept the job of handling your finances. The exceptions to this rule are California, Delaware, Georgia, Michigan, Minnesota, New Hampshire, New York, Pennsylvania, and Vermont. If you live in one of those states make sure you get good advice about having your attorney-in-fact sign your document.

Recording. Only two states (North Carolina and South Carolina) require you to record a power of attorney for it to be durable—that is, for it to remain in effect if you become incapacitated. In all other states you must record your power of attorney only if it gives your attorney-in-fact authority over your real estate. Even if recording is not legally required, you can do so anyway; officials in some financial institutions may be reassured later on by seeing that you took that step.

When Your Document Becomes Effective

There are two kinds of durable powers of attorney for finances: those that take effect immediately and those that do not take effect unless a doctor (or two, if you wish) declares that you can no longer manage your financial affairs. Which kind you should choose depends, in part, on when you want your agent to begin handling tasks for you.

You want someone to take over now. If you want someone to take over some or all of your affairs now, you should make your document effective as soon as you sign it. Then your agent can begin helping you with your financial tasks right away—and can continue to do so if you later become incapacitated.

Even if you give your agent permission to start handling your finances before you become incapacitated, you don't have to turn over complete control. Explain to your agent what you want done, and your agent should follow your wishes carefully. If you want your agent to consult you before taking action, he or she is legally obligated to do so. If you ever become dissatisfied with the arrangement, you can revoke the durable power and end the agent's authority to act for you.

You want your agent to take over only if you become incapacitated. You may feel strongly that your agent should not take over unless you are incapacitated. In this case, you have two options. If you trust your agent to act only when it is absolutely necessary, you can go ahead and make an immediately effective document. Legally, your agent will then have the authority to act on your behalf—but will not do so unless he or she decides that you cannot handle your affairs yourself.

If you are uncomfortable giving your agent authority now, you can add language to your durable power of attorney to make what is known as a "springing" document. It won't take effect until a physician examines you and declares, in writing, that you cannot manage your finances.

There are some real inconveniences involved in creating a springing power of attorney. If you truly trust your agent, you may find that it makes more sense to create a document that takes effect immediately and then make clear to your agent when to take action.

When the Power of Attorney Ends

A durable power of attorney for finances is valid until you revoke it or die, or until there is no one to serve as your agent. Very infrequently, a court invalidates a power of attorney.

You revoke your document. As long as you are of sound mind, you can change or revoke your financial power of attorney at any time, whether or not it has taken effect.

After your death. A durable power of attorney ends when the principal dies. However, if the agent doesn't know of your death and continues to act on your behalf, those actions are still valid.

No agent is available. A durable power of attorney must end if there is no one to serve as the agent. To avoid this, you can name an alternate agent who will serve if your first choice cannot. Furthermore, you can also allow the alternate agent to choose someone else to take over, if it becomes necessary.

A court invalidates the document. Even after you sign a durable power of attorney for finances, if you become incapacitated there is a remote possibility that a disgruntled relative could ask a court to appoint a conservator to manage your financial affairs.

It is rare, but a power of attorney could be ruled invalid if a judge concludes that you were not of sound mind when you signed the durable power of attorney, or that you were the victim of fraud or undue influence. The power of attorney could also be invalidated for a technical error, such as the failure to have your document notarized. If that happens, the judge could appoint a conservator to take over management of your property.

Choosing Your Agent

When you make a durable power of attorney for finances, the most important decision you will face is selecting your agent for finances (sometimes called an "attorney-in-fact"). The person you choose should be someone you trust absolutely and someone with whom you feel confident discussing your plans and needs.

Important Factors to Consider

Your agent may be your spouse or partner, relative, close friend, or any other person in whom you have complete confidence. If there is no one you trust with this great authority, then a financial power of attorney isn't for you. (As mentioned above, if you don't make the document and later become incapacitated, a court will name and supervise the person who manages your affairs. Normally, you'd want to make a financial power of attorney precisely to avoid this outcome—but if there's no one you trust to take on the job, court supervision is probably a good idea.)

In most situations, an agent does not need extensive experience in financial management; common sense, dependability, and complete honesty are enough. If necessary, your agent can get professional help—from an accountant, lawyer, or tax preparer, for example—and pay for it out of your assets. If, however, you want the agent to run your small business or manage extensive investments, be sure you choose someone with sufficient experience to handle the job.

While you need not name someone who lives in the same city or state as you do, proximity can be critical. If you have a long illness, your agent may be called upon to spend weeks or months nearby, opening mail, paying bills, looking after property, and so on.

CAUTION

Family conflicts can disrupt the handling of your affairs. Long-standing feuds among family members may result in objections to your choice of agent or the extent of the authority you delegate. This can wreak havoc with your agent's ability to handle tasks for you. If you foresee such personal conflicts, it's wise to try to defuse them in advance. A discussion with the people who are leery of the power of attorney may help. If you still feel uncomfortable after talking things over, you may want to discuss the troubles with a knowledgeable lawyer. A lawyer can review your documents and might help you feel reassured that your plans will be carried out as you wish.

If You're Married

If you are married, you will probably want to make your spouse your agent unless there is a compelling reason not to. There are powerful legal and practical reasons, in addition to the emotional ones, for appointing your spouse. The main reason is that naming anyone else creates the risk of conflicts between the agent and your spouse over how to manage property that belongs to both spouses.

If your spouse is ill, quite elderly, or simply not equipped to manage your financial affairs, you may have to name someone else as agent. The wisest course is for you and your spouse to agree on who the agent should be, perhaps one of your grown children.

Note that if your spouse is your agent, in many states that designation automatically ends if you get divorced. Wherever you live, you should revoke your power of attorney if you divorce, and create a new one naming a new agent. See "Keeping Your Documents Up to Date," below, for more information.

If You Make a Health Care Directive or Living Trust

If you prepare a document naming someone to oversee your medical care in the event that you cannot (see Chapter 11), it's usually wise to name the same person as both your agent for health care and your agent for finances. If you have created a revocable living trust to avoid

Many Jobs, One Agent

If you prepare each of the legal documents listed below—a health care directive, durable power of attorney for finances, will, and living trust—you will name personal representatives in each document. Naming the same person (and the same alternates) for the following jobs will help to ensure that decisions are made for you with a minimum of confusion and interference.

If you are incapacitated, this document...	... names this representative...	... to handle these duties:
Health Care Directives	Agent for Health Care	Directing your health care
Durable Power of Attorney for Finances	Agent for Finances	Managing your finances
Living Trust	Successor Trustee	Managing trust property during your incapacity
After your death, this document...	**... names this representative...**	**... to handle these duties:**
Will	Executor	Winding up your affairs, including paying debts and distributing property to the people who inherit it
Living Trust	Successor Trustee	Distributing trust property after your death

probate or minimize estate taxes, it is usually wise to name the same person as both your successor trustee and your agent for finances.

If you feel that you must name different people, be certain you name agents who get along well and will be able to work together. You wouldn't, for example, want your agent for finances to interfere with your health care wishes by stalling or resisting payment of medical or insurance bills, two things over which your agent for finances will most likely have control.

Naming More Than One Agent

Though you are legally permitted to name more than one person to manage finances for you, you should name only one agent when you make your power of attorney documents. This is true even if you know two or more people who are suitable candidates and who agree to undertake the job together. There may be problems, brought on by passing time and human nature, with naming people to share the job. In the critical time during which they would be overseeing your wishes and managing your affairs, they might disagree, rendering them ineffective as lobbyists on your behalf. Feuding agents could even end up settling their dispute in court, further delaying and confusing your support.

If you fear that those close to you may feel hurt if you name someone else to represent you, take some time to talk with them to explain your choice. Or, if there are several people you'd feel comfortable naming, you might even let them decide among themselves who the agent will be. If you approve of their choice, you can accept it—and name the others as alternate agents in case the first choice can't serve.

Naming an Alternate Agent

You should name one or more alternate agents to represent you if your first choice is unable to take the job for any reason or resigns after your financial power of attorney takes effect. Alternates serve one at a time, in the order that you specify.

It's a good idea to name at least one alternate agent, but you should be as thoughtful about naming your alternates as you are about picking your first choice: Be sure to name people who will represent your interests well if the need arises.

If You Can't Think of Anyone to Name

If you can't come up with a family member or close friend to name, you may want to consider asking your lawyer, business partner, or banker to serve as agent. If you really know and trust the person, it may be a good option for you. Otherwise, it is better not to make a power of attorney.

Don't name an institution, such as a bank, as agent. Though most state's laws permit it, it is definitely not desirable. Serving as agent is a personal responsibility, and there should be personal connection and trust between you and your agent. If the person you trust most happens to be your banker, appoint that person, not the bank.

Where to Get Help

You can easily prepare your own durable power of attorney for finances with the aid of self-help books or software. A good resource from Nolo is *Quicken WillMaker Plus* (software for Windows), which lets you use your computer to prepare a durable power of attorney for finances. It also allows you to prepare a comprehensive will, health care directives, and a host of other useful legal forms. *Quicken WillMaker Plus* also provides detailed instructions for finalizing your documents according to the laws of your state.

Though it's usually quite simple to prepare your own power of attorney, there are situations in which you may want to enlist a lawyer to help you with your document. This is particularly true if you expect family members to make trouble for your agent. A lawyer can help you weigh your concerns and options and decide whether the document is right for you. No matter what your personal circumstances, you may simply be more comfortable having a lawyer look over your document to be sure it accurately reflects your wishes. If you need help finding a good attorney, see the tips in Appendix B.

In Your Planner

Turn to the Durable Power of Attorney for Finances section of your planner (Section 12). The following guidelines will help you complete the pages there.

Durable Power of Attorney for Finances

Use the first table to provide an overview of your durable power of attorney for finances:

- **Document Title.** You should find the title at the top of your power of attorney document. It may say something simple, such as "General Power of Attorney," or you might find something more convoluted, like "Uniform Statutory Form Power of Attorney." Write in whatever the document says.
- **Date Prepared.** Indicate the date on which you signed the document. This will help your survivors identify the document and avoid confusion.
- **Agent's Name.** Write in the name of the person you named in the document as your agent for finances.
- **Alternate Agents' Names.** Write in the names of any alternate agents you named.
- **Effective Date.** Indicate whether your durable power of attorney took effect as soon as you signed it, or whether it will spring into effect if you later become incapacitated. Or, if for some reason you chose a specific date on which your power of attorney will take effect, write that in.
- **Professional Help.** Indicate whether or not you had professional help with the document—for example, from an attorney, paralegal, or CPA.
- **Professional's Name, Title, and Contact Information.** If someone helped you prepare the document, enter enough information here to help your survivors locate that person if necessary.
- **Location of Original Document.** State where your survivors can find the signed, original copy of the document. (You may be able to include the original document in your planner; see the instructions below.)
- **Locations of Copies of This Document.** List the names of anyone who has a copy of the document, and any place where you've filed a copy. (You should keep at least a copy of each document in your planner, if possible. Again, see the instructions below.)
- **Additional Notes.** Here you can add anything you feel your loved ones should know about the document that they wouldn't be able to figure out from reviewing the document itself. For example, you may want to list any self-help resources you used to prepare your document, or give the reasons why you selected a particular person to be your agent.

EXAMPLES:

I prepared this document myself using *Quicken WillMaker Plus* software.

I have named my daughter Mollie Catherine as agent, because she lives nearby. It will be easiest for Mollie to take on this responsibility, if needed.

Other Financial Powers of Attorney

Here, you'll find several additional tables you can use if you've made nondurable powers of attorney that are currently in effect. If you've made such a document and it will remain in effect for a long period of time—months or a year as opposed to a week or so—you might want to list it here. Your loved ones will then know that the document exists and they can be sure to destroy it if you become incapacitated or die.

The information for nondurable powers of attorney is exactly the same as for your durable power of attorney, above, with one exception. It's a good idea to list the termination date of your nondurable document—that is, whether the power of attorney ends upon your incapacity or death, or at some earlier date.

BINDER

Including powers of attorney in your planner. If you've made an immediately effective power of attorney, you should give the original document to your agent, who will need it to act on your behalf. Make a photocopy of the document and insert it in your planner behind the Durable Power of Attorney for Finances section. If your durable power of attorney takes effect only if you become incapacitated, you should file the original document in your planner and be sure your agent knows how to get to it if necessary. Insert the original document in a pocket divider at the end of the section.

Keeping Your Documents Up to Date

It's a good idea to review your power of attorney documents occasionally—at least once a year—to make sure they still accurately reflect your wishes. Changes in your health may prompt you to change your mind about the kind of help that you want. In addition, you should consider making new documents if:

- you move to another state
- you made and finalized a power of attorney for finances many years ago
- the agent you named to supervise your wishes becomes unable to do so, or
- you get married or divorced.

If you get divorced or your partnership ends, it is best to revoke your durable power of attorney and make a new one. In many states, if your spouse is your agent and you divorce, your ex-spouse's authority is immediately terminated. (If you have named an alternate agent in your power of attorney, that person takes over as agent.) But this is not always true. The safest course of action is to make a new durable power of attorney for finances and name a different agent.

If you make a new power of attorney, be sure to update this section of your planner to reflect the current information.

CHAPTER

13

Organ or Body Donation

Do You Want to Be a Donor? 104

How Donation Works 104

Documenting Your Wishes 106

Where to Get Help 106

In Your Planner 107

Keeping Your Information Up to Date 107

To hear with my heart, to see with my soul,
To be guided by a hand I cannot hold,
To trust in a way that I cannot see,
That's what faith must be.

—MICHAEL CARD, "THAT'S WHAT FAITH MUST BE"

Immediately after your death, your loved ones may be asked whether you wished to donate your organs or your body for medical or scientific purposes. The best thing you can do now is tell those who are close to you—especially your health care agent, close relatives, and friends—how you feel about donation. You can also make some donation arrangements in advance.

This chapter helps you decide whether or not you want to be a donor and tells you how to best document your wishes and arrangements, using your planner and other methods.

SKIP AHEAD

If you've already made decisions about organ or body donation. If you've already made arrangements to donate organs or your body—or if you know for sure that you don't want to be a donor—you can skip right to "In Your Planner" for directions on completing your planner. Then read "Keeping Your Information Up to Date," at the end of the chapter.

Do You Want to Be a Donor?

There is a great need for organ donors in the United States. More than 120,000 Americans are currently waiting for life-saving organ transplant surgery. A million more suffer from injuries or conditions that can be treated with donated tissue or corneas. Although organ donation is on the rise, the need still far exceeds the number of organs donated.

That said, the decision to donate organs or tissues—or your entire body—is a very personal one. Religious, philosophical, or medical reasons may lead you to conclude that donation isn't right for you. Here is some information to help you make the choice.

How Donation Works

How the donation process works depends in large part on whether you want to donate individual organs and tissues—for example, your heart, liver, kidneys, corneas, skin, or whatever organs and tissues are needed at the time—or your entire body. Organs and tissues may be donated for transplants or research, while whole body donations are made to medical schools to help with both research and training.

Whole Body Donations

Most medical schools need donations of whole bodies for research and instruction. The reason these are called "whole body donations" is that the donation will be rejected if any of the organs have been removed from the body.

There will be little or no expense for your estate or survivors if you donate your body. After your death, the medical school will most likely pay to transport your body, as well as for final disposition of your remains. (See "Do I Have to Plan for

Burial or Cremation?" below.) Nevertheless, to avoid any unexpected charges, it's wise to ask the school whether it covers these costs.

Arrangements for a whole body donation must usually be made while you are alive, although some medical schools will accept a body through arrangements made after death with the written permission of the next of kin.

Obviously, if you choose to donate your entire body, you will not be able to plan a funeral with your body present. You may still plan a memorial service, however. (See Chapter 15.)

For information on arranging a whole body donation, see "Where to Get Help," below.

Do I Have to Plan for Burial or Cremation?

If you want to donate your body, what ultimately happens to it depends on the medical school you choose and on your own wishes. Most schools will cremate a donated body and bury or scatter the remains in a specified plot—though some do not provide this service. If you'd like, you can arrange to have your remains returned to your survivors—usually within a year or two. If you want your remains returned to family members or friends for final disposition, you should specify this when arranging the donation. Whatever you decide, you can—and should—include your arrangements and preferences for burial or cremation in your planner. (See Chapter 14.)

In some cases, a whole body donation may be rejected—for example, if you die during surgery or due to certain illnesses. A medical school may even turn away a donation if it doesn't need your body at the time you die. You'll want to have a backup plan for burial or cremation in case the school can't take your body. Be sure to include these wishes in the Burial or Cremation section of your planner. (Again, see Chapter 14.)

Organ and Tissue Donations

Among the organs and tissues now commonly being transplanted are:

- corneas
- hearts
- livers
- kidneys
- skin
- pancreas and lungs
- intestines
- bone
- bone marrow, and
- tendons, ligaments, and other connective tissue.

Tissues and corneas may be accepted from almost anyone and are often used for research purposes. Major organs may or may not be accepted, depending on the circumstances. For example, while there are tens of thousands of patients on waiting lists to receive kidneys, only about 1% of all people who die are compatible donors. One donor, however, can save or help as many as 50 people.

Religious Views and Concerns

Most major religions support organ and body donation. Reverence for life is the basis for almost all religious traditions, and organ donation is viewed as a life-saving act of compassion and generosity. Donated organs must be removed immediately after death, however, and some religions strongly believe that a deceased person's body should remain undisturbed, at least for a number of days, to benefit the consciousness of the deceased person as it separates from the body. If you are uncertain about the right choice for you, it may be helpful to discuss the issue with your religious or spiritual adviser.

For a brief statement of different religious views on organ, tissue, and body donation, you can visit TransWeb: A Resource on Transplantation and Donation at www.transweb.org. Click on FAQ, then see "Does my religion object to donation?"

Before an organ is removed from a donor, doctors must declare that the patient is dead, with no possibility of being revived. Then the body is kept on a respirator to keep blood flowing through the organ until it can be removed and given to a waiting recipient. All of this usually takes about 24 hours.

It will not cost your family anything if you want to donate your organs or tissues. The recipient pays the expenses, usually through insurance, Medicare, or Medicaid.

Organ and tissue donation does not disfigure the body and does not interfere with having a funeral, even an open-casket service.

Documenting Your Wishes

If you've decided to donate your organs or body, you'll need to take some steps to make your desires known. Obviously, you'll want to document your wishes in your planner; this is discussed in detail, below. But there are a number of other important steps you can take to ensure that your wishes are followed.

First, identify yourself as a donor by obtaining a donor card that you carry at all times and by registering online with a donation registry. In most states, your driver's license can also serve as a donor card; the motor vehicles department will give you a supplemental card to carry and will either give you a sticker to place on the front of your license or will print your license with a mark that indicates your desire to be a donor. You can also get a donor card through an organization for organ and tissue donation. Donor organizations provide easy online registration and effective systems for matching up donors with those in need, when the opportunity arises. (See "Where to Get Help," below.)

Second, your health care directive is often a good place to state your wishes regarding organ donation. An increasing number of states are providing a place on their official forms for such instructions. (For more information about health care directives, see Chapter 11.)

Finally, and most important of all, you should discuss your views about organ or body donation with your health care agent (if you've appointed one), close relatives, and friends. Even if you carry a donor card and put your wishes in writing, it is possible that an objection by a close relative could defeat your wishes after your death. The best thing you can do is let those close to you know that you feel strongly about donation.

Where to Get Help

The following resources can help you with your plans to donate your body, organs, or tissues.

Whole Body Donation

If you want to donate your body to a medical school, contact the school of your choice for information. (Keep in mind that some factors will vary from school to school, such as requirements for condition and health of the body, transportation arrangements and costs, embalming, death certificate arrangements, and final disposition of remains. If any of these issues are important to you, remember to ask about them.)

For more information about body donation, especially if there is not a medical school nearby, contact an organization that coordinates donor placement for research and education. Here are three to get you started:

- Anatomy Gifts Registry
  www.anatomygifts.org or 800-300-5433
- MedCure, Inc.
  medcure.org or 866-560-2525
- Science Care, Inc.
  www.sciencecare.com or 800-417-3747.

Organ and Tissue Donation

If you want to register as a donor, you can find your state's online registry at organdonor.gov.

Click on the "Becoming a Donor" link, then click on "Register in your state to be a donor." Or contact Donate Life America at www.donatelife.net or 804-377-3580. Donate Life America is an alliance of donation organizations providing education, instructions, and assistance to those considering organ or tissue donation.

In Your Planner

Turn to the Organ or Body Donation section of your planner (Section 13). The following guidelines will help you complete the pages there.

Begin by checking the box to indicate whether or not you wish to be a donor.

SKIP AHEAD

If you don't want to donate. If you check "No" here, you're done with this section and can go on to the next chapter.

Wishes for Donation

If you want to be a donor, indicate whether you want to donate your whole body, any needed organs or tissues, or specific organs or tissues only. For example, if you know that your heart or other organs would be ineligible for donation but you want to donate your corneas and any needed tissues, you would check the third box and write your instructions in the blank lines.

Arrangements for Donation

Here, you will provide details about any arrangements you have already made to donate your body, organs, or tissues.

- **Receiving Organization's Name, Address, and Telephone Number.** If you have already contacted an institution or organization that will receive your donation—for example, a medical school that will take your whole body—write in the name and contact information here.
- **Location of Documents.** If you have made written arrangements with an institution or organization, indicate where you've filed the documents. (If possible, store the documents in your planner; see the note below.)
- **Additional Notes.** Include any additional donation instructions or information for your survivors.

EXAMPLE:

State Medical College will pick up my body and take it to the school. Within a year, they will cremate my remains and send them to Park View Cemetery, where I have reserved space in a columbarium. See the next section of my planner for more details about my arrangements with Park View, and for information on how I'd like you to handle my body if for any reason the school can't accept it.

BINDER

Including donation arrangements in your planner. If you have made written donation arrangements, hole-punch the papers or slide them into pocket dividers and insert them in your planner binder after the Organ or Body Donation section.

Keeping Your Information Up to Date

When reviewing other information in your planner, take a moment to consider whether your wishes about organ or body donation have changed in any way. If you've made specific arrangements to donate your body or organs, be sure those are current, too—for example, you'll want to double-check the contact information for the receiving institution or organization to make sure it's still correct.

CHAPTER

14

Burial or Cremation

Burial or Cremation? 110

Burial.......... 111

Cremation.......... 112

Embalming.......... 114

Related Decisions 115

Casket or Urn.......... 115

Headstone, Monument, or Burial Marker.......... 116

Epitaph.......... 117

Burial or Cremation Apparel.......... 117

Where to Get Help.......... 117

Making Independent Plans.......... 117

Burial.......... 118

The Cremation Process.......... 119

Product Resources.......... 119

In Your Planner.......... 119

Keeping Your Information Up to Date.......... 123

Peace and rest at length have come, all the day's long toil is past.
And each heart is whispering, "Home, home at last."

—THOMAS HOOD (1799–1845)

The end of life is difficult to comprehend. Thinking about it may make us feel sad, frightened, or even just numb. For this reason alone, almost any competing activity may seem more attractive than deciding what you want to have happen to your body after you die. Yet your willingness to do some planning now will have tremendous value for your loved ones. Without your help, survivors will have to make many difficult and potentially costly choices—all under time pressure while emotions are running strong. Your directions will reduce their anxiety, and perhaps even avert some quarrels, after your death. Beyond this, you may be surprised to find that the planning process is reassuring and satisfying for you, too.

In this chapter, you'll make and record your decisions about whether you wish to be buried or cremated. You'll also make related decisions such as selecting a casket or urn, specifying your wishes for a headstone or marker, deciding on an epitaph, and identifying particular clothing or accessories to dress or accompany your body. (In the next chapter, you will outline your wishes for a funeral or other memorial services, including a reception or other celebration of your life.)

SKIP AHEAD

If you've already made decisions about body disposition. If you've already made plans and arrangements for the handling of your body after death, you may want to skip right to "In Your Planner" for directions on including your directions in your planner. Then turn to "Keep Your Information Up to Date" for information on keeping your planner current.

If You're an Organ Donor

You should make choices about burial or cremation even if you have arranged to have some organs or your entire body donated to a medical institution. (See the previous chapter.) Keep in mind that if one or more of your organs is accepted for donation, the rest of your body must be disposed of or buried. And even if you have arranged to have your entire body donated, there is the possibility the donation may be rejected because of the condition of your body or simply because it is not needed. And finally, after the medical institution has finished using the body for teaching or research, it must be disposed of or buried—usually, between one to two years after it is accepted for donation.

Burial or Cremation?

Your loved ones will want to know whether you want your body to be buried or cremated. You can help even more by making arrangements in advance. The two primary reasons to consider this are emotions and expense.

As mentioned above, if your survivors must make decisions about the disposition of your body, their choices may be hasty and emotional. But if you do some planning now, you can approach the issues methodically and thoughtfully. This will undoubtedly reduce stress for your loved ones and—on a purely practical level—it may save a lot of money. Time-of-need arrangements can be very costly. Consider, too, that everything is likely to be at least a little more expensive by the time you die—so planning ahead is also a hedge against inflation.

If you make arrangements in advance, you can select options that are reasonably priced but still attractive. You can shop around, find what you want, and pay what you can afford. You can talk to more than one service provider, comparing what's included and what it costs.

You may even consider paying a small fee to join a memorial, funeral, or cremation society. You can then choose from an array of products and services at significant cost savings.

Don't worry that by planning ahead you'll lock yourself and your survivors into something inflexible. You can almost always change your plans if you need or want to.

Burial

While cremation is becoming increasingly common, most people still choose to be buried. Depending on your wishes, burial may occur immediately after death or several days later, after a funeral or other memorial service.

The Burial Process

A body may be buried in the ground, generally in a cemetery plot, or aboveground in the chamber of a mausoleum or family crypt. Typically, burial includes containing the body in a casket for viewing and burial. If you prefer to be buried immediately, a casket may not be necessary. (Although required by many individual cemeteries, a casket is not a legal requirement for burials in the United States.)

Embalming is usually not required for burial, even if the body will not be buried for several days. Refrigeration serves the same purpose as embalming. (See "Embalming," below.)

Product or Service	Cost Estimate
Basic Fee Services	
Direct burial services (no viewing or funeral)	$1,000 to $3,600
Funeral director services	$1,750 average
General Services	
Mortuary services—transfer of remains, preparation of obituary, reporting information for death certificate	$500 or more
Mortuary services—embalming, dressing, and shelter of remains	$600 to $1,200
Mortuary services—refrigeration of remains (alternative to embalming)	$50 per day average
Mortuary services and facilities—viewing or visitation, funeral service with clergy, musician, guest register	$1,250 average
Hearse rental and flower transfer from mortuary to gravesite	$550 average
Funeral service booklets	$120 average
Graveside service	$500 average
Cemetery staff for opening and closing grave	$300 to $2,500
Casket or Shroud	
Wood or metal	$500 to $20,000, averaging $2,500
Wood or metal rental	$600 average
Fiberboard or cardboard	$250 average
Burial shroud—fabric with fabric handles for pallbearers	$600 average
Plot, Crypt, or Marker	
In-ground cemetery plot with vault (required by some cemeteries to maintain level landscape)	$2,000 to $12,000
Aboveground cemetery crypt in mausoleum	$3,500 or more
Aboveground individual crypt	$20,000 or more
Aboveground family crypt (8 to 10 caskets)	$2,000,000, more or less
Monument or marker	$600 or more

Burial Costs

Burial can be costly. The national average cost for a traditional funeral, with burial and headstone or monument, is about $10,000. Depending upon the products and services purchased, the pricing of individual service providers, and the array of ceremonies included, burial costs can amount to several times the cost of cremation.

Above are some estimates to help you make your decision.

Cremation

Over 40% of the population chooses cremation rather than burial. For some, the relatively low cost makes the choice a simple one. But there are many reasons why someone may prefer to be cremated—for example, you may wish to have your ashes scattered or kept by a loved one at home.

The Cremation Process

Cremation is the burning of a body at extreme heat, resulting in a fine residue of ash and bone. The cremated remains (also called "cremains") may be buried, scattered, or contained in an urn. A temporary casket is required to contain the body during cremation. Cremation caskets are generally made of unfinished wood, cardboard, pressboard, or canvas. The crematorium supplies the temporary casket. As with burial, embalming of the body is rarely necessary. (See "Embalming," below.)

There are many options for timing cremation and integrating it with memorial services, depending on your wishes. Here are some examples:

- immediate cremation with no services
- immediate cremation, followed by a funeral or memorial service (remains may or may not be present in an urn or other container)
- a wake, visiting period, or traditional funeral service with body and casket present, followed by cremation, or
- a wake or visiting period with body and casket present, followed by cremation and a memorial service without remains present.

If you want a viewing, visitation, wake, or funeral service with your body present, your survivors can rent a casket, either from the mortuary that hosts the memorial services or directly from a retail casket store. Note that under federal law, mortuaries cannot require purchase or rental from their own establishment, and they cannot charge your survivors a fee for using a casket purchased or rented elsewhere.

Complete cremation arrangements usually include local transportation of the body to the crematorium, visitation prior to cremation, a temporary or permanent container for remains, cremation, a memorial service, preparation of obituary and death certificate, and the scattering or other disposition of cremated remains.

Cremation Costs

As with burial, cost may play a part in your decision. Below are some cost estimates.

Product or Service	Cost Estimate
Coordinated by cremation provider	
Direct cremation services—transfer of remains, cremation with temporary casket, basic urn container	$600 to $3,000
Direct cremation with scattering service	$1,000 to $3,500
Coordinated by funeral home	
Funeral director services, including cremation services	$2,200 average
Mortuary services—transfer of remains, preparation of obituary, reporting information for death certificate	$400 or more
Mortuary services and facilities—viewing or visitation and funeral service	$1,250 average
Urn or Niche	
Urn	$300 average
Niche in columbarium, including opening, closing, and marker	$1,000 or more, averaging about $4,500

You Can Go Green

Burial and cremation can be hard on the environment. Embalming chemicals, metal caskets, concrete burial vaults, and cremation emissions take a surprising toll.

It's not difficult to make green arrangements that use biodegradable materials and avoid toxins. Some choices are remarkably simple—and most are significantly less expensive.

- **No embalming.** Embalming fluid contains toxic chemicals—including up to three gallons of formaldehyde. Embalming is rarely required by law or to carry out final wishes.
- **Eco-coffin or biodegradable urn.** You can use a simple wood casket, cardboard box, or fabric shroud for burial. There are many options for biodegradable coffins and urns (for ashes that will be buried), including homemade ones. See "Where to Get Help," below.
- **Home funeral.** While it's more work, your loved ones may find a home funeral to be more satisfying. Most states permit home funerals, but Connecticut, Illinois, Indiana, Louisiana, Michigan, Nebraska, New Jersey, and New York require the involvement of a funeral director. See "Making Independent Plans," below.
- **No in-ground vault.** Vaults are concrete containers that are placed in the ground to surround a casket. They aren't required by law, but many cemeteries demand them to make landscape maintenance easier. Look for a cemetery that doesn't require a vault or find out whether you can legally refuse one.
- **Green cemeteries.** The Green Burial Council has developed a certification process for cemeteries that want to go green. Learn more and locate green facilities at www.greenburialcouncil.org.
- **Cremation conservation.** Cremation uses fewer resources than burial, but it's not entirely clean. If you have amalgam fillings—fillings that contain mercury—in your teeth, you can ask that they be removed before cremation. See the tip below for cashing in your metals.

What to Do With Cremated Remains

If you choose cremation, you'll want to give some thought to what should happen to your remains afterward. For example, cremated remains may be:

- kept in a mausoleum or columbarium niche in a cemetery, church, or even a school—for example, your alma mater, if facilities and space are available
- placed in the ground, either at a cemetery (in a family plot, single plot, or an urn garden) or family property, if state and local laws allow it
- scattered by the cremation provider, family members, or clergy (remains may be scattered in private or during a ceremony; they may be scattered over uninhabited public land, public waterways, or private property—provided that local law and property owners permit it)
- incorporated into an artificial "memorial reef" at sea
- mixed with fireworks, launched into space, or
- kept at home by someone you choose.

If you wish, your cremated remains can be divided among two or more options.

Religious Concerns

Almost all religions accept cremation. Only Islam, Baha'i, Jewish Orthodox, and Eastern Orthodox faiths oppose cremation outright. The Catholic Church lifted its cremation ban in 1963. If you are thinking of choosing cremation and have religious concerns, speak with your spiritual adviser.

Embalming

When making decisions about burial or cremation, questions may arise about embalming. Embalming is a process in which the blood is drained and replacement fluids are pumped into the body to temporarily retard its disintegration. While it has now become a common procedure, embalming is rarely necessary; refrigeration serves the same purpose.

Originally considered barbaric and pagan, embalming first gained popularity during the Civil War, when bodies of the war dead were transported over long distances. When the war ended, embalming was promoted (mostly by those who performed the service) as a hygienic means of briefly preserving the body.

When Embalming Is Required

There is a popular misconception that the law always requires embalming after death. In fact, it is legally required only in some states and only in a few instances, such as:

- when a body will be transported by plane or train from one country or state to another
- where there is a relatively long time—usually a week or more—between the death and burial or cremation, and
- in some cases, where the death occurred because of a communicable disease.

If Your Body Is Not Embalmed

If you choose not to be embalmed, that should have no effect on your final arrangements. Your body will be refrigerated until the time of burial, and, if you choose, you can have a funeral or other service with an open casket.

The only effect of not being embalmed will be that if you opt to be buried, your body will begin to decompose within days instead of weeks.

Embalming Costs

The cost of embalming averages about $750, depending on your location and on the individual setting the rate.

Refrigeration is usually less costly, involving an average daily charge of $50. Some facilities provide refrigeration free of charge.

Burial and Cremation Benefits for Veterans

The federal government provides burial benefits to qualifying veterans at no cost. The benefits include an in-ground, lined gravesite (with opening and closing of grave), a government headstone or burial marker, a burial flag, and a Presidential Memorial Certificate. The gravesite will be located within any of 131 national cemeteries, depending on available space.

If you wish, cremated remains can be buried or placed in a national cemetery columbarium with the honors and benefits described above.

If you prefer to have a private burial, cremation, or services, the Veterans Administration offers benefits that include:

- a headstone or burial marker for a private cemetery, and
- military funeral honors, including a burial flag.

Your survivors will need to make these arrangements after your death, so be sure to familiarize yourself with your options and carefully document your wishes in your planner, including the location of your military papers. (See "In Your Planner," below.) To learn more about burial benefits available to veterans, contact the Department of Veterans Affairs at 800-827-1000 or visit www.cem.va.gov.

Cash in Your Crowns

If your dental work is extracted prior to burial or cremation, your survivors can redeem the metals for cash. In the meantime, you can cash in on any dental metals you have replaced during your life.

Garfield Refining Company buys dental metals, including gold or semiprecious crowns, bridges, and inlays. For more information, visit www.garfieldrefining.com. If you don't have Internet access, contact Garfield Refining Company by mail at 810 East Cayuga Street, Philadelphia, PA 19124-9956, or by telephone at 800-523-0968.

If you like, you can include this information in your planner for your loved ones.

Related Decisions

After you've chosen burial or cremation, there are a number of smaller—but still important—decisions you might want to make. These include choosing:

- a casket or urn
- a headstone, monument, or burial marker
- your epitaph, and
- burial or cremation apparel.

Casket or Urn

Choosing the type of container you want for your body may seem like more than you want to think about right now. Why not leave it up to your survivors to choose something appropriate? Here's a story from a family left with little guidance that illustrates why it makes sense to spend a little time deciding what type of casket or urn you'd prefer:

After a long, very sad night, we wandered through the mortuary displays, weeping and overwhelmed. For starters, it was spooky—and the mortician didn't add much warmth. We were hemmed on all sides by a heavy silence and ponderous, expensive caskets.

We eventually selected a lovely, carved rosewood casket, much like the beautiful antiques Mom had loved. It even had accent rosebuds! The pink satin lining looked soft and rich. We thought Mom would know that we did right by her. She would know that she was loved.

Now, Mom was good with her money and no one's fool. Looking back, I know that had she selected her casket, she would have saved thousands of dollars.

Keep in mind, too, that caskets and urns carry the biggest markup of all funeral goods and services. This is an area where it's particularly smart to educate yourself and do some comparison shopping.

Caskets

If your remains will be buried, you may prefer to have a casket—and the cemetery you've chosen may require it. For immediate burial, a simple container or pine box is all that is necessary. If there will be a service prior to burial with your body present, the type of container is entirely up to you—you may want something luxurious or, if the viewing or service will be at home or in another private place, you may not feel the need for any type of container at all.

If your remains will be cremated but you first want to have a funeral or memorial service with your body present, your survivors may simply rent a casket. (This is not as odd as it may sound; it's done quite frequently.)

Caskets are usually made from wood, metal, fiberglass, plastic, fiberboard, or cardboard, and are available in a wide range of finishes, colors, and styles. For example, the fittings or hinges may be finished in gold or silver, with a shine or antique finish. The inside of the casket is usually lined with cloth, which is also available in different fabrics and colors. The closure may be simple, or it may be fitted with a gasket or protective sealer—providing short-term waterproof and protection capabilities, but at significant additional cost.

A wood or metal casket will cost $2,500 on average, while one made of cardboard or fiberboard will be about $250. As an alternative, a cloth burial shroud with fabric handles for pallbearers will run $200 to $1,000. Casket rental averages $600 for viewing and funeral services. You may want to shop around and compare prices. Under federal law, a funeral home cannot charge you a fee if you provide your own casket, whether homemade or purchased from an outside source.

The resources listed in "Where to Get Help," below, can help you choose and purchase the right casket.

Urns

If your remains will be cremated and scattered, the crematory will provide a temporary container and you won't need an urn. If your cremated remains are to be placed in a columbarium or grave, or given to an individual to keep, your survivors will need to provide a container of some sort.

Cremation urns are available in a wide range of materials and styles, from the popular bronze book replica to colorful porcelain vases. The most common materials are hardwood, marble, stainless steel, pewter, bronze, cloisonné, ceramic, and porcelain. Attractive biodegradable urns are available for burial at sea.

Cremation urns start at about $35 for simple wood and can run as high as $5,000 to $10,000 for materials such as gilded porcelain.

Beyond traditional urns, there are unlimited, creative ways to memorialize cremated remains. Containers can be made from books, musical instruments, fishing rods, or sports equipment. Online companies incorporate cremated remains into hand-blown glass ornaments, stuffed animals, wind chimes, and artificial diamonds, charms, or pendants.

You may want to shop around and review the many options available. The resources listed in "Where to Get Help," below, can help you choose a cremation vessel that is right for you.

Headstone, Monument, or Burial Marker

Headstones and monuments are upright grave markers (picture the traditional rounded tombstone), generally used with in-ground burials in a cemetery. In contrast, burial markers are flat and flush to the ground or other surface (picture a plaque), and may be used with an in-ground burial or affixed to a vault above the ground. Burial markers are often used in mausoleums, columbariums, and family crypts. Also, because of space constraints and maintenance considerations, many cemeteries now prefer burial markers for graves in the ground.

Headstones, monuments, and burial markers come in an almost endless array of shapes and sizes, from the common tombstone to elaborate sculptures and designs. For example, a headstone or burial marker might bear the logo of a fraternal organization, a military insignia, embossed flowers or figures, or a ceramic photograph. Designs are limited only by the constraints of cemetery policy, the craft of the builder, the flexibility of materials, and your budget.

Headstones and monuments are generally made from marble or granite. Both stones come in a variety of colors and shades. With granite, the darkest shades have been shown to provide the best long-term resistance to erosion. Burial markers are made from stone or various metals—such as steel, bronze, or copper.

Headstones and burial markers start at about $400 and run into the thousands. Adding a vase usually costs $100 or more. An individual mausoleum or crypt costs about $20,000, and a family mausoleum (containing eight to ten caskets) can run as much as $2 million.

The resources listed in "Where to Get Help," below, can help you price, choose, and purchase the right headstone, burial marker, or personal mausoleum.

Epitaph

Many people think of an epitaph as just the words or a saying on a grave marker or urn. But an epitaph can include things like symbols or photographs, too. For many, a simple epitaph is sufficient: name, place and date of birth, place and date of death. For others, including a title or brief description of life's work is appealing—for example, Loving Mother, Innocent Lamb of God, or Faithful Servant and Soldier.

If you will be sharing a grave marker with someone—your spouse, for example—you'll probably want to make this decision together. If your spouse has already died and you'll be sharing an existing marker with him or her, remember to consider any epitaph that's already on the marker when you're deciding what yours should be.

You may also want to request that a photograph be added to your grave marker. Photographs are usually reproduced on ceramic and affixed to the face of the grave marker. (This typically costs about $300.) And if you are a member of an organization, you may wish to request that the insignia or symbol of the group be engraved on or affixed to the face of your grave marker. As with the markers themselves, the options are almost limitless—restricted only by the available space and the potential expense. Most monument companies include the cost of a standard inscription in the price of the headstone or marker. If you want a longer inscription or more elaborate design, you will pay an additional cost.

Burial or Cremation Apparel

When a body is prepared for burial or cremation, it is dressed according to the wishes of the family. If you like, you can specify the clothes and accessories in which you'd like your body to be dressed. Depending on your wishes, your body may actually be buried or cremated in these clothes, or they may be removed and given to your executor or loved ones prior to burial or cremation.

For apparel, consider what outfit may be most meaningful to you and to your survivors. You may have a special dress or suit, uniform, scholastic robes, or religious vestments that would be most appropriate. For religious reasons, you may choose to be clothed in a burial shroud.

Accessories might include special jewelry or pins, rosary beads or other religious emblems, emblems of membership, or medals of accomplishment. There may also be items representing your life and your loves that you wish to have buried or cremated with your body—for example, a photograph, a quilt, particular flowers, or a symbol of your profession.

TIP

U.S. flags for veterans. The Department of Veterans Affairs will provide a U.S. flag, at no cost, to drape the casket or accompany the urn of an honorably discharged deceased veteran. For more information, contact the Veterans Administration at 800-827-1000 or visit www.cem.va.gov.

Where to Get Help

The resources listed here provide additional information to help you make decisions related to burial or cremation. Many can help you find local service providers or competitive sources for products. And some can even help you make your arrangements in advance.

Making Independent Plans

If you want to make plans without involving a funeral home or mortuary, turn to these good sources for information:

- ***Final Rights: Reclaiming the American Way of Death,*** by Joshua Slocum and Lisa Carlson (Upper Access, Inc.), a guide to funeral planning that helps family and friends choose (and spend) wisely. As leading consumer advocates in the funeral industry, the authors provide a wealth of information, examples, and state-specific law.
- **Funeral Consumers Alliance (FCA):** www.funerals.org or 802-865-8300. The FCA is a nonprofit organization dedicated to protecting an individual's right to have a meaningful, dignified, and affordable funeral. The organization's website is a rich resource, including a directory of funeral consumer organizations, information on burial and cremation, and resources for purchasing a casket or urn.
- **Home Funeral Directory:** www.homefuneraldirectory.com. This website provides a wealth of information, insights, tips, how-tos, and resources for home funerals.

TIP

Finding your state's laws. You can find your state's burial, cremation, and funeral laws online. To get started, go to www.nolo.com and type "burial and cremation laws," plus your state's name, into the search box at the top of the page.

Burial

The following organizations provide information and resources for better understanding the burial process and making your own arrangements:

- **Federal Trade Commission (FTC):** www.ftc.gov. The FTC provides consumer information on planning and paying for burials and funerals. See the series Shopping for Funeral Services on their website, and download or order the publications *Paying Final Respects: Your Rights When Buying Funeral Goods and Services* and *Shopping for Funeral Services.*
- **Department of Veterans Affairs:** www.cem.va.gov or 800-827-1000. The National Cemetery Administration division of the VA is the place to get information on national cemeteries and other burial benefits for veterans.

Paying for Your Plans

Over the years, memorial and cremation societies have become popular. For a membership fee, these organizations provide information about funeral, cemetery, and cremation providers, offering discounts for products and services purchased in advance of need.

To locate a reputable funeral society in your area, go online to the Funeral Consumers Alliance (www.funerals.org), then click on "Find a Local FCA." For cremation societies, search members of the Internet Cremation Society at www.cremation.org.

Use caution when paying in advance for funeral goods and services. What if you find you can't complete your installment payments or if you want to cancel for a refund? How might inflation change the products and services you've selected? What will your payments cover if you die while traveling? What if you move? Be sure you know the answers to questions like these before you sign a pre-need contract.

As a simple alternative, you might want to estimate the cost of your final arrangements—including burial or cremation, funeral or memorial services, and an obituary—and set aside that amount in a pay-on-death bank account for the executor of your will. In that way, you can retain control over your plans—whether you change your mind, die while traveling, or relocate to another state.

The Cremation Process

The following organizations provide information to help you better understand the cremation process and make your own arrangements:

- **Cremation.com:** This Internet resource provides information about the cremation process, including religious and legal issues, medical issues, making arrangements, and writing your obituary. The site also includes directories of providers and suppliers.
- **Internet Cremation Society:** www.cremation.org. This is a comprehensive cremation resource, including directories of service providers, urns, and scattering services. The website offers links to hundreds of cremation-related companies.

Product Resources

To better familiarize yourself with the options for cremation- and burial-related products, visit some of the websites listed below.

- **CasketXpress and UrnXpress**
  www.casketxpress.com and
  www.urnxpress.com
  800-550-7262 or 800-550-1172
- **Costco**
  www.costco.com (click on "Funeral" tab)
  800-955-2292
- **Funeral Consumers Alliance**
  www.funerals.org
  802-865-8300
- **Monument Builders of North America**
  www.monumentbuilders.org
  800-233-4472
- **Sea Services Corporation**
  www.seaservices.com
  888-551-1277

In Your Planner

Turn to the Burial or Cremation section of your planner (Section 14). The following guidelines will help you complete the pages there.

Disposition of Remains

This section contains two tables, one for burial and one for cremation—you will use only one of them. Check the box next to Burial or Cremation, indicating which of the two you've chosen.

Burial

If you want to be buried, fill in the following information. If you do not feel strongly about certain topics, simply write "family choice" and leave the decision to your survivors.

- **Check One: Immediate/After Services.** Indicate whether you want your body to be buried immediately after your death, or whether you wish to be buried following services—for example, a funeral with your body present.
- **Check One: Embalm/Do Not Embalm.** Indicate whether or not you want your body to be embalmed.
- **Check One: In-Ground/Aboveground.** Indicate whether you wish for your remains to be buried in the ground (in a cemetery plot, for example) or above-ground (such as in a crypt or mausoleum).
- **Burial Organization Contact Information.** Provide the name, address, and telephone number for the organization arranging the burial—for example, a mortuary.
- **Burial Location and Contact Information.** Provide the location and contact information for the place you will be buried—such as the name of the cemetery and plot location. If you will be using a shared plot or crypt—for example, a crypt with your spouse or a family cemetery plot—make note of that.
- **Location of Documents.** If you have made burial arrangements—for instance, with a mortuary or cemetery you've described just above—indicate where you've filed the related documents. (If possible, store the documents in your planner; see the note at the end of this section.)

- **Additional Notes.** Include any additional burial direction or instructions for your survivors. For example, if you are eligible for veterans benefits and want to use them, describe your wishes here.

Cremation

If you want to be cremated, fill in the following information. If you do not feel strongly about certain topics, simply write "family choice" and leave the decision to your survivors.

- **Check One: Immediate/After Services.** Indicate whether you want your remains to be cremated immediately or following services—for example, after a funeral with your body present.
- **Check One: Embalm/Do Not Embalm.** Indicate whether or not you want your body to be embalmed.
- **Check One or All That Apply:** Niche in columbarium, In-ground, Scattered, To individual. Check one or more of these boxes to indicate what should happen to your cremated remains. If you want your remains to be divided, check every box that applies and explain your wishes in Additional Notes, below.
- **Cremation Organization Contact Information.** Write in your preferred cremation service or crematorium, including contact information.
- **Final Location and Contact Information.** Write in the location for your final remains. For example, if you've arranged for a niche in a columbarium, provide the name and contact information for the organization that maintains it. Or, if you want your remains to be interred—that is, buried in the ground—or scattered, provide the location and any related contact information. If you wish for your remains to be given to an individual, write in the person's name and contact information.
- **Location of Documents.** If you have made cremation arrangements—for instance, with a crematory or cemetery you've described just above—indicate where you've filed the related documents. (If possible, store the documents in your planner; see the note at the end of this section.)
- **Additional Notes.** Include any additional cremation direction or instructions for your survivors. For example, if you are eligible for veterans benefits and want to use them, describe your wishes here.

Casket or Urn

Check the box that indicates whether you want a casket, urn, or other container for your remains. If your choices for body disposition don't require a container, check "No" and skip this table.

Now complete the tables, describing your wishes for a casket or urn. Three tables are provided, in case you need to describe more than one container—for example, three urns, if you choose to divide your remains; or a casket and an urn, if you want a rental casket for a funeral but then want your remains to be cremated.

If you do not feel strongly about a particular topic, simply write "family choice" and leave the decision to your survivors.

- **Item.** Indicate the type of container you want. If you want to specify a container other than a casket or urn, check "Other" and write in a brief description of your wishes.
- **Material.** Indicate the material for the container you've chosen and provide a brief description of it. For example, for a casket, you might check "Wood" and then write in "Birch." Following is a chart of typical materials for caskets and urns.
- **Model or Design.** Describe the model (including the model name or number if possible), shape, or design of the container.

EXAMPLES:

Model 7404

Book design

Vase design

Caskets

- Wood (hardwoods such as oak, walnut, or mahogany; or soft woods such as pine or poplar)
- Metal (typically steel, bronze, or copper)
- Fiberglass
- Plastic

Urns

- Wood (hardwoods such as oak, walnut, or mahogany; or soft woods such as pine or poplar)
- Metal (typically stainless steel, pewter, bronze, or copper)
- Stone (such as granite or marble)
- Cloisonné, ceramic, porcelain, or other glass
- Biodegradable (for ocean burial) or other temporary container

- **Exterior Finish.** Describe your wishes for the luster, artwork, color, or other features of the external material or fittings for the container. (If you want an inscription, describe that in the "Epitaph" section, below.)
- **Interior Finish.** Describe your wishes for the color, design, or material of the interior, including any selection of fabric.

EXAMPLES:

Beige crepe (creamy fabric with no shine)

Pink satin (smooth, gloss fabric with a distinct shine)

Royal blue velvet

No fabric

- **Cost Range.** Provide guidelines for the amount to be spent on the item, whether economical, mid-price, or luxury.
- **Additional Notes.** Include any additional notes or directions for your survivors. For example, if you have already purchased the container, make a note of that and include its location and any other information your survivors will need to obtain it.

EXAMPLES:

Ask Joe Stevens of Elbamore to make my casket. Joe will know how—just a simple pine box.

Headstone, Monument, or Burial Marker

Check the box that indicates whether you want a headstone, monument, or burial marker. If your choices for body disposition don't require a marker of any kind, check "No" and skip this table.

Use the table to describe your wishes. If you do not feel strongly about a particular topic, simply write "family choice" and leave the decision to your survivors.

- **Description.** Describe the type of headstone or marker that you want. If you will be using an existing headstone or burial marker (such as one shared with a spouse), make a note of that.

EXAMPLES:

2' upright monument

Shared, existing headstone, with Rebekka Melone (my deceased wife)

Flush marker

Submit VA Form 40-1330, *Application for Standard Government Headstone or Marker,* to the VA National Cemetery Administration, 800-827-1000 or www .cem.va.gov. I've completed the form and filed it at the end of this section for you to use.

The national cemetery arrangements include a headstone or marker, so there is no need to order one separately. You will need to provide epitaph information, however. See my instructions below.

- **Material.** Provide the type of material that you would like to be used. For example, for a headstone or monument, you might write in "marble" or "granite." For a burial marker, your choice may be metal (typically steel, bronze, or copper), marble, or granite.
- **Design.** Describe the shape, motif, or model (including model name or number, if any) that you would like.

EXAMPLES:

Model 56, standard

Bench model, upright headstone with adjoining bench

Winged angel, about 5' tall

- **Finish.** Describe your preference for the luster, cut, and color of the headstone or marker.

EXAMPLES:

Rough-hewn base, sides, and top

Red, or brown-red, polished

Polished figure atop rough-hewn base

- **Additional Notes.** Include any additional notes or direction for your survivors. For example, if you have already purchased the marker, make a note of that and include the location and any other information your survivors will need to obtain it.

Epitaph

In this section, you outline your wishes for your epitaph—that is, the words, symbols, or photographs that will be inscribed or included on your headstone, marker, or urn. Begin by checking the box that indicates whether you want an epitaph. If you have no need for an epitaph, check "No" and skip this table.

Complete the table to describe your wishes for an epitaph. Three tables are provided, in case you need to include more than one inscription—for example, one inscription on an urn and another for a columbarium marker.

If you do not feel strongly about a particular topic, simply write "family choice" and leave the decision to your survivors.

- **Item.** Briefly describe the item to be inscribed with the epitaph—for example, your headstone or urn.
- **Inscription.** If you want something written on the item, write it down exactly as you'd like it to appear.

EXAMPLES:

Liberty, Humanity, Justice, Equality
—Susan Brownell Anthony

That's All Folks!
—Mel Blanc

- **Additional Notes.** Here, add anything else you'd like to include on the item. For example, indicate whether you wish to include a photograph, symbol, or other image. Be sure to make a note about where your survivors can find the photograph or image. (You may also consider including it with your planner; see the note below.)

Burial or Cremation Apparel

Begin by checking the box that indicates whether or not you want to specify clothing, accessories, or other items to accompany your body after death. If you mark "No," you can skip this table. Otherwise continue on and fill in the following information.

- **Clothing, Accessory, or Other Item.** List and describe each item of clothing, each accessory, and every other item that should dress or accompany your body.

EXAMPLES:

Navy blue suit, Valentine's tie from Mary

Black scholastic robe, my Tam O'Shanter on my head, my staff alongside my body

My diamond brooch from Tom for our 50th anniversary

Burial shroud only

- **Location.** For each item, describe where your survivors can find it and provide any necessary access information.

EXAMPLES:

Find my staff in the back right corner of the closet in my study.

My diamond brooch is in the safe; see Section 23 of this planner for access instructions.

- **Remove Before Interment or Cremation.** If you want an item to be returned to your loved ones before your body is buried or cremated, indicate that here. Check "Yes" to note items to be removed before burial or cremation; check "No" for items that should remain with your body.
- **Additional Notes.** Include any other notes or instructions for your survivors.

EXAMPLES:

Please ask the mortuary to keep my hair and makeup simple and light. Don't let them overdo it! (See my color photo in the obituary section.)

Buy a new dress for me: Size 12, blue flowers, something pretty.

BINDER

Including burial or cremation materials in your planner. You can use a hole-punch, pocket divider, or protective sleeves to include relevant documents with this section of your planner. These documents may include arrangements you've made for burial or cremation, application forms or information about veterans benefits, or copies of a photograph or other image you'd like to include with your epitaph.

Keeping Your Information Up to Date

It's a good idea to review your final arrangements occasionally—at least once every few years—to make sure they still accurately reflect your wishes. In particular, review your plans if you move to another state or change your mind about any details related to the disposition of your remains. When you make changes, remember to update this section of your planner.

CHAPTER

15

Funeral and Memorial Services

Types of Memorial Services 126

Viewing, Visitation, or Wake 126

Funeral or Memorial Service 127

Reception or Celebration of Life 129

Where to Get Help 130

In Your Planner 130

Keeping Your Information Up to Date 134

> *Someday on a pier you'll stand, dear,*
> *And I shall sail away.*
> *Please let me go with smiles then*
> *As I did you today.*
>
> —ROMAINE HULSEY MELONE (1879–1967)

If you've ever settled a loved one's affairs after death, you probably know that it can be difficult to plan a funeral or memorial service. Family and friends want to honor the person who has died, but they may not agree on how, and decisions usually have to be made quickly—much more quickly than most people are inclined to act in a time of grief.

Documenting your wishes for memorial services will provide tremendous relief to your loved ones. Your work will provide welcome guidance to them, heading off potential disputes and relieving confusion. This chapter helps by giving you basic information about the three primary types of services and gatherings following a death:

- a viewing, visitation, or wake
- a funeral or memorial service, and
- a reception or celebration of the deceased person's life.

Some people and families choose to have all of these services, some select one or two, and some wish for none. Here, you'll have the opportunity to review all these options and record the choices that feel right for you.

SKIP AHEAD

If you've already made arrangements for a funeral or other memorial service. If you already have plans in place for your after-death services, you may want to skip right to "In Your Planner" for directions on including your instructions in your planner. Then turn to "Keeping Your Information Up to Date," at the end of the chapter.

Types of Memorial Services

Death often involves at least one ceremony and sometimes more. The most common is the funeral, which occurs just prior to burial or cremation—although smaller informal ceremonies, often called wakes or visitations, are also commonly held during the days or hours before burial or cremation occurs. The details of a wake, funeral, or memorial service can vary widely, depending on community custom and the religious, cultural, and personal backgrounds of the deceased person and the survivors.

Viewing, Visitation, or Wake

The viewing, visitation, or wake is an opportunity for family and friends to view your body or to sit with you after you've died. For many, it is a quiet, meditative time for personal reflection. For others, it will be a time to gather with family and friends for remembering, sharing, and honoring your life.

A viewing or visitation is commonly held in the viewing room of a funeral home or mortuary. However, you may wish that your body "lie in honor" in another place, such as your home, a community hall, or a church. It all depends on your wishes and the options available to you.

Traditionally, a wake is a gathering characterized by both sadness and gaiety—a celebration of the life that has passed and a send-off to whatever comes next. A wake is often held in the home of the deceased, but many mortuaries now offer their facilities and services for one- or two-day wakes. A wake can be an important part of the grieving process, giving family and friends an opportunity to come together to comfort each other.

Wakes From Many Cultures

When thinking about a wake, you may want to consider cultural or ancestral history as well as personal desires. For example, a traditional Irish wake lasts from the time of death until the start of the funeral service. The age-old purpose is to raise a ruckus to wake the dead—while faithfully watching to ensure the deceased is truly gone. The gathering includes laying out the body, keening (wailing), sharing of memories, storytelling, prayers, games, music, food, and drink.

Wake traditions from Japan call for a send-off of chanting, burning of incense, and prayers to ease the passage of the deceased's soul into heaven. The Maoris of New Zealand have certain games that are played only during wakes. The Chinese tradition includes a long vigil to protect the deceased, with friends and family sharing stories, keening, playing games or gambling, and remaining watchful through the long hours. The wake is typically followed by a meal of traditional dishes, such as curried goat with raisins (Jamaica) or Dublin coddle (Ireland).

If you want a viewing, visitation, or wake, you may wish to consider:

- where and when the gathering should be held
- who should be invited
- whether you will have a casket and if so, whether it should be open or closed, and
- whether you want music, readings, certain types of food or drink, or other special details for the gathering.

Funeral or Memorial Service

The difference between a funeral and a memorial service is that for a funeral, the body is usually present. Because the remains are not present at a memorial service, plans for memorials are more flexible. Memorial services are often held many months (sometimes even years) after a death.

Most people will want at least one ceremony held after they die but before their remains are buried or cremated, even if it is simple and informal. However, there may be reasons why this type of ceremony is not appropriate. One may be that you live far from most of your friends and family members, and they would have to drop everything and attend a preburial or precremation ceremony at a great personal cost.

Since burial or cremation typically occurs within a few days of death, attending ceremonies held beforehand can be very disruptive. For this reason, many people opt not to have a funeral, but instead prefer a memorial ceremony—usually held days or weeks after the burial or cremation—that is more accessible to more people.

Funerals

A traditional funeral is a brief ceremony, most often held in a funeral home chapel or a church. The body is usually present, either in an open or a closed casket. Beyond that, there are no absolutes or requirements about what constitutes a funeral. If the deceased person adhered to a particular religion, funerals often include a brief mass, blessing, or other services. If you served in the military, you may choose a military funeral. (See the note at the end of this section.) In addition, many organizations—such as fraternal groups or 12-step programs—will conduct services that reflect the nature and values of the organization. If you have been a member of such an organization, a send-off service by your fellow members can be a warm and healing farewell.

In most states, you have the option to conduct a funeral service entirely on your own. Only seven states legally require the use of a funeral director: Connecticut, Indiana, Louisiana, Michigan, Nebraska, New York, and Utah. For help with planning a family-directed service, follow up with the Funeral Consumers Alliance (see Chapter 14 for contact information).

In some traditions, only family members attend the funeral, while friends and the general public are invited to attend other scheduled ceremonies. In other locales and traditions, this is reversed, and the funeral is the less private event.

Some basic concerns you may wish to address when planning a funeral are:

- where and when the ceremony should be held
- who should be invited
- whether clergy should be invited to participate, along with specific names of clergy you would like
- any specific music you would like played, along with the names of the musicians or singers you would like to perform it
- preferences for a eulogy, and the name of the person or people you would like to speak
- whether you want your body or cremated remains present at the ceremony, either in a casket or other container, or whether you would like a picture displayed instead, and
- whether you want to direct survivors to send flowers or memorial donations.

Facilitator

You'll probably want to give particularly careful thought to who should facilitate the service. Given the type of service you would like, who would be best suited to lead it? You might consider your pastor, priest, or other religious leader. A close friend and respected member of your fraternal or support organization might be a good choice. Or you might ask a close relative to preside over your service. Keep in mind that those who are closest to you may find it most difficult to stand and lead a service. It may well be better to have a facilitator who knows you and cares about you, but who is not one of your most intimate friends or family members. Whomever you choose, talk with that person in advance, if possible. Share with them your wishes and be sure they feel comfortable in the role.

Casket

If you choose to have a casket, you can request that the casket be open or closed during services. Accident or disfigurement often means a closed casket, but some choose a closed-casket service for personal reasons.

If there is a casket, you may want visitors to accompany it to the burial site for an additional ceremony or words. The casket may be lowered during the service, or after the gathering disperses. A service may also be held entirely at the burial site. (See below.)

Pallbearers

In some funeral ceremonies, the casket is carried to and from the place where the ceremony is held—and sometimes again carried from a transportation vehicle to a burial site. The people who carry the casket are called pallbearers. If you envision a ceremony in which your casket will be carried, you can use your planner to name the people you would wish to serve as pallbearers.

The number of pallbearers usually ranges from four to eight, but you can name as many or as few as you wish. You may also want to name a few alternates, in case one or more of your first choices can't serve.

Transportation to Grave

You may have a preference about the type of vehicle that will carry your body to the cemetery and burial site from the place where the funeral ceremony is held. This might be a horse-drawn carriage, a favorite antique car, or a stretch limousine.

If you have selected a mortuary to handle some of your arrangements, it may have only one type of vehicle available. If the vehicle customarily provided is not what you would want for yourself, check to be sure the mortuary will allow you to provide your own—and be sure that it will not add its transportation charge to your costs. If this is an important issue for you, check with the mortuary you selected earlier and, if its arrangements about transportation are not satisfactory, shop for another mortuary.

Graveside Ceremonies

In addition to or instead of holding a ceremony prior to burial, it is common to hold a brief ceremony at the burial site at which a religious leader, relative, or family friend says a few prayers or words of farewell. If this is something you want, and have an idea of who should be there, who should speak, and what they should say, you'll want to describe those details in your planner.

TIP

Military funerals. If you are a veteran, the government will present a U.S. flag, play "Taps," and provide other honors at your funeral or memorial service. For more information, see the Military Funeral Honors website at www.cem.va.gov/military_funeral_honors.asp.

Memorial Ceremonies

A memorial ceremony commemorates and celebrates someone who has died. It usually takes place some time after burial or cremation, so the body is not usually present. Memorial ceremonies may be held anywhere—a mortuary, religious building, a home, outdoors, or even in a restaurant.

Memorial ceremonies are more often the choice of those who wish to have an economical, simple, after-death commemoration. While funeral directors, grief counselors, or clergy members may be involved in memorial ceremonies, they are not necessarily the people to consult for objective advice. Many will advocate that traditional funerals—often more costly and less personalized—are most effective in helping survivors through the mourning process. The truth is that most survivors are likely to take the greatest comfort in attending a ceremony that reflects the wishes and personality of the deceased person.

Reception or Celebration of Life

Following your services—particularly if you choose to have a traditional funeral—your loved ones may wish to host a reception for friends and family, a celebration of your life. A reception can bring together local family and friends with those who have traveled a distance for your services, each to share in the remembrance and the loss of you.

A reception is typically held in a community hall or family home, just following services, though you may know of another place that feels more suitable. Aside from where the reception should be held, you may want to consider the following details:

- who should be invited
- what kind of food and beverages should be served, and
- whether you want to request specific music, activities, or entertainment for the gathering.

Where to Get Help

You may wish to get additional help with your funeral or memorial plans. Many of the resources listed in Chapter 14 can help you, especially the book *Final Rights* (if you want to make plans without involving a mortuary or funeral home) and the Funeral Consumers Alliance. The following organizations offer additional assistance:

- Final Passages (www.finalpassages.org or 707-824-0268) provides a guidebook, tips, and resources for planning home funerals.
- Crossings: Caring for Our Own at Death (www.crossings.net or 301-523-3033) provides workshops, coaching, and resources for those planning a home funeral.

There are also a number of books to assist you with funeral planning:

- ***A Good Goodbye: Funeral Planning for Those Who Don't Plan to Die,*** by Gail Rubin (Light Tree Press), with a light touch and a little humor, will guide you through your funeral planning.
- ***Celebrating a Life: Planning Memorial Services and Other Creative Remembrances,*** by Faith Moore (Stewart, Tabori, Chang), is a guide to planning a personal memorial and celebration, reflecting a unique life, life experiences, and legacy.
- ***The Party of Your Life: Get the Funeral You Want by Planning It Yourself,*** by Erika Dillman (Santa Monica Press), will help you explore and plan creative, culinary, musical, and theatrical possibilities for a funeral or end-of-life celebration that reflects your unique interests, achievements, and taste.

In Your Planner

Turn to the Funeral and Memorial Services section of your planner (Section 15). The following guidelines will help you complete the pages there:

Viewing, Visitation, or Wake

Begin by checking the initial box to indicate whether or not you would like your survivors to arrange a viewing, visitation, or wake. If you check "No," you can skip to the next part, "Funeral or Memorial Service."

If you do not feel strongly about a viewing or wake or some of the details, simply write "family choice" and leave the decision to your survivors. Two tables are provided for you to describe two separate events if you wish, such as a wake in the family home and a mortuary viewing.

- **Type of Service.** Name the basic type of service you want, such as viewing, visitation, or wake.
- **Location and Contact Information.** Provide the location that you prefer for the viewing, visitation, or wake, along with necessary contact information.
- **Existing Arrangements and Location of Documents.** Indicate whether you have already made arrangements—for example, for a wake as part of a package of services with a funeral home or mortuary—and provide the location of any related documents. (If possible, you should file the documents in your planner; see the note below.)
- **Body Present: Yes/No.** Indicate whether you want to have your body present at the viewing, visitation, or wake.
- **Casket: Yes/No.** Indicate whether you want a casket for the service. If you want your body to be laid out without a casket, or if you do not want your body to be present, check "No."
- **Casket: Open/Closed.** Indicate whether you want an open or closed casket during the viewing, visitation, or wake.

- **Invitees: Public/Private.** Indicate whether you would like the event to be private (that is, by invitation only) or public (open to all family and friends). If you select "Private," use **Additional Notes**, below, to describe who should be invited.
- **Timing and Days/Hours.** Describe your wishes for the timing of the viewing, visitation, or wake, and for the days and hours of the service.

  EXAMPLES:

  I'd like the wake to last from the moment of my death until the start of the funeral service at McClintock's.

  Viewing in a mortuary viewing room for the two days (or more) prior to my funeral service.

  Visitation at home for the hours leading up to my cremation.

- **Special Requests.** Include any special requests you have, such as music selections, musicians, refreshments, or other activities or observances.

  EXAMPLES:

  Please play and sing these songs during my wake: "Farside Banks of Jordan," "In the Garden," and "On Eagle's Wings."

  Please plan to feast during my wake! I'd like you to serve corned beef and cabbage, parsley potatoes, home-baked breads, and plenty of stout and whiskey! Eat, sing, cry—and remember me!

- **Additional Notes.** Write in any additional information about your wishes for the event.

  EXAMPLES:

  Family and invited friends only. Please note in my obituary that the service is private and only invite my dearest friends: the Habedanck family, the Warths, Saskia and Cornelius Stevenson, the Greenes, and the Stoddens.

  Please have copies of my latest book available in the mortuary viewing room, and insert in each a copy of the note I have filed at the back of this section.

Funeral or Memorial Service

Begin by checking the initial box to indicate whether or not you want your survivors to arrange a funeral or memorial service. If you check "No," you can skip to the next part, "Reception or Celebration of Life."

If you do not feel strongly about a funeral or memorial service, or some of the details of the arrangements, simply write "family choice" and leave the decision to your survivors.

If you want your survivors to hold more than one funeral or memorial service and you want to describe your wishes, photocopy or print (using the eForms) enough planner pages to describe the additional services.

- **Location and Contact Information.** Specify the location and contact information for the place where you'd like the service to be held.
- **Existing Arrangements and Location of Documents.** Indicate whether you have already made arrangements for a funeral or memorial service, and provide the location of any related documents. (If possible, you should file the documents in your planner; see the note below.)
- **Body and Casket Present: Yes/No.** Indicate whether or not you want your body and casket to be present at the service.
- **Casket: Open/Closed.** If your body will be present in a casket, indicate whether you would like the casket to be open or closed for the service.

  EXAMPLE:

  My wish is to have a simple service, Protestant, with hymns that I enjoy, especially "How Great Thou Art" and "Abide With Me." My casket is to be closed. I do not wish to have family or friends looking upon my dead face. Then my wish is to be cremated and taken out to sea, where my former husband, Ronald, and my sister, Betty, are.

- **Other Items.** If you want your loved ones to display other items that represent your life—such as a photograph, posters, or other personal items meaningful to you—check the appropriate boxes and describe the items. Include the location for each item. If you need more space, use **Additional Notes**, below.
- **Flowers.** Describe whether you would like flowers at the service and, if you would, describe your preference for the types or colors of flowers.
- **Invitees: Public/Private.** Indicate whether you would like the event to be private (that is, by invitation only) or public (open to all family and friends). If you select "Private," use **Additional Notes**, below, to describe who should be invited.
- **Timing and Days/Hours.** Indicate your wishes for the timing of the service and for the day or time of day for the funeral or memorial service.

EXAMPLES:

Two to four days after my death, early afternoon

About one month following cremation

On the one-year anniversary of my death

- **Type of Service: Religious/Military/Other.** Check the box for the type of service that you desire, whether religious, military, or other (including a lodge or fraternal organization, 12-step, or something informal). For each choice, add a brief note describing the type of service.

EXAMPLES:

Religious: Presbyterian

Religious: Islamic

Military: U.S. Army

Other: Masonic

Other: Alcoholics Anonymous

- **Service Contact.** Provide contact information for the person or organization that can arrange the type of service you desire. For example, if you would like a service coordinated by your lodge or 12-step group, provide contact information for the organization.

TIP

Arranging for a military funeral. If you are a veteran and you would like a military funeral (see the tip on military funerals, above), write in your planner, "Please ask [the church, funeral home, or other facility coordinating the service] to contact the U.S. Department of Defense to arrange a military funeral." The coordinating facility will make arrangements directly with the Department of Defense.

- **Facilitator.** Identify the person whom you wish to preside over your service, including contact information. Depending on the type of service you have chosen, this person could be clergy (that is, your pastor, priest, rabbi, or other religious leader), a member of your fraternal organization or 12-step program, or a family member or friend.
- **Eulogy.** Identify the people you'd like to have speak at your service, including the name and contact information for each.
- **Music Selections and Musicians.** Include your wishes for specific music to be played or performed during your services. Include your wishes for specific musicians to perform, including vocalists.

EXAMPLES:

I would like bagpipers to play from the mortuary to the burial site.

Please ask John and June to sing "Farside Banks of Jordan," if they are able.

- **Readings.** Describe any readings or recitations you prefer, such as scripture or poetry. If possible, include copies with your planner. (See the note below.) If you wish to specify who is to read or recite, name each person.
- **Pallbearers.** If your casket will be carried to or from your service, name your pallbearers here. Include the name and contact information for up to eight pallbearers, plus two to four alternates.
- **Graveside Ceremony.** Indicate whether you want only a graveside service, a graveside ceremony following a funeral at another location, or no graveside service at all. Add any description or clarifying detail in the space provided.

EXAMPLE:

Please arrange for the release of several white pigeons at the conclusion of the graveside prayer.

- **Transportation to Service.** Describe your wishes for transportation, such as for transporting your body from the funeral to the burial site, or shuttling family between ceremonies.

EXAMPLES:

Transfer casket from mortuary to grave in a horse-drawn carriage.

It's fine to use the mortuary hearse to transport my casket.

Please coordinate rides for family, throughout the day, in our fleet of classic Ford Mustangs. Our Classic Club friends have offered to chauffeur.

- **Additional Notes.** Include any additional requests you may have for funeral or memorial services.

EXAMPLES:

In the pocket divider for this section, I have included photos and a poem that I'd like printed in the funeral service program, to be given to all who attend my service.

Also hold a separate Mass 40 days after my death.

Please also plan an additional memorial service to be held on the one-year anniversary of my death.

TIP

Presidential Memorial Certificate for veterans. Your loved ones may wish to request a Presidential Memorial Certificate, signed by the current president, in gratitude for the service of honorably discharged deceased veterans. In the **Additional Notes** section, suggest that your survivors request a certificate by contacting the Department of Veterans Affairs by mail at Presidential Memorial Certificates (41B3), National Cemetery Administration, 5109 Russell Road, Quantico, VA 22134-3903, or online at www.cem.va.gov. They can also visit any regional office of the Department of Veterans Affairs. They must include copies (not originals) of your discharge papers and death certificate with the request.

Reception or Celebration of Life

Begin by checking the box to indicate whether or not you would like your survivors to arrange a reception or celebration. If you check "No," you can skip to "Keeping Your Information Up to Date," below.

If you do not feel strongly about a reception, or some of the details, simply write "family choice" and leave the decision to your survivors.

- **Location and Contact Information.** Specify the location and contact information for the place you'd like the reception or celebration to be held.

- **Existing Arrangements and Location of Documents.** Indicate whether you have already made arrangements for a reception or celebration of your life, and provide the location of any related documents. (If possible, you should file the documents in your planner; see the note below.)
- **Invitees: Public/Private.** Indicate whether you would like the event to be private (that is, by invitation only) or public (open to all family and friends). If you select "Private," use **Additional Notes**, below, to describe who should be invited.
- **Food and Drink.** If you have particular wishes about the type of food and drink that should—or should not—be served at the gathering, describe those here.

EXAMPLES:

Buffet of salads and good breads. Serve sparkling waters, fruit juice, and coffee. Please—no alcoholic beverages, no meats.

Please serve a hearty afternoon/evening meal of lamb, vegetables, and couscous, with plenty of tea and warm conversation!

- **Additional Notes.** Include any special requests or additional direction you have for the reception or celebration—for example, whether you would like it to include particular pieces of music, readings, or other activities.

EXAMPLES:

If Bonney is able, I would so appreciate her playing the organ at my home during the celebration of my life—especially "The Old Rugged Cross" and "Beer Barrel Polka"!

Please sit down with family and friends and watch some of our wonderful home videos—especially Christmas 1996.

In an envelope at the end of this section, there's a letter I would like Peder to read to all during the reception following my service.

BINDER

Including funeral or memorial service materials in your planner. You can use a hole-punch, pocket divider, or protective sleeves to include relevant documents with this section of your planner. These documents may include arrangements you've made for a wake, visitation, funeral, or other service, application forms or information about a military funeral, or copies of readings for your services.

Keeping Your Information Up to Date

It's a good idea to occasionally review your wishes for services—at least once every few years—to make sure they're still accurate. In particular, review your plans to be sure all contact information is current and that the details of your services are still as you'd like them to be.

CHAPTER

16

Obituary

What to Include in Your Obituary....136

Where to Get Help....137

In Your Planner....137

Keeping Your Obituary Up to Date....139

> *Ancient Egyptians believed that upon death they would be asked two questions and their answers would determine whether they could continue their journey in the afterlife. The first question was, "Did you bring joy?" The second was, "Did you find joy?"*
>
> —LEO BUSCAGLIA (1924–1998)

An obituary is a notice that will be printed online, in newspapers, or in other publications after your death. It lets people know that you have died and provides some biographical information about you. In addition, the obituary may specify the time and place of your funeral or memorial service and include other information, such as wishes for donations to be made in your name. This section of your planner will help your loved ones put together an accurate obituary that reflects your preferences.

SKIP AHEAD

If you've already drafted your obituary. If you've already written an obituary, you may want to skip to "In Your Planner" for directions on including the obituary in your planner. You should also read "Keeping Your Obituary Up to Date," at the end of the chapter.

What to Include in Your Obituary

You may prefer to draft your own obituary and file it in your planner. After your death, your survivors can simply review what you've written to make sure it's current and send it off to be published. Or, rather than drafting a full obituary, you may want to provide specific details that your survivors can use to write an obituary for you. Your planner permits either option. Whichever you choose, you'll want to devote some time to deciding what your obituary should include and where it will be published.

Depending on your needs, your obituary might be brief (called a "death notice"), moderately long, or the length of a full article. In large part, it depends on where your obituary will appear after your death. Many newspapers require obituaries to be very short. On the other hand, if you're well known in your community or the field in which you work, a newspaper or other publication may want to publish a longer obituary or even an article about your life. Following are a couple of examples of brief and moderately long obituaries. For help finding more examples, see "Where to Get Help," below.

EXAMPLE (BRIEF):

Kelly, Roberta C. Born in Chicago on December 27, 1936, passed away in Toledo on December 22, 2013. Services to be held at Toledo Grand Mortuary, December 27, 2013, at 10:00 a.m. Friends welcome.

EXAMPLE (MODERATE):

Kelly, Roberta C. Born in Chicago on December 27, 1936, passed away in Toledo on December 22, 2013. For 49 years, Roberta was the loving wife of the late Samuel E. Kelly. Their three daughters and families survive them: Antonia and William Koenig, Bethany and Sean O'Connor, and Catherine Kelly, all of the greater Chicago area. A graduate of Sequoia Technical Schools, Evanston, Roberta served as

Executive Assistant for Mr. Lawrence Cooper of Cooper & Cooper, Chicago, for more than 20 years. In lieu of flowers, remembrances may be made to the American Heart Association. Services to be held at Toledo Grand Mortuary, December 27, 2013 at 10:00 a.m. Friends are welcome.

When deciding what to include in your obituary, consider the following topics:

- your date and place of birth
- family information, including the names of your spouse, children, grandchildren, parents, and siblings
- details about your education
- employment information
- military service
- memberships in service, community, or recreational organizations
- important awards or achievements
- your primary interests and hobbies
- whether or not you want people to send flowers in your name
- whether or not you want people to make donations to a particular charity or organization in your name, and
- anything else you'd like others to know and remember about your life.

You may also want to select a photograph to include with your obituary. Your planner provides a place for you to indicate which photo you prefer, and its location.

TIP

Guarding sensitive information. Unfortunately, obituaries have become popular sources of information for identity thieves. You may want to use caution when supplying details for a death notice. For example, instead of providing a full birthdate, you might give just the month and year, such as March 1947. For married women, you may choose to omit the maiden name, commonly used to gain access to financial and other critical accounts.

Where Will Your Obituary Be Published?

Until recently, we published our obituaries in newspapers, newsletters, and magazines of our communities, colleges, and workplaces. Today, obituaries are more often published or shared online through memorial sites, email, Facebook, Twitter, LinkedIn, special-interest blogs, or other online communities.

You can still have your obituary published in a traditional newspaper, but doing so can be costly. While a small-town paper may publish an obituary for free, a metropolitan paper may charge $7,500 for six column inches and a photograph for three days. Typically, the newspaper publication will include online publication (for example, at Legacy.com) for a small additional charge. Given these costs, families often publish a short newspaper obituary that links to a longer online memorial they have posted.

Given the array of choices, you may want to think about where you'd like your obituary published and write your wishes in your planner.

Where to Get Help

One of the easiest ways to get help with your obituary is to review obituaries published or posted in locations you are considering. This should give you many ideas for structuring your obituary, as well as examples of what you can include.

In Your Planner

Turn to the Obituary section of your planner (Section 16). The following guidelines will help you complete the pages there.

Begin by checking the appropriate boxes to indicate:

- whether or not you want an obituary, and if so,

- whether you have already drafted one for your survivors to use.

SKIP AHEAD

If you don't want an obituary. If you check "No," you're done with this section and can go on to the next chapter.

If you've already drafted an obituary, all you need to do is specify its location in the space provided, and you're done. You'll want to keep the obituary itself in your planner, if possible. (See the instructions at the end of this section.)

If you haven't prepared your own obituary, complete the rest of Section 16 by filling in the information your survivors will need to write one for you.

Obituary Overview

In this part, specify the following:

- **Obituary Length.** Indicate whether your obituary should be brief, moderate, or article length. (See above for examples.) If you want your survivors to publish different obituaries in different publications—say, a brief obituary in a newspaper and a longer one in a newsletter or magazine—check all the options that apply and include more specific directions in the **Additional Notes** section, below.
- **Photographs.** Indicate whether or not you wish to have photographs published with your obituary and the location of any specific photos you've chosen. If possible, keep the photographs in your planner. (See the directions at the end of this section.)
- **Publications.** List the newspapers, online site, or other publications in which you want your obituary published.

Obituary Details

Here, you'll provide guidance for the content of your obituary. Note that several items in the table contain preprinted cross-references. For example, "Date and Place of Birth" contains the notation, "See Biographical Information." When your planner is complete, the cross-referenced section will contain the required information, so there is no need to duplicate it here.

Review and complete the following items. For those items that do not apply to you, or for which you do not wish to include information, simply note "not applicable" or "family choice."

- **Education.** Include relevant information about your education—including the schools you attended and the year you graduated—or direct your survivors to a résumé or curriculum vitae that you have included elsewhere in your planner.

EXAMPLES:

Certificate, Sequoia Technical Institute, 1984; B.A., College of the Redwoods, 1988.

See my résumé, filed in Section 7 (Employment).

- **Awards and Achievements.** Add detail about awards you have received—for example, the organization that gave you the award, the title of the award, and the date—and other unique achievements.

EXAMPLES:

The Purple Heart, 1952

Pulitzer Prize for Economics, 1998

Volunteer of the Year, City of Sacramento, 2010

Nordstrom Annual Pacesetter, 15 years

- **Interests and Hobbies.** What are your special interests and hobbies?
- **Values.** What do you value most in life? What has been most meaningful?

EXAMPLES:

Like many of my generation, I have learned the value of hard work. I was never careless with my money.

Passion for the arts, love of nature, and great interest in people.

"A kindhearted and caring man of the highest honor, courage, integrity, wisdom, character, and bravery."

"He could be a taskmaster, always insisting on precision and impatient with inferior work."

- **Flowers.** Indicate whether or not you want people to send flowers, and if so, where they should send them. Depending on your wishes for final arrangements, you may want the flowers to be sent to your family, to a funeral home, or to the site you designate for your memorial service. (You can document your wishes for a funeral home and memorial service in Section 15 of the planner, Funeral and Memorial Services.) If you don't want flowers, you can check the box asking that your obituary contain the simple statement, "No flowers, please." Or, you can check the box asking that instead of flowers, donations be made in your name: "In lieu of flowers, please send donations to [the organizations listed below]."
- **Donations or Remembrances.** If you want contributions or remembrances to be made in your name, specify where they should go—for example, the name of the organization or trust—and provide an address and telephone number. Documents related to these donations—such as information about an individual fund or trust established with your college or church—can be filed in this section of your planner. (See the directions at the end of this section.)
- **Other.** If you have additional requests for or restrictions on the content of your obituary, include those notes here.

Additional Notes

Document anything else that your survivors should know about publishing your obituary. For example, if you wish to run two different obituaries in two different publications, describe your wishes. Or if you wish to use an online guest book for condolences from family and friends, describe that here.

EXAMPLES:

To help prevent identity theft, please don't publish my maiden name.

Create an online memorial at Legacy.com, so you can share and enjoy remembrances with friends and family. At the end of this section, I have included a flash drive that contains the content I'd like you to include on the memorial—a short biography, several photographs, and a snippet from our Christmas 2010 video.

BINDER

Including obituary materials in your planner. It will be most convenient for your survivors if you file your selected photographs, draft obituary (whether handwritten, printed, or stored on portable media such as a USB drive), remembrance plans, or other related materials in your planner binder. You can insert the photo in a plastic binder sleeve or hole-punch the obituary and other materials, inserting them into your planner binder immediately following the Obituary section.

Keeping Your Obituary Up to Date

It's a good idea to review your obituary information every year or two, updating important details that may have changed. Changes that may prompt you to revise your obituary include:

- moving (you may want to change the publications in which your obituary should be published)
- marriage, divorce, or the death of a spouse
- the birth of a child or grandchild
- new achievements or awards, or
- different wishes for contributions or remembrances to be made in your name.

CHAPTER

17

Will and Trust

Which Estate Planning Documents Do You Need? 142

You're Young and Without Dependents 142

You're Paired Up, But Not Married 142

You Have Young Children 143

You're Middle-Aged and Financially Comfortable 143

You're Elderly or Ill 143

An Overview of Wills and Trusts 144

Wills 144

Trusts 146

Choosing Your Executor or Successor Trustee 148

Important Factors to Consider 148

Naming More Than One Executor or Trustee 149

Naming Alternates 150

Compensation for Your Executor or Trustee 150

Avoiding Probate 150

Simplified Procedures for Small Estates 151

Revocable Living Trusts 151

Gifts 151

Payable-on-Death Bank Accounts 151

Retirement Accounts 151

Transfer-on-Death Registration of Securities 152

Transfer-on-Death Registration for Vehicles 152

Transfer-on-Death Deeds for Real Estate 152

Joint Ownership 152

Where to Get Help 153

Will You Need a Lawyer? 153

Resources From Nolo 154

In Your Planner 154

Keeping Your Documents Up to Date 156

> *The true meaning of life is to plant trees,*
> *under whose shade you do not expect to sit.*
>
> —NELSON HENDERSON (~1860)

Almost everyone needs a will to be sure that property passes the way they want it to after death. Depending on your situation, you may want to make additional legal documents to carry out your estate plan, such as a living trust.

This chapter provides an overview of basic estate planning documents. It will help you understand how they work, how to make them, and how to include important information about them in your planner.

SKIP AHEAD

If you've already completed your estate plan. If you've already made a will or other estate planning documents, you may want to skip right to "In Your Planner" to learn how to include these documents in your planner. Then read "Keeping Your Documents Up to Date," at the end of the chapter.

Which Estate Planning Documents Do You Need?

Whatever you own at your death is called your estate. So "estate planning" is the process of arranging for what will happen to your property when you die. Estate planning can also involve making arrangements for the care of your young children in the event of your death and taking steps to ensure that your survivors avoid probate court proceedings.

Your estate planning needs depend on your age, health, wealth, and how cautious you are. To decide where to begin, take a look at the life situations discussed below. Don't worry if none of these examples fit perfectly; these are just simple illustrations of typical situations.

You're Young and Without Dependents

If you're young and don't have any dependents, there's not much point in putting a lot of energy into estate planning. Unless your lifestyle is especially risky or you have a serious illness, you're very unlikely to die for a long time.

Consider making a will, however, if you're uncommonly rich, lead a high-risk lifestyle, or if you have possessions or property that you want to leave to a specific person.

TIP

Make a health care directive. You should also make health care directives no matter what your life circumstances—because accidents and unexpected illnesses do happen; see Chapter 11.

You're Paired Up, But Not Married

If you've got a life partner, but are not married to him or her, a will is a must-have document. Without a will, state law dictates where your property goes after your death—typically, your closest relatives will inherit everything. (In a few states, a registered domestic partner may be entitled to inherit property just as a spouse would, but even these protections are not a good substitute for making the right estate planning documents.)

It's also particularly important that you make health care directives and a durable power of attorney for finances; see Chapters 11 and 12 for more information.

You Have Young Children

If you have young children, you should make a will, if only to name a personal guardian for them. (You can do this only in a will, not in any other type of estate planning document.) The person you name would raise the children in the unlikely event that both you and the other parent could not. If you fail to name a guardian, a court will appoint someone if it's ever necessary. You can also use a will or a living trust to name a trusted adult to manage property that a child or young adult inherits from you.

You're Middle-Aged and Financially Comfortable

If you've made it to a comfortable time in life, you will probably want to take some time to reflect on what you will eventually leave behind.

To save your family the cost and hassle of probate court proceedings after your death, think about creating a revocable living trust. While you are alive, you can cancel the trust or change its terms at any time. After your death, a person you've chosen takes control of your trust property and transfers it according to the directions you left in the trust document, without probate. (Other good strategies are discussed in "Avoiding Probate," below.)

If you do decide to make a living trust, you will still need to make a backup will. A will is an essential catchall device for property not transferred to your living trust. Also, in a will you can name someone to be the personal guardian of your minor child—something you cannot do in a living trust.

You're Elderly or Ill

Now is the time to take concrete steps to establish an estate plan. It's also a good time to think about what could happen before your death if you become seriously ill and unable to handle your own affairs.

First, the basics: Consider a probate-avoidance living trust and, if you're coupled and very wealthy, a tax-saving AB trust (discussed below). Write a will, or update an old one.

Then, although no one wants to do it, take a minute to think about the possibility that at some time, you might become unable to handle day-to-day financial matters or make health care decisions. You can make a few simple documents to give someone legal authority to act on your behalf if you can't take care of things yourself. These documents—health care directives and a durable power of attorney for finances—are discussed just below.

TIP

Everyone should consider making health care directives and a durable power of attorney for finances. No matter what your age or health, you should make a health care directive, in which you state in writing the kind of medical care you want to receive if you are unable to speak for yourself and name a trusted person to oversee your wishes. Every day, people are injured in accidents and wind up in hospitals, and if they haven't made their wishes clear, confusion and disagreements about treatment can make it tough for close relatives. You can find more information about health care documents in Chapter 11.

To name someone to handle financial matters for you, you'll need a durable power of attorney for finances. This document gives a person you choose the legal authority to pay bills, deposit checks, and do whatever else is needed to manage your property on your behalf if you cannot.

Almost every adult who owns property can benefit from making a financial power of attorney, but it's critical to make one if you're older, facing a serious illness, or partnered but not married. Financial powers of attorney are covered in detail in Chapter 12.

An Overview of Wills and Trusts

Here's some more information to help you understand how wills and trusts work, and how to make them.

Wills

A will is the simplest legal document you can use to leave your property to others after your death. In it, you name your beneficiaries—that is, the people you want to inherit your property—and you specify the property you want them to receive. You can also use your will to name your executor—the person who will wind up your affairs after death—and to designate someone to care for your young children, if you have any.

When someone dies without a will (in legal jargon, this is called dying "intestate"), state law determines who inherits the deceased person's property. As described by the National Association of Financial and Estate Planning, "Dying intestate is like taking your property and attempting to throw it to your heirs on the other side of a deep chasm, a chasm which is filled with hazards." In other words, if you don't make a will or other estate planning documents, there's little chance that your property will end up where you want it to.

TIP

Include authority over digital assets. Talk to your attorney about using your will to give your executor the authority to access your online accounts and to manage or retrieve related assets or content. You might also be able to use your will to authorize the companies to disclose your information to your executor.

While such access may not be assured, it will certainly help your executor's efforts to secure the valuable contents of your accounts—correspondence, photos and other images, bill-paying history, and other data.

What's more, in the absence of a will, a court will determine who will care for minor children and their property if a surviving parent is unavailable or deemed unfit. If a judge appoints a property guardian, that person's authority to manage property will be limited and delayed by the ongoing involvement of the court. You can use a will to set up much more convenient methods for managing a young person's property.

Finally, property left by a will must usually go through probate court proceedings. To explore methods of avoiding probate for some or all of your property, read about living trusts and other probate-avoidance methods, below.

Legal Requirements

Any adult of sound mind can make a valid will. Beyond that, there are a few technical requirements:

- The document must expressly state that it's your will.
- You must sign and date the will.
- The will must be signed by at least two witnesses. Your witnesses must watch you sign the will, though they don't need to read it. In most states, witnesses must be people who won't inherit anything under the will.

You don't have to have your will notarized. In most states, however, if you and your witnesses sign an affidavit (sworn statement) before a notary public, you can greatly simplify the court procedures required to prove the validity of your will after you die. (This is called making your will "self-proving.")

Your will does not need to be recorded or filed with any government agency. Just keep your will in a safe, accessible place and be sure the person in charge of winding up your affairs (your executor) knows where it is. Your planner will help with these details; see "In Your Planner," below.

Who Gets Your Property—And What Should They Do With It?

While money can be divided equally among your heirs, most other property cannot—and this can lead to family squabbles. For this reason, you should include in your will or other estate plan all property of great value—whether sentimental or financial—that you wish to leave to specific individuals. Consider naming beneficiaries for any cherished heirlooms, artwork, jewelry, vehicles, collectibles, furniture, musical instruments, and all other property that means something to you (or to them).

If you're leaving an item of property to more than one beneficiary, be sure to specify the share they are each to receive—for example, whether you want them to own it in equal shares or whether one beneficiary should take a larger share than the others.

In addition to stating who gets what, you may also find that you have strong feelings about what your beneficiaries should do with particular items of property that you leave behind. For example, you might want them to keep the property in the family and take care of it—whether it is a vacation house or a horse. Or you might leave something to several beneficiaries with the hope that they will sell the property and split the proceeds among themselves. There's a limit to the type of binding instructions you can place on the property you leave in your will, but you are free to express your preferences. The best way to do this is to write a letter to accompany your will that explains your wishes, or use your planner itself to specify your preferences. (See Chapter 27 for instructions on how to do this.)

Property You Can't Leave by Will

In almost all states, you can't use your will to transfer the following kinds of property:

- **Property you hold in joint tenancy with someone else—or in "tenancy by the entirety" or "community property with right of survivorship" with your spouse.** At your death, your share will automatically belong to the surviving co-owner. A will provision leaving your share would have no effect unless all co-owners died simultaneously.
- **Property you've transferred to a living trust.**
- **Proceeds of a life insurance policy for which you've named a beneficiary.**
- **Money in a pension plan, individual retirement account (IRA), 401(k) plan, or other retirement plan.** Instead, you'll name the beneficiary on forms provided by the account administrator.
- **Stocks or bonds held in beneficiary (transfer-on-death or TOD) form.** If you want to change the beneficiary, contact the brokerage company.
- **Money in a payable-on-death bank account.** If you want to name a different beneficiary, just fill out a simple form at the bank.
- **Vehicles held in beneficiary (transfer-on-death) form.** If you want to change your beneficiary, file a new registration document with your state's motor vehicles department.
- **Real estate named in a transfer-on-death deed.** If you want to name a different beneficiary, make a new transfer-on-death deed.

Most of these are common probate-avoidance methods that are discussed in more detail in "Avoiding Probate," below.

RELATED TOPIC

Do you have an ethical will? An ethical will is a statement about the experiences, values, and beliefs that have shaped your life. It is not a legal document and you should not confuse it with the will you use to leave property to others, your health care directive (sometimes called a "living will"), or a living trust. The letter you write to your loved ones using Chapter 1 of this book is a type of ethical will. If you have made a separate ethical will for your survivors, you should file it in Section 1 of your planner, along with your letter.

Handwritten and Oral Wills

Handwritten, unwitnessed wills, called "holographic" wills, are legal in about 25 states. To be valid, a holographic will must be written, dated, and signed in the handwriting of the person making the will. Some states allow you to use a fill-in-the-blanks form if the rest of the will is handwritten and the will is properly dated and signed.

A holographic will is better than nothing if it is valid in your state. But generally, they aren't recommended. Unlike regular wills, no witnesses watch you sign, so if your will ends up before a probate court, the court may be strict when examining it. It's far better, and not too difficult, to make a valid, witnessed will.

Oral wills (sometimes called "nuncupative" wills) are valid in only a few states, and even then they're only accepted under extreme circumstances, such as the willmaker's danger of imminent death while serving in the military. Clearly, you shouldn't rely on oral instructions as a way to leave your property.

Trusts

A trust is an arrangement under which one person, called a trustee, holds legal title to property for another person, called a beneficiary. This section focuses on the most common type of trust—a basic revocable living trust, used to avoid probate court proceedings after your death. It also introduces AB trusts, with which a wealthy couple can save on estate tax.

Basic Living Trusts

A revocable living trust allows property to quickly and efficiently pass to the beneficiaries you name, without the trouble and expense of probate court proceedings. You can make an individual living trust, or if you're married or partnered, you and your spouse can use a shared living trust to handle both co-owned property and the separate property of either spouse.

To create a basic living trust, you make a document called a Declaration of Trust, which is similar to a will. You name yourself as trustee—the person in charge of the trust property. Then you transfer ownership of some or all of your property to yourself in your capacity as trustee. For example, you might sign a deed transferring your house from yourself to yourself "as trustee of the Jane Smith Revocable Living Trust dated July 12, 2014."

Because you're the trustee, you don't give up any control over the property you put in trust. If you and your spouse create a trust together, you will be cotrustees.

In the Declaration of Trust, you name the people or organizations you want to inherit trust property after your death. You can later change your beneficiaries if you wish; you can also revoke the trust at any time.

When you die, the person you named in the trust document to take over—called the successor trustee—transfers ownership of trust property to the people you want to get it. In most cases, the successor trustee can handle the whole thing in a few weeks with some simple paperwork. No probate court proceedings are required.

Not everyone needs a living trust, however. A living trust may be more than you need if:

- **You are young and healthy.** Many younger people decide to go with just a will (and perhaps life insurance, if they have young kids) and prepare a living trust later in life when they own more property and the prospect of death is more imminent.

- **You can more sensibly transfer assets by other probate-avoidance devices.** There are a number of other ways to avoid probate, and some of them may work well for you. (See below.)
- **You have, or may have, complex debt problems.** One of the benefits of probate is that it provides a deadline by which creditors must file claims against an estate. Not so with a living trust. If you expect trouble with debts, you may want the protections of a full probate proceeding.
- **There's no one you trust to oversee your trust after your death.** If you can't name a successor trustee who's truly trustworthy, a living trust isn't right for you.
- **You own little property.** If you don't own much, probate will be unnecessary or relatively inexpensive (see "Avoiding Probate," below). You won't need to bother with a living trust or probate avoidance—a will should do just fine.

Tax-Saving AB Trusts

A basic probate-avoidance living trust has no effect on taxes. More complicated living trusts, however, can sometimes reduce the federal estate tax bill for people with substantial property.

But first, the good news: Most people don't need to think about federal estate tax, which kicks in only when someone dies owning a very large amount of property. The amount of the estate tax exemption depends on the year of death. (For details, see "Federal Estate Tax," in Chapter 24.)

If you're married or coupled and you expect that your estate may owe estate tax, consider creating a living trust that will both avoid probate and also save on federal estate tax. If you don't, there may be a big estate tax bill when the second spouse dies. That's because the surviving spouse's estate will include his or her share of the couple's property plus the property inherited from the deceased spouse.

An AB trust, also known as a living trust with marital life estate, lets a couple pass the maximum amount of property to their children or other beneficiaries after both spouses die, while at the same time ensuring the surviving spouse is financially comfortable during his or her lifetime.

Here's how it works: Instead of leaving property outright to the surviving spouse, each spouse puts most or all of his or her property in an AB trust. When one spouse dies, the surviving spouse can use that property, with certain restrictions, but doesn't own it outright. That's the reason behind the big tax savings: The property isn't subject to estate tax when the second spouse dies, because the second spouse never legally owned it.

When setting up an AB trust, each spouse names final beneficiaries who will receive the trust's property when the surviving spouse dies. Spouses often name the same people—their children—as final beneficiaries, but it's not mandatory.

Not all couples who may owe estate tax need an AB trust. If you're worried about estate taxes, discuss your options with an experienced estate planning attorney or tax advisor.

Complex Trusts

In addition to basic and AB living trusts, there is a host of more complicated trusts that you might want to consider if you're either very wealthy or have special personal circumstances. These include complex, irrevocable trusts that can help wealthy couples save on estate taxes—such as QTIP trusts, generation-skipping trusts, life-insurance trusts, or charitable remainder trusts. You can also make a "spendthrift" trust that will place controls on property that you want to leave to a beneficiary who is not capable of managing money. And "special needs" trusts allow you to leave property to loved ones with disabilities, without jeopardizing their ability to qualify for government benefits.

A discussion of these trusts is beyond the scope of this book; to get more information you'll need to consult one of the resources listed below, or talk with a knowledgeable estate planning lawyer—perhaps both.

Of course you should include in your planner essential information about any trust that you make. See "In Your Planner," below.

Marital Property Agreements

A marital property agreement is a contract you make with your spouse either prior to marriage (a prenuptial or premarital agreement) or after you are married (a postnuptial agreement). The purpose of a marital property agreement is to establish your property rights if you divorce or when one of you dies; these rights usually differ from the rights you would have under state law.

For example, most states provide that a surviving spouse is entitled to claim one-half to one-third of the deceased spouse's property no matter what the deceased spouse's will or other estate plan says. (In community property states, the surviving spouse automatically owns half of the couple's property.) In a marital property agreement, one or both spouses may waive these inheritance rights to ensure that property passes as they wish—for instance, to children from a previous marriage.

If you and your spouse have a marital property agreement, it may affect the way your property passes when one of you dies. It's important to include it in your planner.

Do You Still Need a Will?

Even if you make a trust, a will is an essential backup device for property that you don't transfer to it. For example, if you acquire property shortly before you die, you may not think to transfer ownership of it to your trust—which means that it won't pass under the terms of the trust document. But in your backup will, you can include a clause that names someone to get any property that you haven't left to a particular person or entity.

If you don't have a will, any property that isn't transferred by your living trust or other probate-avoidance device (such as joint tenancy) will go to your closest relatives in an order determined by state law. As discussed earlier, these laws may not distribute property in the way you would have chosen. Additionally, you will want to make a will to name an executor and to name a guardian for your young children, if you have them. You can't do these things with a living trust.

Choosing Your Executor or Successor Trustee

One of the most important decisions you'll make when completing your will or trust is selecting your executor (the person responsible for carrying out the wishes in your will and wrapping up your final affairs) or your successor trustee (the person responsible for managing and distributing the assets in your living trust). For both, you should also choose an alternate, in case your first choice is unable to serve for any reason. Aside from yourself, these are the people for whom you are going to the trouble of preparing this planner.

To simplify things for purposes of this discussion, both the executor and successor trustee are often referred to simply as your "representative."

Important Factors to Consider

Your representative may be your spouse or partner, relative, or close friend. Keep in mind that the responsibilities may be significant, dragging on over a year or more, and through a difficult time of grief and loss for family and friends. Your representative may even have to stand up to beneficiaries or other family members who are driven by their own beliefs and interests, rather than yours. To do a good job, your representative should:

- be sufficiently assertive and honest—that is, capable of honoring your wishes while being accountable to your heirs
- be organized and capable of handling details, because tasks will be many and varied, stretching out over a year or two following your death
- possess solid communication skills, to work with attorneys, tax preparers, financial and real property advisers, and to serve as liaison to your heirs
- have strong interpersonal skills, if you expect him or her to be working with conflicts or difficult personalities, and
- have the time and energy to take on the job.

While you need not name someone who lives in the same city or state as you do, proximity can also be important. Your representative may be called upon to spend weeks, even months, at your home or business, managing your estate, overseeing your wishes, and distributing your property. Some states also impose restrictions on out-of-state (often called "nonresident") executors, so if you want to name an executor who lives in a different state, you should check your state's laws first.

Once you have identified the people you'd like to name, discuss your choice with each to be sure they agree. Go over the job and, as much as possible, familiarize your representatives with your estate and your wishes. Show them your planner and be sure they will be able to obtain all the materials they'll need after your death.

Naming an Institution as Your Representative

Usually, it's a much better idea to name a person to represent you than a bank or other institution. You'll want someone human, with genuine concern, to take care of these important matters.

Ideally, you'll name someone you know, with whom you have a personal and close relationship—perhaps an adult child or sibling. If no one close to you is available or suitable, you could ask your attorney, another attorney recommended by your attorney, a professional in your bank's trust department, or a professional fiduciary sourced through the local bar association.

However, in some circumstances, you may find yourself wanting or needing to name a corporate executor or trustee. This may be true if your estate is very complex—say, you own a business that will need to stay up and running for a while and there isn't anyone you know who can manage it—or if there's absolutely no one you trust to serve as your executor or trustee.

In cases like these, selecting an institution is preferable to failing to name a representative. But be aware that you may have a tough time finding an institution willing to take on the job. It won't be a problem if you're very wealthy, but if your estate is modest, many institutions will turn you away because they won't make enough profit on the deal.

Naming More Than One Executor or Trustee

Though you are legally permitted to name more than one person to execute your will or manage your trust, it's best to name just one. This is true even if you know two or more people who are suitable candidates and who agree to be coexecutors or cotrustees. There may be problems, brought on by passing time and human nature, with naming people to share a representative's job. Disagreements between them could disrupt the handling of your estate. Feuding representatives could even end up taking their dispute to court, further delaying and confusing the management and distribution of your property.

In addition, if you make both a will and a trust, it's usually wise to name the same person as both your executor and your successor trustee. If you feel that you must name different people, be very sure your representatives are likely to get along and work together well.

If you fear that those close to you may feel hurt if you name someone else to represent you, take some time to talk with them to explain your choice. Or, if there are several people you'd feel comfortable naming, you might even let them decide among themselves who the representative will be. If you approve of their choice, you can accept it—and name the others as alternates in case your first choice can't serve.

Naming Alternates

It's important to name one or more alternate executors or trustees, to represent you if your first choice is unable to take the job for any reason or resigns after your death. Alternates serve one at a time, in the order that you specify.

It's a good idea to name at least one alternate executor and trustee, but you should be as thoughtful about naming your alternates as you are about picking your first choice. Be sure to name people who will represent you well if the need arises.

Compensation for Your Executor or Trustee

Executors and trustees are entitled to reasonable compensation for the work they do on your behalf. Just how much depends on what you set out in the will or trust document, and on state law. That said, most representatives don't expect—or accept—any payment unless the job is unusually difficult or long lasting. This is because they are usually close family members who will inherit most of the property, anyway. (There are also tax considerations. If a representative accepts a fee, the money is taxable income for him or her. If the representative is going to inherit the money anyway, it's almost always better to take it as an inheritance, which isn't taxed.)

If you aren't appointing a relative or close friend as your representative, you may want to specify in your will or trust that they are entitled to a reasonable fee for their work. (Even though they could collect the fee under state law no matter what the document says.) Indeed, you may choose someone because of his or her special skills—perhaps your executor can manage your business until it can be sold, or maybe your successor trustee possesses the unique ability to calm a potentially unpleasant family situation—and it's only fair that you offer compensation.

Avoiding Probate

Property left by a will must normally go through probate—that is, the legal process that includes filing a deceased person's will with a court, locating and gathering the assets, paying debts and taxes, and ultimately distributing what's left as the will directs.

For most estates, probate has significant drawbacks. It usually ties up property for months—sometimes even a year or more. And it's expensive. Attorney and court fees can take up to 5% of an estate's value. Fortunately, for most property, probate is also fairly easy to avoid. This section introduces the most common ways to do it. For more details about the methods discussed here, turn to the resources listed in "Where to Get Help," below.

Simplified Procedures for Small Estates

Almost every state now offers shortcuts through probate—or a way around it completely—for "small estates." Each state defines that term differently. Because of the way the laws are written, however, many large estates, worth hundreds of thousands of dollars, are eligible for special transfer procedures that speed property to inheritors.

There are two basic kinds of probate shortcuts for small estates:

Claiming property with affidavits—no court required. If the total value of all the assets you leave behind is less than a certain amount, the people who inherit your personal property—that's anything except real estate—may be able to skip probate entirely. The exact amount depends on state law, and varies widely. If the estate qualifies, an inheritor can prepare a short document stating that he or she is entitled to a certain item of property under a will or state law. This paper, signed under oath, is called an affidavit. When the person or institution holding the property—for example, a bank where the deceased person had an account—receives the affidavit and a copy of the death certificate, it releases the money or other property.

Simplified court procedures. Another option for small estates (again, as defined by state law) is a quicker, simpler version of probate. The probate court is still involved, but it exerts far less control over the settling of the estate. In many states, these procedures are straightforward enough to handle without a lawyer, so they save money as well as time.

Revocable Living Trusts

Living trusts are common probate-avoidance devices. They are discussed above.

Gifts

Giving away property while you're alive helps you avoid probate for a very simple reason: If you don't own it when you die, it doesn't have to go through probate. That reduces probate costs because, as a general rule, the greater the monetary value of the assets that go through probate, the greater the expense. If you give away enough assets, your estate might even qualify for a streamlined "small estate" probate procedure after your death (discussed just above).

If you are considering making several large gifts, you should know that giving more than $14,000 to any one recipient in one calendar year requires filing a federal gift tax return. You won't actually have to pay any tax now, but the amount you give away will reduce your estate tax exemption after death.

Payable-on-Death Bank Accounts

Payable-on-death bank accounts offer one of the easiest ways to keep money—even large sums of it—out of probate. All you need to do is fill out a simple form, provided by the bank, naming the person you want to inherit the money in the account.

At your death, the beneficiary just goes to the bank, shows proof of the death and of his or her identity, and collects whatever funds are in the account. The probate court is never involved.

For more information, see "Bank Accounts," in Chapter 19.

Retirement Accounts

When you open a retirement account such as an IRA or 401(k), the forms you fill out will ask you to name a beneficiary for the account. After your death, whatever funds are left in the account will not have to go through probate; instead, the beneficiary you named can claim the money directly from the account custodian.

For more information about naming beneficiaries for your retirement accounts, see Chapter 20.

Transfer-on-Death Registration of Securities

Almost every state has adopted a law (the Uniform Transfer-on-Death Securities Registration Act) that lets you name someone to inherit your stocks, bonds, or brokerage accounts without probate. It works very much like a payable-on-death bank account.

For more information about naming beneficiaries for transferring securities, see "Brokerage Accounts," in Chapter 19.

Transfer-on-Death Registration for Vehicles

Arizona, Arkansas, California, Connecticut, Delaware, Illinois, Indiana, Kansas, Missouri, Nebraska, Nevada, Ohio, Vermont, and Virginia offer car owners the sensible option of naming a beneficiary, right on their certificate of title or title application, to inherit a vehicle.

To learn more, see Chapter 26.

Transfer-on-Death Deeds for Real Estate

In several states—Arizona, Arkansas, Colorado, District of Columbia, Hawaii, Illinois, Indiana, Kansas, Minnesota, Missouri, Montana, Nebraska, Nevada, New Mexico, North Dakota, Ohio, Oklahoma, Oregon, Virginia, Washington, Wisconsin, and Wyoming—you can transfer real estate without probate by creating what's known as a "transfer-on-death" deed. These deeds must be prepared, signed, notarized, and filed in the county land records office just like a regular deed. The deed should clearly state that it doesn't take effect until death—and you can revoke it any time before then. (Don't try this in any but the handful of states listed here; it won't work.)

For more about real estate, see the next section, "Joint Ownership," and Chapter 25.

Joint Ownership

Several forms of joint ownership—joint tenancy, for example—provide an easy way to avoid probate when the first owner dies. To take title with someone else in a way that avoids probate, you usually don't have to prepare any additional documents. All you do is state, on the paper that shows your ownership (a real estate deed, for example), how you want to hold title.

Joint Tenancy With Right of Survivorship

Property owned in joint tenancy automatically passes, without probate, to the surviving owner(s) when one owner dies. Joint tenancy often works well when couples (married or not) acquire real estate, vehicles, bank accounts, securities, or other valuable property together. Setting up a joint tenancy is easy, and it doesn't cost a penny.

After one joint owner dies, generally all the new owner has to do is fill out a straightforward form and present it, with a death certificate, to the keeper of ownership records: a bank, state motor vehicle department, or county real estate records office.

Joint tenancy is usually a poor estate planning choice when an older person, seeking only to avoid probate, is tempted to put solely owned property into joint tenancy with someone else. Adding another owner this way creates several potential headaches:

- **You're giving away part ownership of the property.** The new owner has rights that you can't take back. For example, the new owner can sell or mortgage his or her share—or lose it to creditors.
- **You may have to file a gift tax return.** If the value of the interest you give to a new co-owner (except your spouse) exceeds $14,000 in one year, you must file a gift

tax return with the IRS (unless you're adding a joint tenant to a bank account to which you deposited the money; in that case, no gift is made until the other person withdraws money). No tax is actually due, however, until you leave or give away a large amount in taxable gifts. (The threshold is changing year-to-year, as the federal estate tax laws evolve.)

- **It may spawn disputes after your death.** Many older people make the mistake of adding someone as a joint tenant to a bank account just for "convenience." They want someone to help them out by depositing checks and paying bills. But after the original owner dies, the co-owner may claim that he or she is entitled, as a surviving joint tenant, to keep the funds remaining in the account. In some instances, maybe that's what the deceased person really intended—it's too late to ask. (If you want to give someone authority to use your money on your behalf, use a power of attorney. See Chapter 12 for more information.)

CAUTION

Check your state's law. A number of states have special rules or restrictions for establishing a joint tenancy. For example, in some states, you must include very specific language on the title document. These requirements aren't hard to meet, but you don't want to overlook them. Check the rules for your state before you proceed.

Tenancy by the Entirety

In some states, married couples often take title not in joint tenancy, but in "tenancy by the entirety" instead. It's very similar to joint tenancy, but can be used only by married couples (or by registered domestic partners in just a couple of states). Both avoid probate in exactly the same way.

Community Property With Right of Survivorship

If you are married and live or own property in Alaska, Arizona, California, Nevada, or Wisconsin, there is another way to co-own property with your spouse: community property with the right of survivorship. If you hold title to property in this way, when one spouse dies, the other automatically owns the asset. Transferring title to the surviving spouse is simple and doesn't require court proceedings.

Where to Get Help

Chances are good that you can make your own basic estate planning documents, without hiring a lawyer. This section helps you decide whether or not you'll need a lawyer's help and provides some good self-help resources for getting more information and making your own documents.

Will You Need a Lawyer?

If your wishes are fairly simple, you probably won't need a lawyer to create your estate planning documents. For example, making a will rarely involves complicated legal rules, and most people can draft their own will with the aid of a good self-help book or software program. You just need to know what you own and who you care about, and have a good resource to guide you.

A basic living trust isn't much more complicated than a will, and you probably won't need to hire a lawyer. With a good self-help resource, you can create a valid Declaration of Trust (the document that creates a trust) yourself. For property that you want to leave through the trust you must also take care of some crucial paperwork—retitling property to the trust. For example, if you want to leave your house through the trust, you must sign a new deed, showing that you now own the house as trustee of your living trust. This paperwork can be tedious, but it is not difficult because living trusts have become so common.

If you have questions that aren't answered by the resource you're relying on, it's worthwhile to see a good lawyer. You usually won't have to turn over the whole project; you can simply ask your questions and then finish making your own will and trust.

On the other hand, if your estate is large or complicated, you may want to consult a good estate planning lawyer and have the lawyer draw up your documents to make sure your plan is sound and your intentions will be carried out as you wish. This may cost a couple of thousand dollars or more, depending on where you live and the complexity of your plan—but if your estate warrants a lawyer's involvement, you can almost certainly afford the help. Here are a few situations in which you should consider talking with a lawyer:

- **Your estate may owe federal estate tax.** See "Federal Estate Tax," in Chapter 24, for more information.
- **Your family situation is complex.** For example, there is tension between a current spouse and children from a former marriage, or one of your primary beneficiaries has a disability and receives government benefits or is too irresponsible to manage an inheritance.
- **The property you leave will require an unusually high degree of care or management.** For example, if you own a business and you haven't already made a sound plan for someone to take over.
- **You want to make a marital property agreement.** You may be able to draft your own agreement, but you will need separate lawyers to review and finalize the document. Otherwise your agreement may not stand up in court.

If you don't already have a good lawyer, see Appendix B. It provides suggestions to help you find a knowledgeable expert.

Resources From Nolo

The following resources from Nolo will help you learn more about estate planning and related matters. You'll also want to visit Nolo's website at www.nolo.com. There, you'll find all the resources listed below, plus hundreds of free articles on estate planning and other essential legal topics.

- **Nolo's Online Will and Living Trust.** You can make your will or living trust online at www.nolo.com. You'll be asked a series of straightforward questions and offered help along the way.
- ***Quicken WillMaker Plus* (software for Windows)** lets you use your computer to prepare a comprehensive will. The program also helps you to prepare a health care directive, a durable power of attorney for finances, and other useful forms.
- ***Plan Your Estate,*** by Denis Clifford, offers in-depth discussion of all significant elements of estate planning, from simple wills to complex tax-saving trusts.
- ***8 Ways to Avoid Probate,*** by Mary Randolph, offers a thorough discussion of the major ways to transfer property at death outside of a will.
- ***Special Needs Trusts: Protect Your Child's Financial Future,*** by Stephen R. Elias and Kevin Urbatsch, shows you how to leave money to a disabled loved one without jeopardizing government benefits.
- ***Prenuptial Agreements: How to Write a Fair & Lasting Contract,*** by Katherine E. Stoner and Shae Irving, helps you prepare your own prenup. It contains detailed clauses for drafting your own agreement and tips on negotiating, communicating, and working with lawyers to finalize your document.

In Your Planner

Turn to the Will and Trust section of your planner (Section 17). The following guidelines will help you complete the pages there.

RELATED TOPIC

In this section, you should list all of your key estate planning documents—that is, your will and any trusts or marital property agreements you have made. You will cover other estate planning issues—such as pay-on-death designations for bank accounts, securities, or vehicles, or beneficiary designations for retirement accounts—in other sections of your planner.

For each document you've made, provide the following information:

- **Document Title.** Fill in the name of the document here. This could be as simple as "Will" or "Living Trust," or you may want to take the title directly from the top of the document, if there is one: "Will of Jackson M. Jones," or "The Ella Bradford Harris Living Trust."
- **Date Prepared.** Indicate the date on which you signed the document. This will help your survivors identify the document and avoid confusion.
- **Professional Help.** Indicate whether or not you had professional help with the document—for example, from an attorney, paralegal, or CPA.
- **Professional's Name, Title, and Contact Information.** If someone helped you prepare the document, enter enough information here to help your survivors locate that person if necessary.
- **Location of Original Document.** State where your survivors can find the signed, original copy of the document. (You may be able to include the original document in your planner; see the instructions below.)
- **Locations of Copies of This Document.** List the names of anyone who has a copy of the document, and any place where you've filed a copy. (You should keep at least a copy of each document in your planner, if possible. Again, see the instructions below.)
- **Executor and Successor Trustee.** Fill in the name of the executor of your will or the successor trustee of your living trust, if you've made one. Also include the names of any alternate representatives you've named.
- **Additional Notes.** Here you can add anything you feel your survivors should know about the document that they wouldn't be able to figure out from reviewing the document itself. For example, you might want to list any self-help resources you used, or explain why you selected someone to be your executor, successor trustee, or guardian of your child.

EXAMPLES:

I prepared my own will using *Quick & Legal Will Book*, by Denis Clifford.

I have chosen my daughter Becky Arnold Jones as executor of my will, and have named my son Tom Arnold as alternate executor. I have complete faith that any of my children could represent me well. However, Becky and Tom live nearby and I feel the task will be less difficult for them for that reason.

With much consideration and discussion—including with many of you—we have selected Chloe and Isaac Smith, our dear friends, as guardians for our children, should the need arise. The Smith children are close in age to our own, and we feel that Chloe and Isaac could best provide a home and family for our children. Please embrace the Smiths as members of our larger family.

BINDER

Including your will, trust, and related documents in your planner. For your convenience and to aid your executor, successor trustee, and survivors, include in your binder at least a photocopy of your will and any trusts or marital property agreements. If you will be storing your entire planner in a secure location at home—for example, in a fireproof safe—you can even tuck the originals into the binder. For photocopies, you can hole-punch the documents and slip them into the binder following this section. For originals, it's best not to mar them with holes. You'll want to get pocket dividers that you can insert after this section, and put the originals into the pockets.

Keeping Your Documents Up to Date

After you've made a will or trust, you will want to conduct an annual review to be sure everything's up to date. Here are some questions to ask yourself when deciding whether it's time to update a document:

- Have you changed your mind about who you want to inherit a significant portion of your property?
- Have you married, found a new life partner, or lost a spouse due to divorce or death?
- Do you have new children or stepchildren?
- Have you acquired or disposed of substantial assets, such as a home or business?
- Are your choices for executor, successor trustee, or children's guardian or property manager still appropriate?
- Do you need to add additional property to your trust, if you've made one?

There are two ways to modify a will: either make a new one or add what's known as a "codicil" to the existing will. A codicil is an amendment or addition to a will revoking part of it or adding a provision, such as a new gift of an item of property. Codicils usually aren't the best way to change a will—they run the risk of creating contradictions or confusion about the will's terms. Because of this, and because a codicil must be dated, signed, and witnessed just like a regular will, it's usually just as easy, and more foolproof, to make a brand-new will. Gather all copies of your old will, destroy them, and replace them with the new will. To be safe, the new will should contain a simple statement like this: "I revoke all wills and codicils that I previously made."

Updating a trust generally means simply adding an amendment to the original document or creating a trust "restatement" that includes the new information. As with your original trust, be sure that you take the necessary steps to transfer new property to the name of the trust. You may even want to carry a wallet card printed with the legal name and date of your trust, so that titling property is easy and becomes second nature.

If appropriate, ask your attorney (or any other professional who helped you with the original documents) to assist with changes to a will, trust, or marital property agreement—or just ask for a review of the changes you've made.

If you make changes to an estate planning document, be sure to make any corresponding changes to Section 17 of your planner.

CHAPTER

18

Insurance

What Kind of Insurance Do You Need? 158

Life Insurance 159

Long-Term Care Insurance 164

Where to Get Help 168

Life Insurance 168

Long-Term Care Insurance 168

In Your Planner 169

Keeping Your Information Up to Date 170

Everything is sweetened by risk.

—ALEXANDER SMITH (1830–1867), "CITY POEM: THE FEAR OF DYING"

An insurance policy is a contract that provides reimbursement for specific losses or injuries in exchange for a periodic payment (called the premium). Insurance policies cover people and property for the costs of loss or injury due to death, illness, accident, fire, flood, and much more. Common insurance types include life, medical and dental, disability, home, and vehicle insurance.

Your planner is a convenient place to summarize and organize your insurance policies so your caretakers and survivors will know what coverage you have and what benefits you're owed. This information will help them request insurance proceeds, and modify or cancel policies.

Before turning to the specifics of your planner, however, you may want to take some time to consider whether you have all the insurance you need. (Or, on the other hand, whether you might do fine with less.) Because you're completing this planner and thinking about end-of-life issues, it makes sense to focus on two types of insurance: life insurance and long-term care insurance.

SKIP AHEAD

If you're well covered. If you've got your insurance act together—you're confident that you've got the right coverage, your policies are up to date, and you're comfortable with your beneficiary designations—you may want to skip right to "In Your Planner" for directions on including insurance information and materials in your planner. Then turn to "Keeping Your Information Up to Date" for tips on keeping your planner current.

What Kind of Insurance Do You Need?

The most common insurance policies are those covering your health (medical, dental, and vision), your home and its contents (homeowners' or renters' insurance), and your vehicles. It's prudent to have these basic policies in place to reduce health care costs and to cover damage or loss to your home or your personal property.

You may also have disability insurance to replace your income if you become severely ill or injured and unable to work. A disability insurance policy can supplement any benefits you receive through your state disability insurance plan, Social Security, or workers' compensation. Your personal situation—the number of people depending on your salary, the amount of your savings, and other available sources of income—will dictate whether disability insurance would be a wise investment for you.

If you're a professional or self-employed, you're probably well aware of the types of policies you need to cover personal liability, malpractice, or errors and omissions. If not, and you own your own business or are a practicing professional or executive who may be subject to personal liability for your actions, it would pay for you to investigate your insurance options.

When it comes to life and long-term care insurance, most people aren't sure whether they need coverage, what types to buy, and how much to purchase. This part of the guide helps you make decisions about these two types of policies.

Beyond the Norm

Don't think for a moment that insurance comes only in the typical forms mentioned here. You can insure almost anything—assuming you're willing to pay the premiums. Here's some not-so-common coverage:

- Alien Abduction
- Asteroid Damage
- Breast Implant Explosion
- Celebration Disruption
- Immaculate Conception
- Impregnation by Aliens
- Injury by Ghosts or Werewolves
- Kidnapping
- Pet Mortality
- Stallion Disability
- Wine Collection Loss.

One woman insured her looks for £100,000. If she is ever rated unattractive by an independent "wolf-whistling builders" panel, the insurance company will pay. And there have been others: Formula One racing champion Fernando Alonso insured his thumbs for $13.3 million, Bruce Springsteen insured his voice for $6 million, a winemaker insured his nose for $7.8 million, and a street artist insured his eyes for $1 million.

Life Insurance

A life insurance policy pays benefits to named beneficiaries when the insured person dies. (Generally the payment is a single lump sum, but there are also policies that pay benefits over time.) The most common reason to purchase life insurance is to provide money for a spouse and children. Less often, people purchase life insurance so that there will be cash on hand to cover expenses after death.

This section sets out the basic types of life insurance, the reasons you may—or may not—need it, and some tips to help you make choices about any policy you do decide to buy.

Types of Life Insurance

The two primary types of life insurance are term and permanent, with many variations available.

Term insurance. Term insurance provides coverage for a specified length of time, such as ten years. If you die while the policy is in effect, term insurance pays your beneficiaries the face value of the policy. Once the term expires, so does the coverage.

Term insurance is less expensive than permanent insurance, because you are simply paying for the life insurance coverage and not for additional benefits (discussed below) you might enjoy with permanent insurance.

Term insurance may be appropriate for younger parents seeking coverage for the number of years that their children will be dependent. It is also a good choice whenever you need insurance for just a short period—for example, to qualify for a business loan.

The benefits of term insurance vary depending on the insurance company. Some policies:

- are automatically renewable, without a medical examination
- offer fixed premiums for the first year
- offer fixed premiums for several years, or
- can be converted into permanent insurance.

Permanent insurance. Permanent insurance is more expensive than term insurance, but it offers certain benefits that term insurance does not. Permanent insurance cannot be canceled as long as you pay the premiums—regardless of your age, your health, or the number of years you have held the policy. A permanent insurance policy is also an investment.

During the early years of your permanent insurance policy, your premiums (reduced a bit by commissions for the agent) go into a reserve account that is invested by the insurance company. As the investment yields returns, a portion of the returns are passed on to you.

Over time, you can let the returns accumulate in your reserve account, you can use them to pay your premiums, or you can borrow against them. If you choose to cancel your policy, your reserve account will be paid to you as "surrender value" on your policy.

The Annuity Alternative

An annuity is another way to establish a future payment stream. Briefly, it's a policy under which the insurance company agrees to pay the beneficiary a certain amount of cash each year (or month), instead of a one-time payout at death. You may be drawn to this idea if you feel that your beneficiary will be unable to manage a single, large payment. However, there may be less expensive—and more flexible—ways to achieve the goal of providing a beneficiary with payments over time. Consider establishing a trust, with a responsible family member or friend serving as trustee and administering its terms. You can establish a simple, ongoing trust for a young person in your will or living trust. (See Chapter 17.) For more complex trusts, you'll want to consult a lawyer.

There are several types of permanent life insurance. Here are the most common:

- **Whole life insurance.** Whole life (also called "straight life") insurance offers fixed coverage, with a uniform payment schedule over the life of the policy. Because the payment amount is fixed, the premium is relatively high in the early years (when your risk of death is lowest) and lower in the later years (when your risk of death increases).
- **Universal life insurance.** Universal life policies combine the best of both term and permanent insurance, and offer additional advantages. Like whole life, universal life builds reserves. But unlike the fixed premium amounts for whole life, the universal life policy allows you to vary the premium or the amount of coverage (or both) from year to year. Also, universal life provides consumer information that is typically not provided with a whole life policy—for example, you'll receive reports showing how your premium is applied: toward the insurance company's overhead expenses, for reserves and policy proceeds, and for your personal reserves or savings.
- **Variable life insurance.** The cash reserves of variable life policies are invested in securities, stocks, and bonds, combining the insurance reserve feature with a mutual fund. Your investment return, therefore, is tied to the performance of the financial markets.
- **Variable universal life insurance.** With variable universal life, you get a policy that combines flexible premium payments and coverage (as described for universal life, above) with the investment opportunity (and risk) of variable life insurance.
- **Single-premium life insurance.** With this type of life insurance, you pay for the policy up front. This requires a single, large payment—$5,000, $10,000, or more, depending on your age and the policy's value. Single-premium insurance may make sense if you are thinking of transferring the policy to a new owner to reduce estate taxes. (See "Transferring Ownership of Life Insurance," below.)
- **Survivorship life insurance.** Survivorship life insurance (also called "second to die" or "joint" insurance) is a single policy that insures two lives, usually spouses. When the first person dies, no proceeds are paid. The policy remains in effect and premiums are still due. Benefits are available only when the second person dies. This type of policy may be attractive to very wealthy couples who expect that substantial

estate taxes will be due when the second spouse dies. Insurance proceeds may be necessary to cover the taxes, particularly if family assets are tied up in a business or real estate—or anything else that's not liquid—and the survivors won't want to sell. (A survivorship policy may also be useful if not all the beneficiaries want to keep the asset: Those that do could use the insurance payment to buy out the others.) Finally, this type of policy may be wise if one spouse is in poor health and other types of life insurance are relatively expensive. Premiums on survivorship policies are often comparatively low.

SEE AN EXPERT

Federal taxes and survivorship life insurance. The federal tax laws governing survivorship life insurance are somewhat ambiguous. Because this is a complex area, you need to check with an estate planning lawyer who knows the latest tax rules. Also, discuss this issue with your insurance agent to ensure that your survivorship policy will have the effect you intend. It may be best to have the policy owned by a life insurance trust. (See "Transferring Ownership of Life Insurance," below.)

- **"First to die" life insurance.** This type of insurance is the reverse of survivorship life. With first to die life insurance, two or more people are insured under a single life insurance policy and proceeds are paid when the first person dies. These policies are particularly useful for business partners. When the first partner dies, the proceeds are paid to the surviving partners or the company. Proceeds can be used to buy out the deceased person's beneficiaries or to make other necessary business adjustments due to the death of an owner.

Additional Life Insurance Benefits

You can often add extra coverage to a standard life insurance policy through what is known as a policy endorsement. The premium will rise as coverage increases. (The reverse is also true: Reduced coverage, through a policy endorsement, can reduce your premiums.) The most common life insurance endorsements are:

- **Accidental Death:** Typically doubles your death benefit (called "double indemnity") if you die from a type of accident covered by the policy.
- **Family Income Benefit:** Guarantees a monthly payment to your family for a specified period of time following your death.
- **Spouse and Children:** Covers not only your life but also the lives of your spouse and/or children.
- **Waiver of Premium:** Protects your policy from being canceled in covered situations, such as disability.
- **Renewal Provision:** Guarantees that your policy will be renewed at the end of its term.
- **Withdrawal Provision:** Allows you to withdraw money from your reserves (reducing the policy coverage by the amount of your withdrawal).

Evaluating Your Need for Life Insurance

Before you buy a life insurance policy, carefully consider whether you really need it. Think about all sources of income that will be available to your survivors. These might include the property you leave behind, proceeds from another policy (such as a group life insurance plan or death benefits through your union), Social Security survivor benefits, or assistance from other family members.

If you are wealthy, or if your relatives are wealthy, you may need little or no life insurance.

Your accumulated wealth will most likely cover immediate and long-term living expenses. On the other hand, if you are struggling just to get by, or if you are young and healthy, you might consider purchasing a term insurance policy. A moderate term policy can provide quick cash to your survivors at relatively low cost to you.

If you're going to buy life insurance, how much do you need? That depends on your plans for the proceeds. You most likely want insurance to provide ready cash for expenses after your death or to provide some money for your spouse or children. Or you may want to leave a sum of money for someone else. Here's a brief look at each goal:

After-Death Expenses

Most people don't need life insurance to cover postdeath expenses such as funeral costs, debts, or taxes. If you're not sure how much your estate is likely to owe, you can make a rough estimate by working through a few chapters of this guide: Chapters 13, 14, and 15 (your final arrangements); 22 (Credit Cards and Debts); and 24 (Taxes). When thinking about final expenses, consider your bank accounts, securities, and other cash assets, and then determine the additional amount (if any) that your survivors will need to cover death-related costs. You may be able to set aside the necessary amount in a joint bank account or a pay-on-death bank account. If you believe that life insurance is your best option for covering expected costs, purchase a policy that will deliver the necessary cash.

Benefits for a Surviving Spouse or Children

If you want to provide money to cover living expenses for your spouse and/or children, you will need to estimate the number of years they will need support and the amount they will need each year. An insurance agent can work with you to forecast the need and arrange an appropriate life insurance policy.

Life and LTC Hybrid Policies

Several companies now offer a hybrid policy, a combination of life insurance and long-term care coverage. The combination policy is increasingly popular as it offers "value protection" on an LTC policy—a policy that, standing alone, is costly but may not be used.

Here's how the combination policy usually works. The policy offers a beneficiary death benefit reduced at time of payout by any long-term care expenses claimed under the policy. If the LTC coverage has not been tapped, the death benefit is paid in full. The premiums for the combination are typically paid in a lump sum when the policy is purchased. While this may sound costly, the fixed, up-front payment protects the insured from oft-climbing premiums for LTC policies. At the same time, potential insureds will find it easier to secure coverage under a combination plan than for standard LTC insurance.

Note that coverage and premiums vary widely by company and policy. They all have two things in common, however: thorny complexity and significant investment. Before you acquire a combination policy, review the terms completely with a financial advisor (not the agent selling the insurance).

If you name minor children as policy beneficiaries, you'll need to name someone to manage the proceeds. (See "Naming Life Insurance Beneficiaries," just below.)

Benefits for Others

If you want to leave money to someone other than your spouse or children, life insurance is one way to do it, though it may not be the best. You'll need to estimate the amount you would like to leave to each person and evaluate the cost of the coverage. A financial planner can help you evaluate your goals and options, while an insurance agent can help you with the details of insurance benefits and costs.

Naming Life Insurance Beneficiaries

When you purchase a life insurance policy, you must name beneficiaries—those who will receive the proceeds after you die. You name the beneficiaries on a form provided by the life insurance company, not in your will or living trust. As long as you own the policy, you can change the beneficiaries as you wish.

Unless you name your own estate as the beneficiary (not recommended), insurance proceeds are paid directly to your beneficiaries without the costs and delays of probate.

Here are a few points to consider when naming policy beneficiaries:

Cash for Postdeath Expenses

As mentioned above, life insurance is rarely necessary for this purpose, but if you want to purchase a policy to provide cash for postdeath expenses, you must take care when naming your beneficiary. If you name your estate, the proceeds may get hung up in probate court. Instead, consider naming your living trust, the executor of your will, or the successor trustee of your living trust as the policy beneficiary. Make it clear to the executor or successor trustee that the proceeds are to be used to cover estate-related expenses after your death. (You can note this in your planner.)

Benefits for a Surviving Spouse or Other Adults

If you purchase life insurance to provide for an adult—such as your surviving spouse—it usually makes sense to name that adult as beneficiary. If you want to name two or more adults as beneficiaries, simply name each adult and specify the percentage of the benefits to be paid to each. You'll also want to specify what should happen if one or more beneficiaries die before you do.

CAUTION

If you live in a community property state. If you live in a community property state (see Chapter 25) and you purchase a life insurance policy with community property funds, your surviving spouse automatically owns one-half of the proceeds when you die—despite other beneficiary designations you make on the policy itself. If you and your spouse agree to different ownership terms, you should document that agreement in a separate form, available from the insurance company.

Benefits for Minor Children

If you purchase life insurance for the benefit of young children, you need to name a competent adult as property manager to manage the proceeds. If you don't, and the children are minors when you die, the probate court will have to appoint someone to do the job. This entails attorneys' fees, court proceedings, and court supervision of the life insurance proceeds. Here are some ways to prevent these costs and hassles:

- Name a trusted adult beneficiary who will use the money for the children's benefit.
- Name the children as policy beneficiaries and name an adult property manager under your state's Uniform Transfers to Minors Act (UTMA). Most insurance companies permit this and have the forms for it.
- If you have a living trust, name the trust as the beneficiary of the policy. In the trust document, name the minor children as beneficiaries of any money the trust receives from the insurance policy. Also establish within the trust a method to impose adult management over the process, which can be either a child's trust or an UTMA custodianship. You will need to give a copy of your living trust to the insurance company.

Transferring Ownership of Life Insurance

If your estate owes federal estate taxes when you die (most estates don't; see the note below), whether or not life insurance proceeds are included in the taxable estate depends on who owns the policy at the time of your death. If you own the policy, the proceeds are included in the federal taxable estate; if someone else owns it, the proceeds are not included.

If you want life insurance proceeds to avoid estate tax, you can transfer ownership of your life insurance policy to another person or entity. There are two ways to do this:

- transfer the policy to another adult (such as the policy beneficiary), or
- create an irrevocable life insurance trust and transfer ownership to the trust.

Transferring ownership of a life insurance policy involves some potentially complex tax issues and a full discussion is beyond the scope of this book. If you're interested in learning more, see the resources listed in "Where to Get Help," below.

RELATED TOPIC

You probably don't need to worry about federal estate taxes. Most people don't need to think about federal estate taxes; they apply to less than 1% of the population—those who die owning a very large amount of property. Some states impose estate and inheritance taxes, however, and your estate may be liable for these. See Chapter 24 for more information.

Long-Term Care Insurance

Long-term care (LTC) insurance pays for the costs of nursing care if the insured person becomes disabled. LTC policies set out the health problems (called "benefit triggers") that the insured must experience before benefits are paid. Policies typically cover costs only up to a policy maximum amount.

There are plenty of disadvantages to these policies, but if you're financially comfortable and can afford the premiums, an LTC policy may help you protect your assets later in life. The following discussion should help you to decide whether LTC insurance is right for you.

Who Needs Long-Term Care Insurance?

LTC insurance doesn't make sense for everyone. As with life insurance, if you're wealthy, you probably don't need it. Although the insurance may provide some financial protection, those with plenty of money can generally afford the long-term care they will require. On the other hand (and unlike life insurance), LTC insurance is rarely a good investment for those with little money; as there are probably more important things to do with the funds that you have. (And if you're truly stretched, government programs will most likely provide some benefits. See "Government Assistance: A Last Resort," below.)

If you're on middle ground—financially comfortable, but not rich—LTC insurance may do a good job of helping you protect your assets and your family. Explore your options, and the associated costs, as early as age 55. The premiums will be lower today than if you wait. Here's why:

- The younger you are when you secure your policy, the lower the associated premiums will be.
- The sooner you purchase your policy, the less likely you will have to factor in a preexisting condition—and the associated difficulty and cost of securing coverage.
- The premiums for LTC insurance are rising, due to reduced competition in the industry—that is, fewer insurance companies offering policies—and demands for increasing company profits.

As a rough guideline, LTC insurance is probably for you if, when you're in your 80s, you expect to:

- own your home
- have less than $500,000 on hand, and
- receive about $50,000 in annual income.

This is especially true if you view the policy not as a particularly attractive investment, but as a method to safeguard your assets—and you choose a policy that provides the broad coverage that you might need.

Government Assistance: A Last Resort

Two public programs help to offset the need for LTC insurance by providing care benefits. The benefits are limited, however, and may not help you that much—if at all.

Medicare, managed by the U.S. Department of Health and Human Services, provides benefits if you are transferred to a skilled nursing facility following a hospital stay of three days or longer. If you are transferred on the second day, you will not receive Medicare benefits. And if you are not transferred to a skilled nursing facility, you may not see any benefits at all. If you do qualify, Medicare will pay for nursing facility care for up to 100 days.

Medicaid is administered by each state. Medicaid will cover the costs of long-term care in different types of care facilities, but only for those without other financial options.

The Costs of Long-Term Care Insurance

The cost of LTC insurance will depend on your age, your health, and the benefits provided. Your age when you secure a policy accounts for much of the premium difference. As a rough estimate, for standard $200 daily coverage over three years, you could expect to pay an annual premium of about $2,500 at age 60, $3,500 at age 70, and $8,800 at age 80.

When evaluating LTC insurance rates, a generally accepted rule of thumb is that the monthly premium should not exceed 5% of your monthly income. Be cautious in your evaluation; as the years roll by, it is possible that the ratio may change—rates will increase and your income will probably decline.

It is worth noting that some companies now offer policies with a "step-down" feature that allows you to reduce coverage while also reducing your premiums. This feature can be very attractive when facing rate hikes in LTC insurance premiums.

Another appealing feature is the "waiver of premium" provision offered with some policies. This provision allows you to stop paying premiums—usually 30 to 90 days after you begin to collect long-term care benefits. Waiver of premiums generally applies to residential care benefits and not to home care.

Many policies state that your premiums will never increase due to your age or the number of benefit claims you make. But insurance companies may seek (and obtain) across-the-board rate increases from state insurance commissions. Currently, rate increases for LTC insurance are occurring in almost every state. Before you buy a policy, compare rate increases by different companies over the past five years. A company with low year-to-year increases will most likely provide the best value for your coverage.

Choosing the Right Long-Term Care Coverage

The long-term care you will require (if any) may take many different forms. Care may range from periodic care in your home, to assisted living, to 24-hour monitored care in a nursing facility. Care benefits and covered facilities range from policy to policy. You will probably want to secure the broadest, most flexible coverage available. When evaluating LTC policies, compare the benefits for each type of covered care—and note how long the benefits last. You want to make sure you're covered if you end up needing years of care.

Residential Care Coverage

Look for a policy that covers as many types of residential care facilities as possible. A good LTC policy will:

- cover "custodial care"—that is, basic room and board plus personal services such as help with feeding, dressing, and bathing
- pay benefits if you live in any facility licensed by the state as a custodial care facility
- not restrict benefits to stays in "nursing facilities"
- not limit the size (the minimum number of beds) for a covered facility, and
- not limit benefits only to stays in Medicare- or Medicaid-certified facilities.

The Chances of Needing a Nursing Home

There's a reasonable chance that you will someday spend at least a little time in a nursing facility. Of people aged 65 or older, one-third of all men and two-thirds of all women will most likely require nursing home care. However, of those who enter a nursing facility, almost half stay six months or less, with about 25% staying longer than three years.

If you do require nursing home care, it may be costly. According to recent reports by MetLife and Genworth, the national average daily rate for a private room in a nursing home is about $235; a semiprivate room is about $210. For assisted living, the national average base rate is about $3,425 per month.

There are a couple of reasons why a good custodial care facility might not seek Medicare or Medicaid certification. First, because some facilities do not provide skilled nursing care, the certification is not required. Second, because some facilities do not wish to accept reduced payments through Medicaid, the facilities do not seek certification.

Many companies now offer policies that cover both nursing facilities and assisted living residences. And some policies are even more flexible, providing benefits for either residential care or home care, rather than making you select one or the other.

Home Care Coverage

You may be interested in a policy that covers residential care only, or one that covers both residential and home care. If you have sound alternatives for help in your home—such as close family members who may visit or live with you, or who will open their home to you—home care coverage will probably be important to you.

Home care coverage may include intensive nursing and physical therapy, help with daily living activities, and shopping or housecleaning services. When purchasing home care coverage, be sure to seek the broadest range of coverage available. A good policy will:

- include skilled nursing care and services from other professional medical providers, such as physical or speech therapy
- cover services from nonmedical personal care providers (whether from a licensed home care agency, an independent certified aide, or any other person you choose) to help with activities of daily living, including eating, bathing, dressing, moving around, using the toilet, monitoring medications, light shopping, helping with meals and cleanup, laundry, telephone calls, and paperwork
- provide some coverage for home services, such as housecleaning, grocery shopping, and meal preparation, if a home care health aide provides personal assistance
- cover care provided in the home and in licensed community care facilities (such as adult day care centers), and
- provide for respite care (short-term, temporary care that gives your regular caretakers—usually family members—a chance to rest), and hospice care.

Inflation Protection

Make sure your long-term care policy includes inflation protection. While a benefit of $200 per day may seem reasonable now, because of inflation and the increasing cost of health care, that amount may not be nearly enough ten or 15 years from now. Good inflation protection may raise the initial cost of a policy by 25%, but a policy without it may be a total waste of money.

Avoiding Conditions and Exclusions

Carefully review the conditions and exclusions of any LTC policy you consider. In particular, pay attention to the following:

Requiring a Prior Hospital Stay

Some policies pay benefits for long-term care only if the care begins shortly after a stay in a hospital or skilled nursing facility. Often, however, long-term care is necessary without such a stay—for example, in cases of chronic illness, Alzheimer's, or sheer frailty. Most states have banned this extreme coverage condition, but some have not. Avoid policies that include it.

Permanent Exclusions

Some policies exclude coverage for specified illnesses or conditions. If you need care for one of the excluded conditions, you will receive no benefits—regardless of the length or type of care you require. Some common exclusions are alcohol and chemical dependency, certain heart diseases, certain forms of cancer and diabetes, HIV-related illnesses, mental illness, and nervous disorders. Avoid policies that contain a lengthy list of exclusions—even if you do not have any of the specified illnesses or conditions. In the years that you hold the policy, you may develop an excluded illness or condition—and you will not get any benefits from the policy.

Preexisting Conditions

Some LTC policies won't provide benefits if your care is due to an illness or condition that was diagnosed or treated within the recent past, generally six months to two years prior to writing the policy. The exclusion works different ways under different policies. You should find one with the shortest exclusion periods available or seek a policy that does not carry the exclusion at all.

If you have certain preexisting health conditions—for example, if you have had a stroke or heart attack, are cognitively or physically impaired, have high blood pressure or diabetes, are obese, or simply are more than 80 years old—it may be difficult for you to purchase an LTC policy. Work with an insurance agent to find out whether you have options.

Benefit Triggers

LTC policies define health problems that you must experience (called "benefit triggers") before benefits will be paid. The most common benefit trigger in LTC policies is the "inability to perform without assistance" those activities that make up your daily life. Policies list certain activities—such as bathing, dressing, eating, using the toilet, walking, getting out of bed, taking medication, or continence. Policies typically pay benefits only when you are unable to perform a certain number of activities on your own. When considering a policy, ensure that:

- assistance with very few activities (such as two out of a listed three, or a maximum of three in a list of seven) constitute the benefit trigger
- bathing and dressing are included in the list of activities, because these are usually the first tasks to require assistance
- you will be considered unable to perform an activity without assistance even if you can do it sometimes with supervision

- benefits will be paid if you have "cognitive impairment" or diminished mental capabilities (not simply physical capabilities), as with Alzheimer's or other dementia requiring long-term care, and
- benefits do not require "severe" cognitive impairment, as this standard is very difficult to meet.

In some LTC policies, the benefit trigger requires that your care be "medically necessary due to an illness or injury." Avoid a policy with similar wording, as the "illness or injury" definition may be prohibitively narrow. Such wording rules out coverage benefits for simple frailty, the most common condition requiring long-term care. Also, your ability to perform daily activities may be severely diminished, but not through a clear diagnosis of an illness or injury—and, again, your LTC benefits would not cover your condition. Furthermore, it is sometimes difficult to determine the start and end of an illness or injury—and your need for long-term care and benefits will be caught up in this indeterminate (and probably, for you, unfavorable) definition.

Some policies require a doctor's statement, certifying that the insured person cannot perform the specified activities without assistance. This written statement will serve as the benefit trigger. Make sure the policy you consider allows your personal physician to provide the initial determination, even if the insurance company requires a second opinion by a doctor they appoint.

There are many places you can go to get more information about long-term care insurance. Some of the best are listed in the next section of this chapter.

Where to Get Help

If you want to learn more about insurance, start with Nolo's website at www.nolo.com. There, you'll find lots of free information on estate planning, retirement, and elder care, including articles on life insurance and long-term care insurance.

For some direction on finding reputable professionals—financial planners, insurance agents, and lawyers—to help you sort through your insurance alternatives, see Appendix B.

Life Insurance

A number of companies provide life insurance information and free quotes, helping you to estimate costs and compare policies from different insurers. Take a look at:

- InsWeb
  www.insweb.com
- Select Quote Life
  www.selectquote.com
  800-670-3213
- QuickQuote
  www.quickquote.com
  800-867-2404

For additional information, turn to one of these books:

- *New Life Insurance Investment Advisor: Achieving Financial Security for You and Your Family Through Today's Insurance Products*, by Ben G. Baldwin (McGraw-Hill Trade), a complete life-insurance consumer handbook.
- *Questions and Answers on Life Insurance: The Life Insurance Toolbook*, by Tony Steuer (Life Insurance Sage Press), a comprehensive and clear resource for professionals and consumers alike.

Long-Term Care Insurance

You can find good information about long-term care insurance online and in books. You might start by visiting one of these websites:

- **Clark Howard: www.clarkhoward.com.** Check the Clark Howard website for up-to-date, brief articles, and tips (select Clark's Topics, then click on Insurance)—for example, a list of insurance companies that are rated financially sound.

- ***Consumer Reports*: www.ConsumerReports.org.** *Consumer Reports* regularly publishes comparisons and evaluations of LTC policies. You can also find the magazine at your local library.
- **LongTermCare.gov.** Through this website, the U.S. Department of Health and Human Services provides information, links to resources, and locator assistance for insurance and providers, including overview of Medicare and Medicaid long-term care coverage.

If you need more information, *Long-Term Care: How to Plan & Pay for It*, by Joseph Matthews (Nolo), can help you figure out what kind of care you'll need and how to make it affordable. In addition to LTC insurance, the book explains Medicare and other government benefits.

Medicare and Medicaid

Medicare provides lots of information about long-term care, including nursing home comparisons for your area and explanations of various benefit programs. In particular, you might want to review the publication, *Medicare & You.* Visit Medicare online at www.medicare.gov or call them at 800-633-4227.

Medicaid is administered by each state. To contact the Medicaid program for the state in which you live, search for your state's Medicaid website or contact them by telephone. The name of the Medicaid department varies from state to state. Some common department names are Health, Health and Human Services, Social and Health Services, and Public Aid. You can find contact information by checking the state government listings in your telephone book or by searching online.

In Your Planner

Turn to the Insurance section of your planner (Section 18). Follow these guidelines to complete the pages there.

When completing this section, you should list each insurance policy that you own or that covers you or your property. These may include policies for health, your home and its contents, vehicles, umbrella liability, professional liability (such as errors and omissions, malpractice, or personal liability), disability, life, accidental death, and long-term care. Be sure to include less-typical types of coverage, such as death benefits you may have through your union or under your long-term care policy, credit protection coverage on a credit card, or accidental death insurance provided through one of your credit card companies.

In addition to policies you own that cover your life or property, you should list any policies owned by others that cover you—for example, disability coverage through your employer, health coverage through a spouse's employer, or a life insurance policy someone else owns that covers your life. Conversely, remember to list any policies you own that cover someone else—such as medical insurance through your employer that covers your family, or a life insurance policy you own that covers another person.

- **Type of Policy and Policy Number.** List each policy under the corresponding type in the first column of the table, and provide the policy number. If you have multiple policies of a given type, include each one. (And don't worry if you don't have an insurance policy for each category included here; most people won't.) You can use the "Other" category for any policies you have that don't fit anywhere else. These may include credit card insurance (coverage that pays off your balance or certain large purchases if you die) or mortgage insurance.

- **Insurance Company Name and Contact Information.** Include the name and contact information for the insurance company and your agent, if you have one.
- **Policy Owner.** Write in the name of the policy owner. If you don't own the policy yourself, include contact information for the policy owner.
- **Description of Coverage and Status.** Briefly describe who or what the policy covers—for example, provide the name of the person covered by the policy, a property address, or a list of personal property. Also, if you have any comments about the current status of the policy, note that here. For example, indicate whether there is an outstanding loan against the policy or current claim for which you are receiving benefits.

  EXAMPLES:

  Covers Roderick Harris (self); I took out a $4,500 policy loan on December 1, 2004

  Covers Edward G. Keeble (father)

  Covers Rochelle Garcia (self); payments in process

  Covers 433 41st Avenue, Sun City, FL, with Policy endorsement for art and jewelry

- **Location of Policy.** Describe the location of the policy documents. (If possible, keep your policies with your planner; see the note just below.)

Additional Notes

Include any other background or direction your survivors may need.

BINDER

Including insurance documents in your planner. You can use your planner binder to organize and store your current insurance policies and related claim or loan documents. You may also want to include appraisal certificates or other records of property value in the Insurance section of your planner. You can hole-punch your documents and insert them into the binder following this section, or use pocket divider pages.

Keeping Your Information Up to Date

Here are some changes that may trigger updates to this section of your planner:

- you acquire or cancel policies
- you qualify for benefits and payments are in process, or
- you change your beneficiary designations—for example, if you marry, divorce, or have a new child.

CHAPTER

19

Bank and Brokerage Accounts

Making Your Accounts Accessible 172

Avoiding Probate for Bank and Brokerage Accounts 173

Bank Accounts 173

Brokerage Accounts 173

Where to Get Help 174

In Your Planner 174

Keeping Your Information Up to Date 175

> *A billion here, a billion there, pretty soon it adds up to real money.*
>
> —SENATOR EVERETT DIRKSEN (1896–1969)

There are several good reasons to include your bank and brokerage accounts in your planner. One of them is just for you: When you review your accounts, you may find that you want to make some changes. For example, you may decide to simplify and consolidate your accounts, brush up your investments by changing or diversifying your holdings, or change beneficiary designations to match your estate planning goals.

Other advantages fall to your caretakers and survivors: If you become incapacitated, your agent for finances will need detailed financial information to handle your bills and investments. To wrap up your estate after you die, your executor or successor trustee will need to know exactly what bank and brokerage accounts you own.

In your planner, you'll summarize every account you hold with a financial institution—including checking, savings, and money market accounts, plus accounts for stocks, bonds, and mutual funds. You can also include relevant account materials in your planner.

Before turning to these details, however, this chapter tells you how to be sure someone can manage your accounts for you if you become incapacitated, and gives you some tips on passing your account assets to loved ones upon your death, without probate.

TIP

If your checks are lost or stolen. After you have completed this section of your planner, you will have a complete record of your checking accounts. If checks are lost, stolen, or misused, contact your bank to report the problem and take steps to protect your accounts. Also contact the major check verification companies so that retailers who use their services will not accept the reported checks. Contact information for the major check verification companies is preprinted in the Bank and Brokerage Accounts section of your planner.

SKIP AHEAD

If you've already named beneficiaries for your accounts. If your beneficiary designations are clear and complete, you may want to skip right to "In Your Planner" for directions on including your account information and documents in your planner. Then read "Keeping Your Information Up to Date," at the end of the chapter.

Making Your Accounts Accessible

If you become incapacitated, you'll want someone to take care of your finances for you. There are three basic ways to make your accounts accessible to someone you trust. The first is by far the most important option to consider.

Durable Power of Attorney for Finances

This is the best way to ensure that someone will be on hand to manage your finances if you become incapacitated. The document gives a trusted person you name the power to manage all your accounts and investments, pay bills, and take care of any other financial matters that arise. (See Chapter 12 for details.)

Living Trust

If you've transferred any financial accounts to a living trust and you become incapacitated before your death, your successor trustee is permitted to manage the accounts in your trust. (See Chapter 17 for more information about living trusts.) But it's unlikely that you'll put everything you own into your living trust. A durable power of attorney will permit someone to manage other property, too.

Joint Accounts

If you become incapacitated, a joint account owner can of course use account funds to pay bills for you—but that person isn't authorized to handle other account-related tasks, such as endorsing your checks and depositing them into the account. You'll want to make a durable power of attorney for finances to ensure that someone has complete authority to handle your affairs.

Don't Make a Joint Account Just to Avoid Probate

If you own financial accounts with someone else, the surviving owner(s) will take possession of the accounts when you die, without probate. But be cautious about setting up joint ownership only to avoid the costs and delays of probate. Adding a joint owner to an account may create all kinds of headaches—from giving up control of some of your assets to potential gift tax concerns. If avoiding probate is your primary concern, it's better to use the pay-on-death method, discussed in this section.

Avoiding Probate for Bank and Brokerage Accounts

There is an easy and effective method—called a "pay-on-death" designation—that you can use to avoid probate for bank and brokerage accounts. You can use it to name a beneficiary who will get the property immediately upon your death.

Bank Accounts

Pay-on-death (POD) bank accounts—sometimes called informal bank account trusts, revocable trust accounts, or Totten trusts—are one of the simplest ways to keep money out of probate. All you need to do is fill out a form provided by the bank, naming the person(s) you want to inherit the money in the account at your death.

As long as you are alive, the beneficiary you named has no rights to the money in the account. You can spend it, name a different beneficiary, or close the account altogether.

At your death, the beneficiary just goes to the bank, shows proof of your death and of his or her identity, and collects whatever funds are in the account.

CAUTION

States that impose estate or inheritance taxes. In states with these taxes, the bank may require proof that the taxes will be or have been paid. Ask your bank about it. A bank representative should be able to tell you about any requirements and explain what evidence it will accept as proof of tax payment.

When the first owner of a joint account dies, the funds in the account become the property of the surviving owner without probate. A POD designation on a joint account takes effect only when the second owner dies.

Brokerage Accounts

In almost every state, there is a law (the Uniform Transfer-on-Death Securities Registration Act) that lets you name someone to inherit your stocks, bonds, or brokerage accounts without probate.

A transfer-on-death (TOD) designation works very much like a pay-on-death bank account. You take ownership of your account in what's called "beneficiary form." For a securities account, your broker can give you the necessary paperwork. For individual stocks or bonds, contact the company's transfer agent. (A transfer agent is a business that is authorized by a corporation to transfer ownership of its stock from one person to another.)

After you have registered ownership this way, the beneficiary has no rights to the securities as long as you are alive. You are free to sell them, give them away, or name a different beneficiary.

On your death, the beneficiary can claim the securities by providing proof of death and some identification to the broker or transfer agent.

If you change your mind about who you want to inherit properties with joint, POD, or TOD designations, you will need to change the document in which you named the co-owner or beneficiary.

TIP

Stocks on hand and U.S. savings bonds. If you hold individual, paper stock certificates (rather than stock secured electronically at your brokerage), you may want to plan ahead for ownership transfer. You can add a transfer-on-death beneficiary; contact your broker or the stock company's transfer agent. Or you can easily transfer holding to your brokerage, into an account that will determine ownership transfer on your death. Similarly, if you have savings bonds in your name only, you might want to add beneficiary designations on each. For help, see "Registering an EE Bond or I Bond" at www.treasurydirect.gov.

Where to Get Help

Chapter 17 of this guide contains more suggestions to help you avoid probate. Beyond this book, you may want to browse Nolo's website, at www.nolo.com, for free articles and information on estate planning, including probate avoidance. For a thorough discussion of the subject, see *8 Ways to Avoid Probate,* by Mary Randolph (Nolo).

In Your Planner

Turn to the Bank and Brokerage Accounts section of your planner (Section 19). The following guidelines will help you complete the pages there.

When you complete this section, be sure to include all your bank accounts, such as checking and savings accounts, certificates of deposit, and money market accounts. Also list any accounts that you hold with brokerage firms, such as stock (or equities), bonds, notes, mutual funds, or money funds. And don't forget accounts held for the benefit of others, such as a 529 or Coverdell education savings account (formerly called an Education IRA).

RELATED TOPIC

Don't list retirement accounts or cash under the mattress here. List retirement benefits in Section 20 of your planner. Similarly, if you have cash, municipal bonds, stock certificates, or other financial assets that are stored at home or somewhere other than at a financial institution, identify these assets in Section 27 of your planner.

- **Financial Institution Contact Information.** Provide the name of the bank or firm that holds the account, the address of your branch, a telephone number, and the name of your broker or adviser (if you have one).
- **Account Number, Description of Assets, and Pay- or Transfer-on-Death Beneficiary.** List your account number and the type of account or assets—for example, checking, savings, money market, stock, bonds, or mutual fund. If you have completed a pay- or transfer-on-death beneficiary designation for a bank or brokerage account, note that and list the beneficiary here.

EXAMPLES:

POD: Aubrey Anne Swanson

TOD: Dan Jones

- **Debit Card and Online Access.** If you have a debit or ATM card for the account, note "Debit" or "ATM," list the card number, and include your PIN or password. If you access the account online, note that, too, and provide your user name and password.

EXAMPLES:

Debit: 2222 3333 4444 5555;
PIN: 123456

ATM: 1111 2222 3333 4444;
PIN: 224466

Online: sswanson; PW: cygnet

- **Location of Checkbook, Check Stock, and Statements.** Provide the location of your checkbooks, additional check stock, and statements for the account. If you do your banking online or receive your account statements via email, make a note of that.

EXAMPLES:

Checkbook in upper-left desk drawer, statements in a lower-left file, check stock in back of lower drawer.

Checkbook is in my purse, statements are in desk file. Extra checks in home safe (see Section 23).

I receive bank statements electronically; see account and password detail in Secured Places and Passwords.

I don't have a paper checkbook. I keep track of my checking account in *Quicken*, on my PC. See Section 23 for access information.

Additional Notes

If you have any other information about your bank or brokerage accounts, include it here.

BINDER

Including account materials in your planner. Depending upon the volume and nature of the materials, your planner binder can be a convenient place to store items related to this section—such as recent account statements or seldom-used ATM or debit cards. Insert items in pocket divider pages or plastic binder pouches, or hole-punch documents and insert them directly into the binder following this section.

Keeping Your Information Up to Date

Review your account information at least once a year to ensure that your records are complete and accurate. Be mindful of simple transactions that will trigger updates to your planner records, such as:

- opening a new account or closing an old one
- setting up or changing online account management, or
- changing storage locations for your checkbooks, check stock, or statements.

CHAPTER

20

Retirement Plans and Pensions

Planning for Your Retirement 178

What Happens to Retirement Accounts When You Die? 178

Probate and Taxes 179

Naming Beneficiaries for Your Retirement Accounts 179

Where to Get Help 181

Retirement Planning 181

Individual Retirement Plans and Pensions 181

In Your Planner 182

Keeping Your Information Up to Date 183

> *Experience achieves more with less energy and time.*
>
> —BERNARD M. BARUCH (1870–1965)

There are many good reasons to make a record of your retirement plans. If you become incapacitated, the person in charge of your affairs will have to manage your retirement accounts for you. (See Chapter 12 for more information about using a durable power of attorney for finances to name this person and establish his or her powers.) And when you die, your survivors will need to notify the plan administrators of your death and file claims for any outstanding benefits.

In your planner, you can document information about both the retirement and pension benefits you're receiving now and those you expect later. You'll provide contact information and a description of each plan or account. You can also file related documents—such as plan descriptions or account statements—with your planner.

Before you start recording information in your planner, however, you may want to take a little time to think about retirement in a larger sense: Are you currently pursuing the best options and strategies to help you thrive during your retirement years? And if you die leaving money in your retirement plans, how will you transfer those assets to others? If you aren't sure about the answers to these questions, this chapter provides some helpful resources.

SKIP AHEAD

If your retirement and pension documents are in order. If you have all your retirement plan documents on hand and you're comfortable with your beneficiary designations for each plan, you may want to skip right to "In Your Planner" for directions on completing your planner. Then read "Keeping Your Information Up to Date," at the end of the chapter.

Planning for Your Retirement

You're probably already expecting retirement benefits in some form—whether from an employer-sponsored retirement plan, a pension, an individual retirement account, or Social Security. But sitting down to record information about these benefits in your planner may cause you to wonder whether your overall retirement strategy is in good shape.

Developing a comprehensive plan for a satisfying retirement will take some work. The process requires diligent research, careful evaluation, and quite a few educated guesses, because it is riddled with the uncertainties of at least two futures: your own and the economy's. Nevertheless, few responsible souls would argue that it's wise to leave your future entirely up to chance. If you haven't yet made a plan, this may be the right time to do so.

While a detailed discussion of retirement planning is beyond the scope of this book, you can turn to "Where to Get Help," below, for many good resources to get you started.

What Happens to Retirement Accounts When You Die?

Whether employer-sponsored or individual, retirement plans continue to grow in popularity and are fast becoming a significant asset for many people. If you have retirement accounts, there's a chance that there will be money remaining in them when you die. This section briefly explains what happens to your retirement benefits at death, and how to leave any remaining retirement account assets to others.

Probate and Taxes

The good news is that your retirement funds won't get stuck in probate. Your estate and inheritors may not be able to entirely avoid paying taxes on the money, however.

Probate

For retirement accounts, you can name a beneficiary directly on the account paperwork—in other words, you shouldn't use your will or other estate planning documents for this purpose. The money will pass to the beneficiaries you name, without probate. If pension payments are due to your survivors, they will be paid to them directly, without probate.

Taxes

If your estate is subject to estate taxes, any balance remaining in retirement accounts will be counted as part of your taxable estate. (But remember that there are exemptions to the estate tax. With the marital deduction, for example, the money will not be taxed if you leave it directly to your spouse. See Chapter 24 for more information about estate taxes.)

The beneficiary of amounts remaining in a retirement plan funded with pretax money—such as a traditional IRA, 401(k), or 403(b)—will have to pay income tax on the money as he or she withdraws it from the account. That's because the money was exempt from income tax when the account was funded. On the other hand, the beneficiary of amounts remaining in a Roth IRA will not have to pay income tax on the money, because taxes were paid before the money was deposited into the account.

Naming Beneficiaries for Your Retirement Accounts

You can name a beneficiary for each of your retirement accounts, including individual retirement arrangements. If you have vested rights in a pension plan, you can name a beneficiary to inherit your pension rights.

Your Spouse May Have a Right to Your Money

For some retirement plans, the law requires you to name your spouse as the beneficiary. The specific rules differ from plan to plan:

- With a 401(k) or 403(b) plan, and for most pension plans, you must name your spouse as the sole beneficiary, unless your spouse signs a written waiver. However, retirement and pension plans for employees of government and church organizations are exempt from this requirement; these employees are free to name other beneficiaries without obtaining a spouse's written waiver.
- For IRAs and employer profit-sharing retirement plans, you may name anyone you choose as beneficiary. However, in community property states (see Chapter 25), your spouse has a legal right to half of the money that you earned during marriage. If you live in a community property state and want to name someone other than your spouse as beneficiary, your spouse should sign a document that waives rights to any portion of the retirement plan, including giving up any community property interest in the money.

Here are some of the basic rules about naming various individuals or entities as beneficiaries of a retirement plan—your spouse, others (such as family or friends), your living trust, or an irrevocable trust.

Your Spouse

Most married people name their spouse as the beneficiary of their retirement plans. As described above, for many types of plans and in a number of states, your spouse has an absolute right to some or all of the money in a retirement plan unless he or she signs a waiver giving up that right. If you're married and you don't want to leave all your retirement benefits to your spouse, make sure you know what the law requires in your situation.

If you name your spouse as a plan beneficiary, he or she will be entitled to rights and tax breaks that other beneficiaries are not. For example, a beneficiary spouse can:

- take the inherited amount, free of taxes, and roll it into a traditional IRA or a qualified employer plan
- postpone minimum distributions until age 70½, or
- choose to be treated as the IRA beneficiary, not the owner.

Your spouse will be able to get advice and select the most appropriate option when the time comes.

Other Individuals

Aside from the rules for married folks, described above, you can name other family, friends, or organizations as beneficiaries of your retirement or pension funds. When a nonspouse beneficiary receives the asset, the beneficiary should do both of the following:

- Take the inherited amount, free of taxes, and roll it directly to an IRA that is titled in your name for their benefit—for example, "John Doe, IRA, deceased October 1, 2014, for the benefit of Jane Doe Smith."
- Extend the minimum distribution schedule to cover the beneficiary's lifetime (assuming the beneficiary is younger than you), provided that withdrawals begin as required, in the year following your death.

Naming Multiple and Alternate Beneficiaries

If you like, you can name more than one beneficiary for a retirement account. You can specify how you want the remaining money divided among your beneficiaries when you die, such as a percentage to each. You can also name alternates for each of your beneficiaries.

Living Trusts

If you've set up a living trust (see Chapter 17), you may wonder whether you can name your trust as the beneficiary of a retirement account. This is generally not a good idea, for several reasons.

- Retirement funds are already exempt from probate, so there's no need to leave them to your trust for that purpose.
- If you are married and you name your trust as the beneficiary, your spouse will not be able to take advantage of a tax-free rollover to a personal IRA. (This is true even if your spouse is the sole beneficiary of your living trust.) Nonspouse beneficiaries are similarly limited.
- When you die, amounts remaining in the plan may have to be withdrawn and distributed within five years—again, raising the tax bill. While this is sometimes the case with individual beneficiaries, it is almost always the case when the beneficiary is a trust.

Irrevocable Trusts

Naming an irrevocable trust as beneficiary may make sense if you wish to structure a payment stream for children or other beneficiaries incapable of managing their own money. In this case, you would name the trustee of the trust as the beneficiary of the retirement plan.

SEE AN EXPERT

Setting up an irrevocable trust. Designing an irrevocable trust that will provide benefits exactly as you want is a complicated task. If you wish to create such a trust and transfer retirement funds to it, seek help from a knowledgeable lawyer. See Appendix B for help finding one.

Where to Get Help

There are many reliable resources that provide information about retirement plans, pension plans, and retirement planning. Here are a few to get you started.

Retirement Planning

Several good books can help you to develop or refine your retirement plan.

- ***The AARP Retirement Survival Guide: How to Make Smart Financial Decisions in Good Times and Bad,*** by Julie Jason (Sterling), is a good, high-level resource for those planning to retire and recently retired, providing particular insights for working with professional advisors and those selling financial products.
- ***The Bogleheads' Guide to Retirement Planning,*** by Taylor Larimore, Mel Lindauer, Richard A. Ferri, and Laura F. Dogu, foreword by John C. Bogle (Wiley), written by a nonprofit consortium of investors (adherents of John Bogle, founder of Vanguard Group), rewards the reader with sound information, tips, and humor on topics ranging from health insurance, to divorce, to finding the right advisor for you.
- ***How to Retire Happy, Wild, and Free: Retirement Wisdom That You Won't Get From Your Financial Advisor,*** by Ernie J. Zelinski (Visions International Publishing), is a lively primer to enjoying your retirement years—from managing your finances to living out your dreams.

Websites for Retirement Planning

- About Retirement Planning http://retireplan.about.com
- Kiplinger's Retirement Report www.kiplinger.com/fronts/channels/retirement
- U.S. Department of Labor, Employee Benefits Security Administration, www.dol.gov/ebsa/publications (see Retirement)
- Wells Fargo "My Retirement Plan" www.wellsfargo.com/myretirementplan

Individual Retirement Plans and Pensions

Even if you're confident about your overall retirement strategy, you may still have some questions about a particular plan or pension. For a thorough explanation of the rules governing different types of retirement plans, including withdrawals made by beneficiaries, see *IRAs, 401(k)s & Other Retirement Plans: Taking Your Money Out*, by Twila Slesnick and John C. Suttle (Nolo), or *Managing Retirement Wealth: An Expert Guide to Personal Portfolio Management in Good Times and Bad*, by Julie Jason (Sterling).

In addition, these sources can help:

IRAs

For more information about individual retirement accounts, you can request detailed publications from the IRS (see below for the website address and phone number). In particular, look for Publication 590, *Individual Retirement Arrangements (IRAs),* and Publication 560, *Retirement Plans for Small Business (SEP, SIMPLE, and Qualified Plans)* (retirement plans for the self-employed).

Pensions

For more information on pension plans and how they work, turn to the following resources:

- **IRS: www.irs.gov or 800-876-1715.** See Publication 575, *Pension and Annuity Income*, for a discussion of tax treatment of distributions received from pension and annuity plans, including calculating the tax-free portion of payments and rolling over certain distributions.
- **AARP: www.aarp.org or 888-687-2277.** AARP publishes helpful articles about pensions. To find the most current articles, type "pension" in the search engine on the AARP home page.
- **The Pension Rights Center: www.pensionrights.org or 888-420-6550.** The Pension Rights Center provides information, counseling, and referrals for additional help if you're seeking benefits under a pension.

Tax information

For an overview of the tax rules for retirement plan distributions, Social Security (also discussed in the next chapter), selling your home, reverse mortgages, and more, take a look at IRS Publication 554, *Tax Guide for Seniors* (see above for the website address and phone number).

SEE AN EXPERT

If you need more help developing a retirement strategy, understanding a pension or retirement plan, or seeking retirement benefits, consult a reputable financial planner, a pension-plan expert, or a knowledgeable lawyer. Appendix B provides suggestions for finding good experts.

In Your Planner

Turn to the Retirement Plans and Pensions section of your planner (Section 20). The following guidelines will help you complete the pages there:

RELATED TOPIC

Don't include education savings plans or Social Security benefits here. Government benefits of all kinds, including Social Security, are covered in the next section of your planner. Education savings plans, such as 529 or Coverdell accounts, are covered in the prior section, Bank and Brokerage Accounts.

Employer Retirement and Pension Plans

Describe retirement or pension plans provided through an employer. Include plans that are already paying retirement benefits to you and those that will pay you or your beneficiaries in the future.

- **Company Contact Information.** Include the name of the company or organization that manages the retirement or pension plan, the address, telephone number, and the name of your contact or adviser (if any).
- **Description, Status of Plan, and Beneficiary.** Provide a brief summary of the plan benefits and status, and the beneficiaries you have named for the plan.

EXAMPLES:

401(k) Plan, balance $59,243.34 as of December 31, 2014, no distribution to date. Beneficiaries: Roderick H. Harris (primary), Carol Schmitt (secondary).

B&O Pension; no payout to date. Beneficiaries: Louise (wife) (primary), and Donald (son) (secondary)

Acme Retirement; monthly payments in progress (I receive checks in the mail). Beneficiaries: Benjamin (primary), Best Friends Sanctuary (secondary)

Pension; monthly payment by direct deposit to First Bank checking account 0789-444333

- **Account Number.** Provide the account or identification number for the retirement or pension plan.
- **Location of Statements.** Indicate where you file your plan statements.

EXAMPLES:

See B&O Pension file in desk.

Statements in Acme Retirement file in top drawer of file cabinet (left of my desk).

Recent statement at back of this section.

Additional Notes

Include any additional information about your employer-sponsored retirement plans or pensions. If you have set up an online account (and password) for managing a plan, note that here.

EXAMPLES:

I often file the Acme Retirement monthly check with my current bills, until I have time to make the deposit. Check the Current Bills file (in the front, bottom drawer of my desk) to find any checks not yet deposited.

I manage my 401(k) at accutrak.com (username: C_Harris, password: harris2302).

Individual Retirement Accounts and Plans

Describe your individual retirement accounts, including traditional or Roth IRAs, Keogh plans, and SEP-IRAs.

- **Financial Institution Contact Information.** Provide the name of the financial institution that manages the account, the address of your branch, the telephone number, and your contact or adviser (if any).
- **Description, Status of Plan, and Beneficiary.** Describe the plan and the status of your benefits, and note the names of the beneficiaries of the plan.

EXAMPLES:

Health Care Investment III and Triune II mutual funds; no withdrawals yet. Beneficiaries: Laura, Shane, Amanda (children).

Acme stock, Global mutual fund, and money market account; monthly direct-deposit to Wells Fargo checking account 0835-858535; Michael and Matthew (nephews) are beneficiaries.

- **Account Number.** Provide the account or identification number for the plan.
- **Location of Statements.** Indicate where you file your account statements.

EXAMPLES:

See Vanguard file in desk drawer.

Last statement in planner.

Additional Notes

Include any additional information about your individual retirement accounts or plans. If you have set up an online account (and password) for managing a plan, note that here.

BINDER

Including retirement and pension documents in your planner. You can file related materials, such as account statements, in your planner binder. It will probably be easiest to hole-punch the documents and insert them directly into the binder, immediately following the Retirement Plans and Pensions section.

Keeping Your Information Up to Date

Your agent or executor will need an up-to-date overview of your assets, contact information, and the current status of each account.

Remember to update your planner if you:

- acquire a new plan
- no longer qualify for a plan, or consolidate plans
- establish an online account to manage your plan, or
- change the location for plan statements.

CHAPTER

21

Government Benefits

About Social Security 186

Where to Get Help 188

Social Security 188

Other Government Benefit Programs 189

In Your Planner 189

Keeping Your Information Up to Date 191

> *One who knows that enough is enough will always have enough.*
>
> —LAO-TZU (570–490 BC)

Government benefits come in many forms. The federal government provides dozens of assistance programs for those who are eligible—from benefits for retirees to medical services for those with special needs, from support for adoptive and foster families to assistance for those with low incomes. At the state level, benefits vary from state to state. The most common state benefit is assistance for low-income families, which provides cash, medical care, and reduced costs for food, housing, and utilities.

In your planner, you can describe any government benefits that you are currently receiving, benefits that may be due to you in the future, and any benefits due to your survivors. You can also describe the location of related paperwork.

SKIP AHEAD

If you already have government benefits paperwork. If you already have current paperwork or statements detailing your government benefits, and if you're clear about the status of your benefits, you may want to skip right to "In Your Planner" for directions on including information and documents in your planner. Then turn to "Keeping Your Information Up to Date" for tips on keeping your planner current.

The first part of this chapter provides basic information about Social Security benefits—the program that concerns most people. To learn more about other government assistance programs, see "Where to Get Help," below.

About Social Security

Despite concerns about its viability, the Social Security Administration (SSA) continues to deliver extensive benefit programs to almost every family in this country. Through programs for older Americans, disabled workers, and dependents, Social Security currently provides monthly benefits to about 62 million people. Briefly, here's how it works.

Employees pay a combination of Social Security and Medicare taxes on earned income, called FICA tax (named after the Federal Insurance Contributions Act). Employers pay a matching FICA amount for each employee. Self-employed individuals pay Social Security and Medicare taxes at twice the rate of employees, though they're permitted to deduct half of the self-employment tax as a business expense.

Social Security tax money is pooled in a trust fund that provides retirement and disability benefits to individuals and eligible family members. Medicare taxes are pooled in a trust fund that offsets hospital and related medical costs for Medicare beneficiaries.

The Social Security Administration provides four basic types of benefits: retirement, disability, family, and survivor benefits. Each of these benefits is briefly discussed below.

Medicare provides health insurance for people aged 65 or older and for many people with disabilities. The Medicare program is briefly described in Chapter 18, Insurance. If you are eligible for Medicare, you should document that information in the Insurance section of your planner.

Retirement Benefits

Financial advisers suggest that retirees need about 70% of their work income to live comfortably after retirement. According to SSA guidelines, Social Security retirement benefits are intended to replace about 40% of the average wage earner's income after retiring. The remaining amount is expected to come from employer retirement or pension plans, individual retirement arrangements, and other savings and investments.

In January 2014, the average monthly Social Security benefit for a retired worker was $1,294, and for a retired couple, $2,111. There is no guarantee of your retirement payout or of the specific amount—but it is expected that the Social Security Administration will remain solvent and that money will be there when you're eligible for it.

Social Security retirement benefits are available to qualifying individuals when they reach retirement age. Any qualifying person may elect to start receiving payments as early as age 62. On the flip side, you can elect to delay retirement, receiving larger payments beginning at age 70.

If you continue to work and receive Social Security retirement benefits at the same time, your earnings may be reduced until you reach a certain age. After that age, you can earn as much as you want and still receive your full Social Security retirement benefit. For more information about how other retirement income affects your Social Security benefits, see "Where to Get Help," below.

If you're approaching retirement age and thinking about filing for Social Security retirement benefits, make an appointment with the SSA (see "Where to Get Help," below) and spend some time talking with a Social Security representative about your payment options. Make this call at least several months before you plan to retire.

Disability Benefits

The SSA provides disability benefits to people who can no longer work because of a condition that is expected to last at least one year or to result in death. The eligibility guidelines for SSA disability differ from those of private disability or state disability plans. While you may be eligible for benefits under a state or private plan, you may not be eligible under SSA.

If you become disabled, contact the SSA and apply for benefits as soon as you can. It may take several months to process your claim.

TIP

Additional assistance from Supplemental Security Income (SSI). In addition to Social Security retirement and disability benefits, people who are 65 or older, or who are blind or disabled, may be eligible for payments through the Supplemental Security Income (SSI) program. SSI is managed by Social Security but funded by general revenues, not Social Security taxes. To find out more about SSI, see "Where to Get Help," below.

Family Benefits

When you become eligible for Social Security retirement or disability benefits, your family members may also become eligible for benefits. Eligible family members will receive monthly payments—as much as half of the retirement or disability amount paid to you.

Benefits can be paid to your spouse when he or she is:

- age 62 or older, or
- any age, if he or she is caring for your child—and the child is under the age of 16 or is disabled and receiving Social Security benefits on your SSA record.

Benefits can be paid to your children if they are unmarried and:

- younger than 18 years old, or
- between 18 and 19, but attending secondary school full time, or
- age 18 or older and severely disabled, with a disability that started before age 22.

If you are divorced, benefits may also be paid to your ex-spouse. To qualify, your ex must:

- be at least 62 years old
- have been married to you for ten or more years
- have been divorced from you for two or more years
- be unmarried, and
- be ineligible for equal or greater Social Security benefits based on his or her own work or someone else's work.

Survivors Benefits

Your survivors may be eligible for benefits when you die. Eligible survivors will receive monthly payments—as much as the full retirement amount that would have been paid to you.

Your spouse qualifies for benefits if he or she is:

- at least 60 years old, or
- at least 50 years old and disabled, or
- any age, if he or she is caring for your child—and the child is under age 16 or disabled and receiving Social Security benefits.

SEE AN EXPERT

Retirement benefits for surviving spouses. If you are receiving retirement benefits based on the account of your deceased spouse, you'll have choices to make when you reach age 62 and become eligible to start collecting Social Security benefits based on your own earnings record. To maximize your benefits, you'll want to discuss your options with someone who is familiar with the complex SSA guidelines. Call the SSA and ask a representative to help you.

In addition, your children can receive survivor benefits if they are unmarried and:

- under the age of 18, or
- between 18 and 19, but attending elementary or secondary school full time, or
- age 18 or older and severely disabled, with a disability that started before age 22.

Other eligible survivors may include your dependent parents, surviving divorced spouse, and, under some circumstances, stepchildren, adopted children, and grandchildren.

In addition to ongoing survivor benefits, your spouse or minor children may be eligible for a one-time payment of $255 upon your death.

Your Social Security Number

Your Social Security number (SSN) is an important link between you, your employment records, taxes, and future benefits. It's also one of the most sensitive pieces of information used to establish credit. Guard it carefully:

- Store your card securely and do not carry it in your wallet or purse.
- Don't give your SSN to anyone, unless the source is trustworthy and the need for the information is clear. If you do provide your SSN, request that it—along with other sensitive personal information—be kept confidential.

If your Social Security card is lost or damaged, you can contact the SSA (see below) to request a replacement card.

Where to Get Help

Here are some resources to help you learn more about Social Security and other government benefit programs.

Social Security

In 2013, the Social Security Administration permanently discontinued its routine annual mailing of individual statements. Now, you can create an online account to access your SSA earnings and benefits information. After you create an account, you can verify your earnings record, update your account information (such as for an address change), estimate future benefits, apply for benefits, modify your direct deposit arrangements, or request a benefit-verification letter (if needed to provide proof of income). To get started, go to www.socialsecurity.gov/myaccount.

The SSA website also offers an easy online Retirement Estimator at www.socialsecurity.gov/retire2. There, you enter information about yourself and your recent earnings, and the estimator will display your estimated benefits at age 62, your full retirement age (also showing that age for you), and age 70. This information is also calculated for you when you're logged into your SSA online account.

Social Security Publications

The following publications may be particularly interesting or helpful to you. You can access them on the SSA website or request them over the phone:

- *Understanding the Benefits*, Publication No. 05-10024 (a comprehensive guide to all SSA benefits)
- *Retirement Benefits*, Publication No. 05-10035
- *How Work Affects Your Benefits*, Publication No. 05-10069
- *Disability Benefits*, Publication No. 05-10029
- *Supplemental Security Income (SSI)*, Publication No. 05-11000, and
- *Survivors Benefits*, Publication No. 05-10084.

There are many additional publications available from the SSA, including several related to work and earnings—for state and local government employees, the self-employed, those working for nonprofit organizations, farmers, farmworkers, and those serving in the military. Follow up with the SSA to find those most relevant to you.

For more information about Social Security benefits, contact the Social Security Administration: www.ssa.gov or 800-772-1213. You can also visit your local Social Security office. (Find your local office on the SSA website, by calling the main SSA number, or by looking it up in the government pages of your phone book.) If you plan to visit your local office, it's a good idea to call ahead and schedule an appointment.

Finally, if you're still looking for answers, you may want to check out *Social Security, Medicare & Government Pensions: Get the Most Out of Your Retirement & Medical Benefits,* by Joseph Matthews with Dorothy Matthews Berman (Nolo). It explains how to find out what you and your family members can expect to receive from Social Security.

Other Government Benefit Programs

If you want information about government benefit programs other than Social Security, start by visiting the Benefits website at www.benefits.gov. Benefits provides a seamless tool to help you to find, research, and contact both federal and state government benefit agencies. You can also use the website to find eligibility requirements and application instructions for various benefits.

In Your Planner

Turn to the Government Benefits section of your planner (Section 21). The following guidelines will help you fill in the pages there.

Social Security Benefits

Provide a summary of all your Social Security benefits, including those based on your earnings or disability that go to your family members and any benefits that you expect to receive in the future. Don't bother listing universal benefits, such as the one-time death benefit to which your survivors will probably be entitled. Instead, describe those that are specific to you—for example, retirement benefits based on the earnings record of you or your spouse.

RELATED TOPIC

Don't list Medicare benefits here.

If you receive Medicare benefits, document that information in the Insurance section of your planner (Section 18).

- **Account Name and SSN.** For each program, identify the account name and Social Security number for the benefit you are receiving (or expect to receive in the future). For retirement or disability benefits, the account name and SSN may be your own or the wage earner's. For family or survivor benefits, the account name and SSN will be the wage earner's, whether retired, disabled, or deceased.
- **Account Access, Status, and Payment.** Describe online access for the account, if any (including account name or identification, password). Describe status of the account (especially whether the SSA is currently paying benefits), the amount, and the method for current payments.

  EXAMPLES:

  ACCT l0v3SSA, PW t000day!, no payments to date

  Claim in process; expect payments to begin in October 2015

  Monthly payments by direct deposit to SAS Bancorp checking account

- **Location of Documents.** Provide the location of your SSA statements or other benefit paperwork. If possible, you should file at least one recent statement in your planner. (See the note below.)

Other Government Benefits

Describe other federal, state, and local programs from which you are currently receiving benefits or are eligible to receive benefits from in the future.

- **Program Name and Contact Information.** Write the name of the benefit program and the contact information for the office that manages your benefits. If there is a particular person that serves as your contact—such as an account manager or benefits administrator—name that person and provide his or her direct telephone number, email address, or other contact information.
- **Program Description.** Briefly describe the program and the type of benefits it provides to you—such as cash assistance, reduced costs for food or home utilities, or loan repayment assistance.
- **Account Name and Identification.** Identify the account name and any identification—such as a Social Security or other account number—for the benefit you are receiving or expect to receive in the future. The account name and identification may be another person's (sometimes called the "qualifying" person) or your own.
- **Account Access, Status, and Payment.** Describe your online access for the account, if any, the status of benefits (especially if you are receiving payments), and the amount and method for any current payments.

  EXAMPLES:

  Application submitted; no payments to date

  Claim in process; expect payments to begin in September 2015

  Monthly credits applied to account; see instructions filed at the end of this section

  Monthly payments by direct deposit, National Bank checking

- **Location of Documents.** Provide the location of your program statements or other benefits paperwork. Depending on the volume of material, it may make sense to file the documents directly in your planner. (See the note just below.)

Additional Notes

Provide any additional details or directions about your government benefits, including your account name and password if you manage an account online.

BINDER

Including government benefits paperwork in your planner. You can file important government benefits documents in your planner binder. Hole-punch your benefit statements and insert them directly into your planner binder immediately following the Government Benefits section. Or, if there is paperwork that you can't or don't want to hole-punch, use pocket dividers or plastic sleeves.

Keeping Your Information Up to Date

Remember to update your planner if any of the following occur:

- you acquire a new benefit
- you no longer qualify for a benefit
- you establish an online profile to manage your account, or
- you change the location where you file statements or other benefits paperwork.

CHAPTER

22

Credit Cards and Debts

Evaluating and Reducing Debt ... 194

STEP 1: Review Your Income and Expenses ... 195

STEP 2: Review Your Credit Cards and Loans ... 195

STEP 3: Make a Budget ... 195

Where to Get Help ... 197

Major Credit Bureaus ... 197

Shopping for a Credit Card ... 197

Making a Budget and Getting Out of Debt ... 197

Avoiding or Reporting Identity Theft ... 198

In Your Planner ... 198

Bill Storage and Payment ... 198

Keeping Your Information Up to Date ... 200

> *Annual income twenty pounds,*
> *annual expenditure nineteen six, result happiness.*
> *Annual income twenty pounds,*
> *annual expenditure twenty pound ought and six, result misery.*
>
> —CHARLES DICKENS (1812–1870), DAVID COPPERFIELD

If you become incapacitated, your loved ones or agent for finances will need to pay your routine bills. After your death, your executor will need to take care of your outstanding bills and debts. They will need immediate access to information about what you owe—and how you pay. Ironically, if you have simplified your life with automatic bill payment, you may have further obscured the process for your survivors. Your planner is the place to make your methods known.

Your planner lets you organize information about your current bills, debts, credit cards, and record-keeping habits. For you, it is a valuable reference. (For instance, if your credit cards are lost or stolen, you'll have important contact information at your fingertips.) Ultimately, your planner will provide valuable direction to your loved ones.

TIP

If a credit card is lost or stolen. After you have completed this section of your planner, you will have a complete record of the credit cards that you own. In the event of a loss, important contact information is preprinted in your planner. Turn to the Credit Card and Debts section (Section 22) if you need to contact the major credit reporting bureaus, Federal Trade Commission, or Social Security Administration.

As you prepare to complete this section of your planner, you might find that it's a good time to assess your overall financial situation by taking a look at the number and type of credit cards you're holding and the amount of debt you're carrying. You may be able to make changes that will be of long-term value to you and your family. If you want to take that step, this chapter starts out with some suggestions to help you.

SKIP AHEAD

If your finances are in good shape. If you have a good handle on your finances and you're comfortable with the terms of your credit cards and outstanding loans, you may want to skip right to "In Your Planner" to document your information in your planner. Then turn to "Keeping Your Information Up to Date" for tips to keep your planner current.

Evaluating and Reducing Debt

Your ability to manage credit and debts is a function of several factors: your income, your expenses, how much you owe, how much it costs you (the interest rates), and your personal commitment and discipline. If you have fallen into a cycle of spending more than you have and borrowing to make up the difference, you'll need to make an effort to break the pattern. The three basic steps outlined here can help you get a handle on your outstanding debt and set in place an approach that will save you money for the rest of your life.

STEP 1: Review Your Income and Expenses

Set aside a few hours to review your monthly net income and all of your outstanding bills and debts. Start by gathering together the materials that show your income (including take-home pay, family support that you receive, and all other income sources you can think of), statements for your current bills and loans, and paper and pencil.

Calculate your monthly net income, then deduct amounts for bare necessities—housing, utilities, groceries, transportation, child support or alimony payments, and other essentials. Next, total the minimum monthly amounts due on all of your current bills and loans. Compare your net income less essentials to the total minimum due for bills and loans. Ideally, you'll find you have sufficient income to pay the total minimum due, plus additional income to begin to tackle your debt burden.

If you find you have insufficient income to pay the minimum due on your outstanding debts, seek some additional help. Follow up with a credit counselor or other resources described in "Where to Get Help," below.

If you do have additional income available to tackle debt, increase your monthly payment for the bills and loans that carry the highest interest rates.

CAUTION

Watch out for fees. As you evaluate your income and expenses, take note of any bills for which you have been charged extra fees, such as those for late payments or exceeding your credit limit. These fees are typically very expensive and will wreak havoc on your budget. This may seem obvious, but many people throw away money because they forget to pay bills on time or fail to keep track of their credit card limits. Setting up a timely bill-paying schedule and giving your maxed-out credit cards a rest can save you a bundle.

STEP 2: Review Your Credit Cards and Loans

Every credit card and loan comes with its own terms, including the interest rate, annual fee, and grace period before you must pay interest on a charge. Some of your credit cards may also return benefits to you, such as an annual rebate, retail discounts, or free travel.

Take a close look at each of your credit cards and loans. Review the basic terms offered and the various fees assessed, and identify the cards and loans with the least favorable terms. If you have credit cards or loans with high interest rates or annual fees, plan to pay them off in full and cancel the accounts. If you have more than one debt with unfavorable terms, pick the worst one and put as much money as you can toward the balance until you've paid it off, while paying the minimum amount on your other accounts. Then tackle the second worst offender, and so on.

Ultimately, plan to use only the credit card (or take out only the loan) that delivers the most advantageous terms available to you. You may wish to cancel retailer credit cards and use a major credit card for your purchases. (Or, you may want to securely store that retailer credit card and bring it out only when the retailer runs cardholder-only promotions.)

These days, there are a wide variety of major credit cards with varying terms. For an effective tool to compare credit card programs and apply for a card, see "Where to Get Help," below.

STEP 3: Make a Budget

Once you have these short-term steps behind you, you will want to develop an annual budget. With a sound budget in place, you can more closely evaluate your income and expenses, and you can better plan for periodic expenses such as household or auto maintenance, insurance premiums, and property taxes.

Avoiding Identity Theft

Once you've got a credit card with excellent terms, hang on to it—along with all other sensitive information about you and your finances. Identity theft is a serious matter and an increasingly popular crime. An identity thief steals important information—your name, address, telephone numbers, bank account or credit card numbers, or your Social Security number—and uses that information to apply for more credit cards or loans, open accounts, or to go on spending sprees. Here are some ways you can avoid becoming a victim:

- **Secure personal records.** Keep your personal information safe at home. At work, verify that your personnel records are securely maintained.
- **Shred sensitive materials before you put them in the trash.** Combing through trash is one of an identity thief's best strategies.
- **Watch your wallet.** Keep your wallet in a safe place at all times—at home, at work, and in stores and restaurants.
- **Limit your load.** Carry only the personal identification and credit and debit cards that you need. Store little-used items in a secure location, such as in your planner.
- **Secure your Social Security number.** Keep your Social Security card safe, and give out your SSN only when absolutely necessary.
- **Check your credit report.** Review your report every four months. Investigate unrecognized activity.
- **Use passwords.** Place passwords on your accounts and devices (such as cellular telephones) using codes that are not easily guessed or found. Store your passwords securely in Section 23 of your planner or using password-management software.
- **Guard against theft.** Any time you are asked to provide personal information by telephone, through the mail, or over the Internet, be wary. Call the organization's customer service number and validate the exchange before you provide any personal information.
- **Protect your PC.** Take steps to protect information on your computer by using a firewall and secure browser. Don't download files from strangers, do maintain current virus protection, password-protect sensitive information, and avoid automatic log-in processes. Keep your operating system up to date, including the latest security patches.

If you do lose important items or if you suspect that your information has been used to commit fraud or theft, take the following steps immediately:

1. Contact the national credit reporting bureaus.
2. File a police report.
3. File a complaint with the FTC.
4. Contact the Social Security Administration.
5. Close suspect accounts.

See "Avoiding or Reporting Identity Theft," below, for more information.

There are several good products (including books, software, and online services) available to help you develop and maintain a budget. Some of these are listed in "Where to Get Help," below.

Where to Get Help

For general information about debt and credit, visit Nolo's website, at www.nolo.com. You'll find free articles on managing debt and much more. For more details, you can turn to the following resources.

Major Credit Bureaus

The national credit reporting bureaus—Equifax, Experian, and TransUnion—offer tips and resources for managing your personal debt. Under a new law, you can order a free copy of your credit report from each bureau every year. It's a good idea to take advantage of this offer. Check your report with each agency to be sure it's up to date and free of errors.

It is best to order your credit report from one of the three bureaus every four months. That way, you can spread your free reviews over 12 months.

Use www.annualcreditreport.com to request free copies of your credit report from all three credit bureaus.

Shopping for a Credit Card

The Internet makes it easy to shop for a major credit card. Look for a reputable site that lists and compares rates for different companies. Here are some good tools for your search:

- ASAP Credit Card
  www.asapcreditcard.com
- Bankrate, Inc.
  www.bankrate.com/credit-cards.aspx

Making a Budget and Getting Out of Debt

The following resources can help you to develop a budget and reduce your debt. If you want to start with free information on the Internet, here are some good websites:

- Clark Howard—Save More, Spend Less and Avoid Rip-Offs
  www.ClarkHoward.com
  Click on the "Clark's Topics" link, then "Personal Finance & Credit."
- Dave Ramsey—Learn how to take control of your money and change your future
  www.DaveRamsey.com
  Click on "Get Started."
- The Motley Fool—To Educate, Amuse & Enrich
  www.fool.com
  Click on the "How to Invest" tab, then "Personal Finance."

If you want to take your work a step further, the following books provide information about personal financial management, including creating a budget and reducing your debt.

- ***The Total Money Makeover: A Proven Plan for Financial Fitness,*** by Dave Ramsey (Thomas Nelson), provides a step-by-step process for getting out of debt, improving financial security, and saving for the future.
- ***How to Get Out of Debt, Stay Out of Debt, and Live Prosperously,*** by Jerrold Mundis (Bantam), based on the principles of 12-step programs, includes examples, anecdotes, and direction for digging out and staying out of debt.
- ***Clark Howard's Living Large in Lean Times: 250+ Ways to Buy Smarter, Spend Smarter, and Save Money,*** by Clark Howard, Mark Meltzer, and Theo Thimou (Avery Trade), written by a sharp, pragmatic entrepreneur

(and host of popular radio and TV shows), *Living Large* delivers a wealth of buying and saving tips on everything from cars to travel.

Avoiding or Reporting Identity Theft

For more information about identity theft, turn to the following sources:

- Federal Trade Commission
  www.ftc.gov or 877-438-4338
  Online, select "Tips & Advice," "For Consumers," then "Privacy & Identity."
- Social Security Administration
  www.ssa.gov or 800-772-1213
  See especially Publication No. 05-10064, *Identity Theft and Your Social Security Number.*

In Your Planner

Turn to the Credit Cards and Debts section of your planner (Section 22). The following guidelines will help you complete the pages there.

Bill Storage and Payment

Here's where you provide information about your bills and bill-paying practices. Include both your "paper" bills—the ones that you probably receive by mail—as well as those you receive electronically.

- **Location of Pending Bills.** Describe where you store paper bills until you pay them.

  EXAMPLES:

  See the cherrywood box at the far left side of my home desk.

  "Current Bills" file, front/lower-left desk drawer.

In the following table, provide information about all of your bills, paper and electronic. Include bills you pay by check or money order, those paid online by you, those paid automatically by preauthorized charge to your credit card, and any bills paid by automatic debit to your bank account.

- **Payee.** Identify the company or individual who receives the payment.

  EXAMPLES:

  PG&E

  WSJ Online

  MetroCard

- **Account Number.** Insert your account number with this payee.
- **Notice.** Describe how the payee sends you a bill.

  EXAMPLES:

  US Mail

  Email

  Annual notice based on loan agreement. See "Ace Mortgage" file in file cabinet.

- **Frequency and Amount.** Write in how often you receive the bill and an estimate of how much you pay each time, so that your agent or executor knows what to expect.
- **Method of Payment.** Describe the steps that you take to make payments. Include your login name and password (if any), source of funds, and any other details your agent or executor will need to make the payment for you or to recognize an automatic payment.

  EXAMPLES:

  Pay via Wells Fargo bill pay, see Section 19 for login information.

  Pay on AT&T website. Login name: mharrison58; PW: 3pj%K867KE.

  Pay by check from WFB Checking -2222.

  Automatically charged to Chase Visa -5678.

- **Record of Payment.** Describe the location of payment records and any details necessary to research payment of a particular bill.

  EXAMPLES:

  I keep payment records (filed by payee) in filing cabinet to left of my desk.

Find payment records in Quicken on my computer. See Section 23 for login.

Additional Notes

Include any other information about your bills that might be helpful to your survivors.

Credit Cards

List all credit cards that you own. Include major credit cards (such as Visa and American Express) and retailer or merchant credit cards (such as those issued by Sears, Gap, or Union 76). Provide the information as printed on each credit card (from the face and the back) or from a billing statement for the card.

RELATED TOPIC

Don't list debit or ATM cards here. Instead, record information about debit or ATM cards in the Bank and Brokerage Accounts section of your planner (Section 19), along with other information about the associated accounts.

- **Issuer.** List the name of the issuing company —for example, Sears, American Express.
- **Account Number and Access.** Write in the account number as it is printed on the face of the card or statement. If you have an online account for this card, also include your account name and password here.
- **Customer Service Telephone.** Include the customer service telephone number (also printed on the back of the card or on the statement) for the issuing company.

Additional Notes

If you have additional information about your credit cards that might be helpful to your survivors, include it here.

Debts I Owe to Others

If you have debts other than those described above, list them here. Include all of your debts—loans made to you, judgments against you (including child support or alimony payments), loans on which you are a cosigner, or other responsibilities you have.

- **Creditor Name and Contact Information.** List the person or company to which you owe the debt. Include an address, phone number, email address, website, and any other useful information.
- **Amount.** Write the total amount of the debt.
- **Terms of Debt and Status of Payment.** Describe the terms of the debt—including the interest rate, if any, and payment schedule—and the status of repayment.

EXAMPLES:

Due in full on February 1, 2019; payment has not begun.

Monthly child support until Audrey turns 18 (March 2017).

No-interest loan; payments started August 1, 2013, $100 per month.

Interest on balance is 6% per year; payment is $1,000 per year plus interest on the outstanding balance; first annual payment made July 1, 2012.

- **Location of Documents.** Provide the location of any loan documents or notes.

Additional Notes

Include any additional information about the debts that you owe to others.

Debts Others Owe to Me

If anyone owes you money, you should complete this table. Include all debts due to you—loans you've made, judgments in your favor (including child support or alimony payments), or other amounts due from others.

- **Name and Contact Information.** List the person, company, or organization that owes money to you. Include the address, phone number, email address, website, and any other useful information.

- **Amount.** Write in the total amount of the debt.
- **Terms of Debt and Status of Payment.** Describe the terms of the debt—including the repayment schedule and interest rate—and the status of repayment.
- **Location of Documents.** Provide the location of any loan documents or notes.

Additional Notes

Include any additional information about debts that others owe that might be helpful to your survivors. If you want to reduce or forgive a debt upon your incapacity or death, you can note that here—but make it official by forgiving the debt in your will.

BINDER

Including your credit card and debt materials in your planner. You can file materials related to your credit cards and debts in your planner binder. For example, you can store items such as infrequently used credit cards in a plastic binder pouch in your binder, or hole-punch documents (such as copies of loan agreements) and insert them directly into your planner binder immediately following the Credit Cards and Debts section.

Keeping Your Information Up to Date

Information in this section of your planner may change frequently. In particular, be sure to update your records if you:

- initiate automatic or online bill payments for one or more routine expenses
- receive a personal loan or make a loan to someone else
- agree to be a cosigner on a new loan
- get a new credit card or cancel an old one, or
- change your login information for an online account.

CHAPTER

23

Secured Places and Passwords

Who Has Access to Your Safe Deposit Box? 203

In Your Planner 204

Keeping Your Information Up to Date 207

> *Any sufficiently advanced technology is indistinguishable from magic.*
>
> —SIR ARTHUR C. CLARKE (1917–2008)

Technology continues to wend its way into our daily lives. We are increasingly reliant on password-protected electronic products and services—from cell phones and computers to electronic budgeting and banking, from email accounts to alarms for our homes and cars. And, while more tangible than many electronic services, our other secured places—safe deposit boxes, filing cabinets, and the like—may be locked up with keys or combination locks, or simply with our own secrecy.

Most of us rarely think about our passwords, access codes, combinations, and keys. Using them becomes second nature to us. Yet for your agent, executor, or other survivors, electronic and physical locks may be formidable barriers—potentially keeping them from the property they must manage on your behalf.

Your planner provides a central place to list account names, passwords, combinations, and PINs. You may also want to store copies of keys with your planner. The planner can help you stay organized, while also providing your survivors with the critical information they'll need later.

Before turning to the instructions for completing your planner, this chapter provides a little bit of information about safe deposit boxes—a common secured place that can cause difficulties for your caretakers and survivors unless you think carefully about what you put in the box and who has access to it.

Using a Password Manager Instead

As an alternative to using the first table in Section 23 of your planner—Products, Services, and Passwords—you could use password-management software to document and store your passwords. In password-management software, you can store user names, passwords, codes, combinations, and PINs, and identify the location of physical keys for various products and services.

You can easily research and compare available products online. Go to these websites: PC Magazine (pcmag.com), CNET (cnet.com), Kim Komando (komando.com), or Consumer Reports (consumerreports.org), then search for "password manager."

If you use software to track your access codes, leave clear instructions for your loved ones in this section of your planner—the name of the password-manager software, where it is stored (that is, online, on your computer, or on another device), whether a special hardware key or device is required to access (and the location of that key or device), the steps to access the software, and then how to access the stored information. (Make sure the password manager you choose doesn't require a personal key, such as your thumbprint!) And be sure to complete the rest of Section 23.

Who Has Access to Your Safe Deposit Box?

For most protected places and accounts, whomever you trust with the password, access code, combination, or key can get into them. But there's one notable exception: safe deposit boxes. Normally, access to your safe deposit box is limited to you and anyone who co-owns (or "co-rents") the box with you. This rule changes if you become incapacitated or die.

Should You Name a Co-Owner?

Depending on your circumstances or the contents of your safe deposit box, you may wish to give one or more people the authority to access your box now—so they need not go through the hassles of gaining access to it later. It's easy to add a co-owner to a box: Usually you and the other person simply visit the bank to add the new co-owner to the authorization card.

Before you do this, however, consider the risks. As soon as you grant the authority, the person you've named will be able to examine the contents of your safe deposit box at any time, adding or removing items at will. Unless you trust the person completely, it's better to make a durable power of attorney for finances—and rely on the built-in protections of the financial institution's access rules.

During Your Incapacity

If you are incapacitated, access is limited to co-owners plus your agent under a durable power of attorney for finances, if the document grants the power to manage the contents of your safe deposit boxes.

If no one is authorized to access your box and you haven't made a durable power of attorney for finances, your box can't be opened without a court order.

After Your Death

Who can get into a safe deposit box after you die depends on state law. In some states, a co-owner can continue to access the box and your executor or successor trustee can easily gain access. (Your executor or successor trustee will need to present a certified copy of your death certificate and a copy of the will or trust showing that he or she is the named executor or trustee.) In other states, however, when one owner dies, the safe deposit box is sealed while the state taxing authority assesses the value of its contents. This can take several weeks.

So how can you use a safe deposit box, yet be sure your survivors can reach the information and assets they need when you die? First, find out whether your state requires safe deposit boxes to be sealed at the time of your death; the bank should be able to tell you.

If the Box Won't Be Sealed

If your state does not require boxes to be sealed, what to do depends on whether or not there are co-owners on the box.

- **Boxes with co-owners.** Even if you have co-owners on the box, do not use it to store any documents or assets that your survivors will need during the first week following your death. (For example, you should never store your burial instructions in your safe deposit box.) Remember that if the bank is closed—say, for a long weekend—even your co-owners won't be able to reach your box or its contents.
- **Boxes without co-owners.** Your executor or successor trustee will have access to the box after you die—but not until they have secured a certified copy of the death certificate. (If you are the only owner of the box and have not appointed an executor or successor trustee, your survivors will have to secure a court order to gain access to the box.) For this reason, it is best not to store any documents or

assets that your survivors will need for the first three or four weeks after your death.

If the Box Will Be Sealed

In states that seal safe deposit boxes when an owner dies, even co-owners are kept out. If survivors need to access the box during this period, they will need to get a court order. A court order may be granted if survivors are searching for a will, trust, or burial instructions—or when they simply want to take inventory of the property in the box, without removing anything.

Access to Your Safe Deposit Box

Here is a summary of who can access your safe deposit box and when they will be able to open it.

If you are incapacitated...	A co-owner on the safe deposit box
	Your agent under a durable power of attorney for finances (if you grant safe deposit box access in the document)
	Anyone who seeks, and is granted, a court order to open the box
After your death...	A co-owner on the safe deposit box*
	Your executor, after presenting a certified copy of the death certificate*
	Your successor trustee under a living trust, after presenting a certified copy of the death certificate*
	Anyone who seeks, and is granted, a court order to access the box

* In a state that seals safe deposit boxes upon the owner's death, access will be delayed for several weeks until the state taxing authority completes an assessment of the box contents.

After the taxing authority reviews the contents of the box, access will be granted to co-owners and your executor or successor trustee. If you are the only owner of the box and have not appointed an executor or successor trustee, your survivors will have to obtain a court order to gain access to the box.

If you live in a state that seals safe deposit boxes, don't use your box to store anything that your survivors might need during the first month or two after your death. Store these items in another secure location.

RELATED TOPIC

More recommendations for storing your planner. If you want to store certain sections of your planner in your safe deposit box, see Completing Your Planner, at the beginning of this book. You will find a list of the sections you can more easily store in your safe deposit box and the sections that should be stored securely at home.

In Your Planner

Turn to the Secured Places and Passwords section of your planner (Section 23). The following guidelines will help you complete the pages there.

Products, Services, and Passwords

List each product and service for which you have a user name and password, access code, combination, key, or personal identification number (PIN). (Don't list PINs for bank accounts here; see the note below.)

Here are examples of common items and services that you should list:

- cell phone
- tablet or iPad
- personal computer
- Internet service provider
- Web hosting service
- email accounts

- online services or groups
- blogs
- software applications
- ebook reader
- ipod
- home alarm system
- garage key code
- car alarm system
- home safe
- mailbox
- gates
- storage unit combination, and
- lockers, drawers, or cabinets.

RELATED TOPIC

Don't include online billing or banking information, or ATM cards here. List account names and passwords in the Bank and Brokerage Accounts section of your planner (Section 19). If you have set up automatic bill-pay for particular debts, describe these arrangements in the Credit Cards and Debts section of your planner (Section 22).

- **Product or Service.** For each product, list the make, model, and type of product. For each service, list the organization name and type of service.

  EXAMPLES:

  Kaiser medical account (www.kp.org)

  AT&T (Internet service provider)

  Facebook.com

  connect.legacy.com support group

  Netflix account

  GoDaddy.com

  Mailbox #12 (at end of court)

- **Account Name, User Name, or Account Number.** Provide the account name, user name, or account number (if any) for the particular product or service. For online services and software, the account name is often some version of your own name.

- **Password, Combination, or PIN.** List the password, combination number, access code, or Personal Identification Number (PIN) for the product or service.

  EXAMPLES:

  Mollie

  pls4sas

  52-31-28

  30173

- **Location of Key.** Describe the location of the corresponding physical key for the product, if there is one (such as the key for your home safe, mailbox, or gates).

  EXAMPLES:

  Box by telephone

  Key chain (purse)

  Key chain (key rack in laundry room)

Common Passwords

You may have frequently used passwords, such as the name of your dog or your son's birthdate. If you do, including them here may help your survivors if you forget to list an account in the table above. Write any common passwords in the lines provided.

Additional Notes

Include any additional background or direction about your products, services, or passwords that your survivors may need. In particular, describe how you want your loved ones to use, update, maintain, or cancel online services, especially social networking sites—such as Facebook, Twitter, LinkedIn, Google+, or Match.

Safe Deposit Boxes

Describe each box that you currently rent.

- **Bank Name and Contact Information.** Include the name, address, and telephone number of the bank where your box is located.

- **People With Authorized Access.** List anyone who already has authorized access because they have visited the financial institution with you, submitted identification, and signed the authorization card. Do not include bank employees who provide routine access to the box.
- **Box Number and Location of Keys.** Provide the safe deposit box number—as printed on the box and on the keys—and the locations where you store your safe deposit box keys. For each box, you probably have two keys; if you store each key separately, describe both locations.

EXAMPLES:

#3125: Key on key chain (purse), key on marked card in pencil drawer of desk

#555: Both keys in storage pouch at back of this section

#1234 and #2345: Primary keys in front of desk drawer, secondary keys in planner (taped to card at end of section)

- **Description of Contents.** Briefly describe the contents of the safe deposit box.

EXAMPLES:

Jewelry (diamond brooch, necklace, and earrings; ruby and diamond bracelet), stock certificates (General Electric), and Smith & Wesson revolver

Cash, savings bonds, video of home and property (for insurance), and original documents (adoption/citizenship papers, marriage certificate)

Additional Notes

Include any additional notes for your survivors about your safe deposit boxes.

Other Keys

List any keys not included above, along with their locations. Include keys for your primary residence, vacation or rental properties, vehicles, employment, and for other uses. Include those for everyday use, those tucked away, and those stored as spares.

- **Purpose.** Describe the purpose for the key or where the key is used. Note the property where it is used, if applicable.

EXAMPLES:

Key to home mailbox

Keys to San Antonio home, doors and gates

Kristi & Suzanne's house key

Lock on hot tub gate

- **Location.** Describe where the key is located or stored.

EXAMPLES:

Key chain (pocket or top of dresser)

Key rack by back door

Box in back of kitchen junk drawer

Under flowerpot on side porch

Other Assets, Other Locations

Finally, what property do you have safely stored or secreted away? What little-known places or arrangements do you need to document or map out for your agent, executor, and loved ones? Do you have property on loan from others?

Consider including the following:

- any financial assets—cash, coins, stocks, bonds, notes, or other certificates of value—that are not stored at a bank, brokerage, or other financial institution
- other valuable items that your survivors may not find without your direction—such as items on loan to others, items you have hidden away, or items stored in a public storage facility, and
- any valuable information that is only in your head—directions to valuables, favorite recipes, the secrets of your magic tricks, and the like.
- **Item and Description.** Describe the item or assets.

EXAMPLES:

General Electric preferred stock certificate, U.S. savings bond, and $5,000 in Mid-State Water Utility bearer bonds

Gold coins

Grandpa's rifles

Mink stole and sable coat

Pie crust recipe

- **Location of Asset.** Describe the location of the item, including the address, if applicable, and any necessary access information (such as keys or combinations).

EXAMPLES:

Locked in home safe

Tucked under my mattress

Buried 2' NW of the apple tree in my backyard, about 3' deep

Lock box under back deck, key on my key chain

Arctic Furs Storage, 17 Washington Square, New York, NY 10011, 333-444-5555

Recipe included in planner, following this section

- **Location of Documents.** Identify any documents related to the item—such as purchase or appraisal records, related contracts, or a storage agreement—and describe where the documents are filed. (If possible, file the related documents in your planner; see the note below.)

EXAMPLES:

Locked in home safe

Storage agreement in desk (lower-left drawer), "Arctic Furs Storage" file

Typed up and filed at back of this section

Please return to Aubrey Swanson, 555 Miller Road, Oakton, VA 22124, 555-555-5555

Additional Notes

Include any additional background or direction your survivors may need.

EXAMPLES:

Once you locate this item, please refer to Section 27. I have described specific care instructions there.

I have outlined the steps for maintaining the pumps and generator, along with overall instructions for the well, pump house, and water tower. See my notes in Section 25 (Real Estate).

BINDER

Including related materials in your planner. If you have documents related to items of property you described in this section of your planner—such as appraisal certificates or purchase records—you can file them in your planner binder. Also include contracts for storage of valuables or maps for locating particular items. Your planner binder is also a great place to store your safe deposit box keys or spare keys. Use a combination of pocket divider pages, plastic sleeves, and plastic zippered pockets to file and protect these important items.

Keeping Your Information Up to Date

Small changes or omissions in this section may keep your survivors from your property—or at least increase the number of hoops they must jump through to get access. In particular, update your planner if you:

- acquire a new product or service—such as a computer, cell phone, email account, or software—that can be used only with an account number, user name, or password
- change a product or service—such as establishing a new email account or purchasing a home safe
- rent a new safe deposit box, or move the contents of an existing box to a new bank, or
- stash away valuable property in a location unknown to others.

CHAPTER 24

Taxes

Tax Basics 210

Estate and Inheritance Taxes 211

Federal Estate Tax 211

State Estate and Inheritance Taxes 212

Where to Get Help 212

In Your Planner 212

Keeping Your Information Up to Date 214

Unquestionably, there is progress. The average American now pays out twice as much in taxes as he formerly got in wages.

—H. L. MENCKEN (1880–1956)

You just can't escape taxes. If you are incapacitated—and even after your death—those in charge of your affairs must make sure that your tax bills are paid.

In the Taxes section of your planner, you can provide important information about your tax records and recommend a tax professional in case your agent or executor needs help preparing and filing your returns.

Before turning to the specifics of how to complete your planner, this chapter provides an overview of taxes that must be paid at the end of life.

SKIP AHEAD

If your tax information is ready to go. If you're familiar with the kinds of taxes that may be due at your death and you're ready to provide information for your caretakers and survivors, turn right to "In Your Planner" to start completing your planner.

Tax Basics

When it comes to taxes, there are three distinct end-of-life phases: the phase leading up to your death, the period following your death, and the point at which your estate is distributed to your beneficiaries. For each phase, the tax picture is a little different.

Prior to Death

If you are incapacitated, your agent for finances, spouse, or another person close to you will file federal or state income tax returns on your behalf (if you receive at least the minimum amount of income, as set by law).

If your death is sudden or follows a short illness, you may still owe federal or state income tax on any unreported income to that point. In that case, your executor or successor trustee (if you have made a living trust) is responsible for filing necessary tax returns on income you earned while you were alive.

After Death

For the year of your death, and for each year until your estate is fully distributed to your inheritors, your executor or trustee may have to file income tax returns for your estate or trust. Again, the returns are due only if your estate or trust receives a minimum amount of income—such as interest, dividends, rents, royalties, business income, or capital gains from asset sales—as set by applicable federal or state law.

Distribution of Estate

Once a full accounting of your estate is complete (or probate proceedings are finished), your executor or trustee will file any necessary estate and inheritance tax returns, depending upon the size of your estate and the state in which you live. (Inheritance tax returns may instead be filed by individual beneficiaries, rather than coordinated by the executor or trustee.)

Most of us are less familiar with estate and inheritance taxes than we are with routine income taxes. The discussion that follows lays out some basic guidelines to help you better understand these taxes.

Estate and Inheritance Taxes

If your estate is worth more than a specified amount, your executor will have to file a federal estate tax return. State estate or inheritance taxes may be due as well.

Federal Estate Tax

Most Americans do not need to worry about the federal estate tax because their estates are not large enough to trigger estate taxes. In 2014, only estates worth more than $5,340,000 owe federal estate tax. This amount will increase with inflation.

The federal estate tax law also provides "portability" between spouses, which gives married couples additional tax advantages. With portability, when the second spouse dies, that estate can tack on any "unused" personal exemption amount from the first spouse's estate. This means that the second spouse to die could leave up to $10.68 million, without owing estate tax. To preserve this benefit, the surviving spouse must file IRS Form 706 within nine months of the first spouse's death. For more information, see "Where to Get Help," below.

If you're wealthy enough to be concerned about federal estate taxes, you should consult an accountant or estate planning attorney to answer your questions and discuss tax planning.

If you do plan to leave a very large estate, there are a number of situations in which some of your property may be exempt from the tax. The most important of these is known as the "marital deduction." Put simply, all property left to a spouse is exempt from federal estate tax, no matter how much the property is worth. (The spouse must be a U.S. citizen, however. There are limits on how much tax-exempt property you can leave to a noncitizen spouse.) Other estate tax exemptions include:

- gifts to charities
- funeral expenses
- estate expenses, such as probate fees
- any claims against the estate, and
- a percentage of state or foreign estate or inheritance taxes.

If the value of your estate is above the estate tax exemption, your executor must file a tax return within nine months from the date of death, or the estate will face penalty and interest charges.

Avoiding Federal Estate Tax

Aside from the exemptions mentioned in this section, there are a few ways to reduce your estate and avoid estate tax. Here are some of the most popular:

- **Tax-free gifts**, which allow you to give up to $14,000 per calendar year per recipient without paying gift tax. You can also pay someone's tuition or medical bills, or give to a charity, without paying gift tax on the amount. This reduces the size of your estate and the eventual estate tax bill.
- **An AB trust**, where spouses leave their property in trust for their children, but give the surviving spouse the right to use it for life. This keeps the second spouse's taxable estate half the size it would be if the property were left entirely to the surviving spouse. See Chapter 17 for more on this type of trust.
- **A "QTIP" trust**, which enables couples to postpone estate taxes until the second spouse dies.
- **Charitable trusts**, which involve making a sizable gift to a tax-exempt charity.
- **Life insurance trusts**, which let you take the value of life insurance proceeds out of your estate.

For more information, see the resources listed in "Where to Get Help," below.

State Estate and Inheritance Taxes

In addition to federal estate tax, you may need to consider whether your estate will owe state estate or inheritance taxes.

Like the federal tax, state estate taxes are based on the gross value of the estate. Not all states have estate taxes, however for many of those that do, the state exemption amount is often lower than the federal exemption amount. An estate may therefore owe state estate tax, but not federal estate tax. Furthermore, if the deceased person lived in one state and owned real estate in another, an estate may owe estate taxes to more than one state. Property left to a surviving spouse, however, is exempt from state estate tax, just as it is exempt from federal estate tax.

In addition, a handful of states impose an inheritance tax on individual beneficiaries. The tax rate depends on who inherits the property; usually, spouses and other close relatives pay nothing or a low rate, and other exemptions apply.

States That Impose Estate or Inheritance Taxes

Estate Tax	
Connecticut	Minnesota
Delaware	New York
District of Columbia	Oregon
Hawaii	Rhode Island
Illinois	Tennessee*
Maine	Vermont
Massachusetts	Washington
Inheritance Tax	
Iowa	Nebraska
Kentucky	Pennsylvania
Both Estate and Inheritance Tax	
Maryland	New Jersey

*Called an "inheritance tax," but is an estate tax. Will be phased out by 2016. (Tennessee)

While each beneficiary is responsible for paying any inheritance tax due on the property you leave him or her, it is usually more efficient for the executor or trustee to coordinate the overall tax payment.

Where to Get Help

Nolo's website (www.nolo.com) provides a number of free articles on estate and inheritance taxes. If you want more information about the basics, it's a good place to start.

For detailed information and rates for federal estate taxes, you can go right to the IRS website at www.irs.gov. Once there, click on "Forms and Publications." In particular, see Publication 559, *Survivors, Executors, and Administrators.*

For more information about state estate and inheritance taxes, contact the state department of taxation or controller's office, or find the information online at the state tax office's website.

In addition, the following Nolo books provide in-depth discussions of estate taxes:

- ***Plan Your Estate,*** by Denis Clifford, explains estate and inheritance taxes and sets out the most popular strategies for avoiding or reducing them.
- ***The Executor's Guide: Settling a Loved One's Estate or Trust,*** by Mary Randolph, is a comprehensive manual for those charged with wrapping up a loved one's affairs. It provides a solid overview of final taxes and the process of filing returns after death.

In Your Planner

Turn to the Taxes section of your planner (Section 24). The following guidelines will help you complete the pages there.

Tax Professionals

List the individuals or firms who have helped with your tax returns in the past, or those you recommend to your agent for finances, executor, or trustee for preparing future returns. Include attorneys, accountants, or other professionals that can help with tax work. If you feel that preparing your returns will be simple, and that it won't require professional assistance, make a note of that. If you do not have a preference, simply write "family choice."

- **Name of Person or Firm.** Write the full name of the professional or firm.
- **Contact Information.** Provide contact information, including address, telephone, and email address, if available.
- **Notes.** Describe the nature of the work performed for you by the professional or firm, and what you recommend the professional or firm do in the future.

Location of Tax Records

Here, describe where you keep your income tax records—for both the current and prior years. You probably don't store current-year information with your old returns, so note the respective locations carefully.

- **Location of Current-Year Records.** Describe where you file your current-year tax records, including necessary access or contact information.

  EXAMPLES:

  Information for current-year return is filed in "[Year] Taxes" file folder, left-hand drawer of my desk. Open the pencil drawer to release the side drawers.

  Records for my next income tax return are in the "Current Taxes" folder, top drawer of beige file cabinet, SW corner of my office.

- **Location of Prior-Year Records.** Describe the location where you store your prior-year income tax returns, including necessary access or contact information.

  EXAMPLES:

  Prior-year returns in records box on bottom shelf, NW corner of garage

  Old tax returns in bottom-left drawer (at the back) of desk

  Prior returns stored in records box in Acme Storage rental space. See Section 27 of this planner, Other Income and Personal Property, for location and access instructions

How Long Should You Keep Tax Records?

Keep your tax returns and supporting documents —such as W-2 and 1099 forms, and receipts and canceled checks for deductible items—for at least three years after you file. For example, if you filed on April 15, 2014 for tax year 2013, keep those records until at least April 16, 2017. In general, the IRS has up to three years to initiate an audit.

To be completely safe, you'll want to keep your records for seven years. The IRS can audit you for up to six years after you filed a return if it suspects that you underreported your income by 25% or more. And it has seven years to check up on you if you've filed a claim for a loss from worthless securities.

For those who file a fraudulent return—or fail to file a return at all—the IRS recommends that you maintain your records indefinitely. In these circumstances, there is no time limit during which the IRS must audit you.

Keep records showing purchases of real estate, stocks, and other investments for at least three years after you sell the asset. If you are audited, you must be able to show your taxable gain or loss.

Even when you no longer need records for tax purposes, you may need them for an insurance company or creditors. Before you dispose of records, ensure that you don't need to keep them for some other reason.

For more information, see Publication 552, *Recordkeeping for Individuals*, available from the IRS at www.irs.gov.

Additional Notes

If you have additional information or direction regarding your income tax records or their locations, include it here. Also include any additional directions you may have about preparing estate or inheritance tax returns.

EXAMPLES:

If the beige file cabinet is locked, see Section 23 of this planner, Secured Places and Passwords, for access information.

I have listed my attorney under Tax Professionals above. If she needs help with the estate tax return, she'll call in a competent CPA or other professional. She's great; trust her.

BINDER

Including tax materials in your planner. Depending on the nature and volume of material, you may want to file tax-related items in your planner binder. You can hole-punch documents such as old tax returns, inserting them directly into your planner binder. For receipts or notes that might be easily lost, you can use pocket dividers, plastic binder sleeves, or plastic pouches.

Keeping Your Information Up to Date

Remember to update this section of your planner if you:

- want to recommend different tax professionals, or
- change the location in which you store your current or prior-year tax records.

At the same time, comb through your old tax records and toss those that are out of date. Follow the guidelines in "How Long Should You Keep Tax Records?" above.

CHAPTER

25

Real Estate

Ways to Own Property 216

Sole Ownership 216

Shared Ownership 216

Special Rules for Married Couples 218

Common Law States 218

Community Property States 219

Where to Get Help 220

In Your Planner 220

Keeping Your Information Up to Date 223

> *Mid pleasures and palaces though we may roam,*
> *Be it ever so humble, there's no place like home.*
>
> —JOHN HOWARD PAYNE (1791–1852)

Your planner helps you organize your real estate records for yourself and your survivors. You can list all properties that you own or rent—for example, your home, a vacation time-share, or a storage space that you lease from someone else. You can also include related materials with your planner. These may include rental or lease agreements, time-share agreements, property deeds, or materials related to the care and maintenance of individual properties. (While individual service providers for your properties are listed in Section 10, you'll describe maintenance details here.)

Before you get to the instructions for completing your planner, however, you'll find a discussion about different ways to own real estate and how state law can affect property ownership. Knowing how you own property (for instance, in joint tenancy or as tenants in common), and the state law that controls it, is important—especially when it comes time to pass that property to others.

If you're not sure how you own a particular piece of real estate, the following discussion can help you sort out your records.

SKIP AHEAD

If you have no questions about property ownership. If you are clear and comfortable with the ways in which you hold title to your property, you may want to skip right to "In Your Planner" for directions on including a property summary and related documents in your planner. Then turn to "Keeping Your Information Up to Date" for tips on keeping your planner current.

Ways to Own Property

If you own property and you want to name beneficiaries to receive it after you die, you need to know what is yours to leave—and set up your ownership (title) documents and estate plan to carry out your intentions. Here are the ways you can hold title to property and, for each, the way the property passes to survivors.

Sole Ownership

If you own property in your own name, without co-owners, you are generally free to leave it to others in any way you like. However, if you are married, or in a registered domestic partnership in a couple of states, your spouse or partner may be entitled to a share of your property. (See "Special Rules for Married Couples," below.)

Shared Ownership

You may own property with one or more other people. Shared property ownership can take several forms:

Tenancy in Common

Two or more people can own property as tenants in common. Spouses, partners, relatives (for example, two sisters or a mother and son), or nonfamily associates often own property in this way.

Tenants in common can own any percentage of the TIC property—for example 7% or 70%. At your death, you can leave your interest in TIC property to anyone you choose. Again, however, spouses or partners may have some rights in the property.

Joint Tenancy With Right of Survivorship

Joint tenancy is another frequently used form of shared ownership for two or more people. Joint tenancy differs from tenancy in common in a few important ways. Under a joint tenancy, each owner must take an equal share of the property. During life, a joint tenant is free to give away or sell his or her interest in the property. But when one joint tenant dies, the property automatically goes to the surviving owners—no matter what the deceased person's will or other estate planning document states. The property transfer is not subject to probate proceedings.

While many people use it for real estate, you can usually hold many types of property in joint tenancy—including vehicles and bank accounts.

A joint tenancy can be created only with a written ownership document that uses language identifying the owners as "joint tenants," "joint tenants with right of survivorship," or other language required by state law.

CAUTION

State rules and restrictions. A few states have special rules or restrictions for establishing a joint tenancy. For example, Alaska permits this kind of ownership only for real estate and only between husbands and wives, as tenants by the entirety (see below). Check the rules for your state before you try to set up joint tenancy ownership.

Tenancy by the Entirety

Tenancy by the entirety is very similar to joint tenancy, but is available only to married couples in about half the states—or to registered domestic partners in just a couple of states. It also offers a couple of potential advantages that joint tenancy property does not:

- During life, one owner is not permitted to transfer his or her share of property without the consent of the other.
- The creditors of one owner may have a more difficult time seizing the property to collect on a debt.

Like a joint tenancy, a tenancy by the entirety must be created in writing.

Community Property

In community property states, any real estate spouses earn or acquire during marriage is normally shared community property—meaning that each spouse owns half. (There are a few exceptions to this rule—for example, property received by gift or inheritance. See "Community Property States," below, for more information.) Community property is also available to registered domestic partners in California. At death, each spouse is usually free to leave his or her half of the property to anyone at all.

TIP

Transfer-on-death deeds for real estate. In several states—Arizona, Arkansas, Colorado, District of Columbia, Hawaii, Illinois, Indiana, Kansas, Minnesota, Missouri, Montana, Nebraska, Nevada, New Mexico, North Dakota, Ohio, Oklahoma, Oregon, Virginia, Washington, Wisconsin, and Wyoming—you can transfer real estate without probate by creating what's known as a "transfer-on-death" deed. These deeds must be prepared, signed, notarized, and filed in the county land records office just like a regular deed. The deed should clearly state that it doesn't take effect until death—and you can revoke it any time before then. (Don't try this in any but the handful of states listed here; it won't work.)

TIP

Community property with right of survivorship. This fairly new form of community property is identical to traditional community property with one exception: On the death of a spouse or partner, the survivor automatically inherits the deceased person's share, just like joint tenancy. Community property with right of survivorship is currently available in six community property states—Alaska, Arizona,

California, Idaho, Nevada, and Wisconsin. (It's called "survivorship community property" in Alaska and "survivorship marital property" in Wisconsin.)

Special Rules for Married Couples

If you are married and you want to leave everything to your spouse, as many people do, you don't need to worry about what belongs to each of you. But if you want to divide your property among several beneficiaries, you need to know just what's yours to leave. This depends on whether your state follows the "common law" or "community property" system of property ownership. The community property states are Arizona, California, Idaho, Louisiana, Nevada, New Mexico, Texas, Washington, and Wisconsin. (In Alaska, spouses can sign an agreement making certain assets community property.) All other states are common law states.

A Note for Domestic Partners

If you have registered your relationship with your state—whether as a domestic partnership, reciprocal beneficiary relationship, or civil union —you, too, should read this section. Many of the provisions will apply to you. For example, if you live in California, you can take advantage of the community property system. If you register your union in Vermont or Hawaii, you can use the tenancy by the entirety form of ownership (discussed above) and the state's inheritance laws will protect you if your partner dies before you do. Because each state's domestic partnership law is so different, however, we can't set out all the specifics here. If you have questions about property ownership or inheritance rights, it's wise to talk with a lawyer in your state who's familiar with these laws.

Common Law States

In common law states, it's usually easy to tell who owns what. If only your name is on the deed, registration document, or other title paper, the property is yours. You are free to leave it to whomever you choose, subject to your spouse's right to claim a certain share after your death. (See "Your Spouse's Right to Inherit," below.)

If you and your spouse both have your names on the title document, you each own a half-interest. Your freedom to give away or leave that half-interest depends on how you and your spouse share ownership. If you own the property as joint tenants with the right of survivorship or in tenancy by the entirety, it automatically goes to the surviving spouse when one spouse dies—even if the deceased spouse's will says something different. If you instead own the property as tenants in common, then you can leave your half to someone other than your spouse if you wish.

Your Spouse's Right to Inherit

To protect spouses from being disinherited, common law states give a surviving spouse the right to claim a portion of the deceased spouse's estate, no matter what the will or other estate planning documents provide.

These provisions kick in only if the survivor goes to court and claims the share allowed by law. If a surviving spouse doesn't object to receiving less, the deceased spouse's estate plan is honored as written.

If you don't plan to leave at least half of your property to your spouse in your will, and you have not provided generously for your spouse outside of your will, you should head off disputes by getting your spouse's signed waiver of his or her right to inherit more from you. Consult a lawyer to ensure the documents are done right.

Community Property States

If you live in a community property state (listed above), the rules are more complicated.

Community property is a method for defining the ownership of property acquired during marriage. Generally, in community property states, all earnings during marriage and all property acquired with those earnings are considered community property, owned equally by husband and wife. Likewise, all debts incurred during marriage are debts of the couple. Separate property and each spouse's half of the community property may be left to whomever the owner wishes. But if there's no will, the surviving spouse takes all of the community property.

Here's a brief rundown on what's usually considered community property—and what's kept separate:

Community Property	Separate Property
Money either spouse earns during marriage	Property owned by one spouse before marriage
Property bought with money either spouse earns during marriage	Property given to just one spouse
Separate property that has become so mixed with community property that it cannot be identified	Property inherited by just one spouse

These rules apply no matter whose name is on the title document to a particular piece of property. For example, a married woman in a community property state may own a car in only her name—but legally, her husband may own a half-interest. The table below shows some other examples.

Property	Classification	Reason
An heirloom your partner inherited during your marriage	Your spouse's separate property	Property inherited by one spouse alone is separate property
A car you owned before marriage	Your separate property	Property owned by one spouse before marriage is separate property
A family home, for which the deed states that you and your wife own as "husband and wife" and which was bought with your earnings	Community property	It was bought with community property income (income earned during the marriage) and is owned as "husband and wife"
A checking account owned and used by you and your spouse, into which you put a $5,000 inheritance 20 years ago	Community property	The $5,000 (which was your separate property) has become so mixed (commingled) with community property funds that it has become community property

Couples don't have to accept the rules about what is community property and what is not. They can sign a written agreement that makes some or all community property the separate property of one partner, or that makes separate property into community property. These marital property agreements are commonly made prior to marrying or creating a domestic partnership, and are usually called "prenuptial agreements" (prenups) or "premarital agreements." (You can find more information below.)

Where to Get Help

For general information about holding title to property in your state, contact your state's real estate department. It can tell you which types of ownership are available and the requirements for holding and transferring title. You can also get answers to questions about what happens to an owner's share after death.

You can easily locate the real estate office for your state by using the online directory maintained by the Association of Real Estate License Law Officials, at www.arello.org. Click on "Resources" and then select "Regulatory Agencies." You can also find the state office information by checking the yellow pages of your phone book. The office is usually listed under real estate or housing in the state government listings.

If you need more information about your title documents, or if you want to change the way you hold property, follow up with a real estate title company in your area. To change the form of property ownership, you will need to prepare a new deed and file it with the land records office in the county where the property is located. (If you live in California, you can turn to *Deeds for California Real Estate*, by Mary Randolph (Nolo), which provides all the forms and instructions you need to transfer property in the Golden State.)

CAUTION

If you want to change ownership forms. Changing the way you own property may involve tax and other consequences. *Plan Your Estate*, by Denis Clifford (Nolo), explains many of the rules—but you may want to consult an attorney or tax accountant before you settle on a course of action. If you need help finding a good expert, turn to Appendix B for tips.

Resources for Couples

The following books are particularly helpful for couples—straight or gay, married or not:

- ***Prenuptial Agreements: How to Write a Fair & Lasting Contract,*** by Katherine E. Stoner and Shae Irving (Nolo), helps you understand the property ownership rules for married couples in your state. If you want to draft your own rules, the book helps you write an agreement and work with a lawyer to finalize it.
- ***Living Together: A Legal Guide for Unmarried Couples,*** by Toni Ihara, Ralph Warner, and Frederick Hertz (Nolo), helps unmarried couples understand property ownership rules and write property-sharing agreements.
- ***A Legal Guide for Lesbian & Gay Couples,*** by Denis Clifford, Frederick Hertz, and Emily Doskow (Nolo), helps same-sex couples sort out property ownership questions and write up agreements about who owns what.

In Your Planner

Turn to the Real Estate section of your planner (Section 25). The following guidelines will help you fill in the pages there.

RELATED TOPIC

Business property. If you own, rent, or lease property for business purposes, describe that property in Section 8, Business Interests. In this section, describe all other property.

Property I Own

Include all real estate that you own, whether by yourself or with others. This may include your home (if you own it), vacation properties, property for which you've cosigned a loan, properties that you own but lease or rent to others, and undeveloped land.

- **Property Address.** Include the complete street address or other location description for each property.
- **Weeks/Year Occupancy.** If, for income tax purposes, you track the number of weeks you spend at the address in a given year, enter that information here. (The number you enter here should correspond to your state tax estimates.) If you maintain just one residence, traveling to other states only for temporary purposes (such as vacation or business), your resident status is probably clear, and you can skip this item.
- **Mortgage Company Contact Information.** If the property is mortgaged, provide the lender's name, address, and telephone number for each loan against the property. If you have an email address, include that, too.
- **Current Occupants and Contact Information.** If you rent or lease the property to others, include their names and contact information.
- **Location of Documents.** Describe the location of ownership documents and any rental agreements your tenants have signed. (If possible, include these documents with your planner; see the note below.)

Instructions for Care of Property I Own

Provide any background or direction about the care that you provide for the property.

RELATED TOPIC

Listing service providers. In this section, provide information or instructions about the care and maintenance of property that you own. If you employ regular service providers for certain tasks or responsibilities, list them in Section 10 (Service Providers).

- **Property Address.** Include the complete address or location for the property (just as you wrote it in the prior table).
- **Property Care.** Include your notes, instructions, requests, or concerns regarding care for individual properties.

EXAMPLES:

The hot tub has a dedicated breaker on the outside north wall of the house.

The map to the septic tank is included at the back of this section. Also see my instructions for troubleshooting problems at the end of this section.

Additional Notes

Include other information, directions, or concerns regarding property you own.

EXAMPLES:

For years, Rod Harris (530-555-3333) has grazed his cattle on our Tehema County land—verbal agreement, no cost. Please get in touch with him when I'm gone.

Cheryl and Tom (123 Sixth Street) have been excellent tenants. If you now want to sell the home, please offer them a good price and see if they're interested in buying.

We hold a reverse mortgage on our home; see the loan documents for details.

The Sunset Avenue garage conversion was done without any permits. You will probably have to remove the improvements when you sell the home.

ABC Properties, Inc., Fallen Rock, has repeatedly expressed interest in buying the property, if we ever want to sell. Give them a call, if you're interested.

Property I Rent or Lease

Describe both your primary residence, if you rent it, as well as other properties that you rent or lease (such as vacation rentals or farmland). Such rental or lease commitments may include property that you rent or lease for your own use, that you sublet to others, or for which you have cosigned someone else's rental or lease agreement.

- **Property Address.** Include the complete street address or other location description for each property.
- **Weeks/Year Occupancy.** If, for income tax purposes, you track the number of weeks you spend at the address in a given year, enter that information here. (The number you enter here should correspond to your state tax estimates.) If you maintain just one residence, traveling to other states only for temporary purposes (such as vacation or business), your resident status is probably clear, and you can skip this item.
- **Landlord's Contact Information.** Provide the name, address, and telephone number for the landlord or rental agent. If you have an email address, include that, too.
- **Term of Rental or Lease.** Briefly describe the terms of your rental or lease for each address—for example, one-year lease or month-to-month rental.
- **Location of Documents.** Describe the location of related documents, such as rental or lease documents. (If possible, include these documents with your planner; see the note below.)

Instructions for Care of Leased or Rented Property

Describe any care that you provide for the property.

- **Property Address.** Include the complete address or location for the property (just as you wrote it in the prior table).
- **Property Care.** Include your notes, instructions, requests, or concerns regarding care for individual properties.

EXAMPLES:

The electrical panel is on the east outside wall of the garage, inside the gate.

There is a portable generator in the tool shed. Use this to pump the well if there is a power outage. Instructions are in the back of this section.

Under the lease terms, I maintain the land—seasonal mowing and clearing debris, brush, and fallen trees. I contract this work to Joe Derby; see Section 10 of this planner (Service Providers).

Additional Notes

Include other information, directions, or concerns regarding your rented or leased property.

EXAMPLES:

There are a sofa and two chairs in my personal storage space that belong to the landlord.

Our landlord lives in the back and uses our laundry setup in our garage (and we save $100 per month on rent). Her laundry supplies are in our garage.

BINDER

Including real estate documents in your planner. You can organize and file documents such as rental and lease agreements, time-share agreements, deeds, and other related documents in the Real Estate section of your planner binder. Pocket divider pages or plastic sleeves work well for this purpose, or you can hole-punch documents and insert them directly into the binder after this section.

Keeping Your Information Up to Date

Review your real estate ownership documents if:

- you move to another state—in particular, if you move from a common law state to a community property state, or vice versa, or
- you get a divorce, are married, or widowed.

In these cases, you will want to evaluate the way that you hold title to your property, the survivorship rights associated with title, and the beneficiaries you have named for the property. Ensure that your property will pass to beneficiaries according to your wishes. Update your planner with any changes you make.

Also, you will want to update your planner if:

- you invest in new property or sell your share in an existing property
- your information or instructions for property care change, or
- you get new tenants for property that you own.

CHAPTER

26

Vehicles

Leaving Your Vehicles to Others 226

Transfer-on-Death Registration 226

Other Nonprobate Transfer Methods for Vehicles 227

Where to Get Help 227

In Your Planner 227

Keeping Your Information Up to Date 228

Well, she ain't into cars or pickup trucks—but if it runs like a Deere, man, her eyes light up.

—PAUL OVERSTREET AND JIM COLLINS, "SHE THINKS MY TRACTOR'S SEXY"

You can use your planner to create a record of vehicles that you own or lease. These may include:

- cars or trucks
- recreational vehicles or trailers
- boats
- snowmobiles or jet skis
- farming or other heavy equipment
- utility vehicles or golf carts
- motorcycles or scooters, or
- airplanes.

Your planner lets you describe purchase or lease information, the location of your vehicles, and the location of related documents. These documents may include title certificates, loan or lease agreements, service or maintenance records, garage or docking agreements, or certificates of appraisal. For easy reference, you can file these documents in your planner.

Before turning to the instructions for completing your planner, this chapter provides some guidance on leaving your vehicles to others at your death.

SKIP AHEAD

If you have your vehicle documents on hand and your beneficiary designations are clear. If you have the important documents relating to your vehicles (both owned and leased) and you know how your vehicles will be transferred after your death, you can skip to "In Your Planner" for directions on completing your planner. Then review "Keeping Your Information Up to Date" for tips on keeping your planner current.

Leaving Your Vehicles to Others

Vehicles are usually registered in the name of one or more owners. If you're the only owner and you die, the vehicle passes to whomever you've named to receive it—or according to state law if you haven't named a beneficiary. If a vehicle is registered to two or more owners, the surviving owner or owners automatically inherit the deceased person's share.

Many states offer simple ways to transfer vehicles to new owners after a death, often bypassing the probate process.

Transfer-on-Death Registration

This convenient way to transfer vehicles is currently available in Arizona, Arkansas, California, Connecticut, Delaware, Illinois, Indiana, Kansas, Missouri, Nebraska, Nevada, Ohio, Vermont, and Virginia. If you own your vehicle and register it in transfer-on-death form, the title certificate will list the name of the beneficiary who will automatically own the vehicle after your death—without probate court proceedings. The beneficiary you name has no rights to the vehicle as long as you are alive. You are free to sell it or give it away, or name someone else as the beneficiary. To arrange this type of transfer, contact your state's motor vehicles department and ask for a certificate of car ownership (title) in "beneficiary form."

Other Nonprobate Transfer Methods for Vehicles

A number of states have established simple ways to transfer vehicles after a death. However, these methods may be available only to surviving spouses or for vehicles of little value. To find out what's available in your state, contact the state motor vehicles agency. (You can find your department of motor vehicles website by following the directions just below.)

Where to Get Help

If you want to retitle a vehicle, whether to add a co-owner or a transfer-on-death designation, you can find more information on your state's motor vehicles department website or by visiting your local motor vehicles department office. To find the link to your state's department, visit www.dmv-department-of-motor-vehicles.com.

In Your Planner

Turn to the Vehicles section of your planner (Section 26). The following guidelines will help you complete the pages there.

Be sure to list all of your vehicles in this section, whether owned or leased. Include every vehicle you can think of—automobiles, trucks, recreational vehicles, boats, airplanes, farming and other heavy equipment, golf carts, motorcycles, scooters, and so on.

Vehicles I Own

Describe each vehicle in which you are sole or part owner (including any for which you are a cosigner). Include those that you use yourself and any that others use—for example, a car that you co-own with your spouse, even though you both think of it as your spouse's car.

- **Vehicle Type.** Identify the vehicle type, including the make, model, and year of manufacture. You should also provide the vehicle identification number (VIN), as printed on your vehicle registration certificate or stamped on the vehicle itself.

EXAMPLES:

Toyota Prius 2012 (VIN JTDKB20U653019999)

John Deere 4010 Compact Tractor 2002
(Serial # LV4010H111222)

VW Rialta RV 2005
(VIN WV3AB47023H013333)

- **Creditor Contact Information.** If you owe money on the vehicle, provide contact information for the company or individual that holds the loan.
- **Garage or Storage Location.** Describe the location for each vehicle, whether at your home or another site.

EXAMPLES:

Home garage

Barn

Ace's Storage, 444 Rural Road,
Hometown, CA 94333, 510-555-1234

Berth #D07 at Hays Marina & Docking,
4 Harbor Road, Hays Harbor, WA 98765,
360-444-6666

- **Transfer-on-Death Beneficiary.** If you have named a transfer-on-death beneficiary for the vehicle, list that person here.
- **Location of Documents.** Describe the location of certificates of title, garage or docking agreements, lease agreements (that is, if you've leased the vehicle to someone else; vehicles that you lease from others are covered below), and other related documents. (If possible, file these documents in your planner; see the note below.)

TIP

If you don't have your title slip. If the original certificate of title has been lost, stolen, or mutilated, you should apply for a replacement or duplicate. Contact your state's motor vehicles department for information. (See "Where to Get Help," above, for contact information.)

Additional Notes

Provide any other details or instructions. If you have passwords or access codes for your vehicles, include them here.

EXAMPLES:

My neighbor John Truitt (530-555-1124) helped pay for the John Deere tractor. He paid 25% of the purchase price, and in exchange he comes up and uses it about two days a week.

Bobby has the paperwork for the car; I served as cosigner so he could get the loan.

Sometimes we rent out the RV for weekends; see the rate sheet and contract at the back of this section.

Key for Mustang wheel locks is on my keychain.

Security codes for Honda Ridgeline:
doors = 1228, navi home = 0210, radio = 1230.

Vehicles I Lease

Document all vehicles that you currently lease. Be sure to include any vehicles that are leased in your name, but are used by others.

- **Vehicle Type.** Identify the vehicle type, including the make, model, and the year of manufacture. You should also provide the vehicle identification number (VIN), as printed on your vehicle registration certificate or stamped on the vehicle itself.
- **Leaseholder Contact Information.** Include contact information for the company or individual that holds the lease.
- **Garage or Storage Location.** Describe the location for each vehicle, whether at your home or another site.
- **Location of Documents.** Indicate the location of lease agreement contracts and other relevant documents, including garage or docking agreements.

Additional Notes

Provide any other details or instructions.

BINDER

Including vehicle documents in your planner. You can organize and file your current loan, lease, or ownership agreements in the Vehicles section of your planner binder. If you have garage or docking agreements, you can easily file them here, too. Three-hole-punch the documents and insert them directly in your planner binder after this section, or use pocket divider pages or plastic binder sleeves.

Keeping Your Information Up to Date

When you review your planner, be sure to make changes to this section if you:

- acquire new vehicles or dispose of old ones
- change a lease agreement
- pay off a vehicle, or
- change the garage or other storage arrangements.

CHAPTER

27

Other Income and Personal Property

In Your Planner....................230

Keeping Your Information Up to Date....................233

Riches may enable us to confer favours, but to confer them with propriety and grace requires a something that riches cannot give.

—CHARLES CALEB COLTON (1780–1832)

While you've already described many sources of income in your planner—such as your employment, bank and brokerage accounts, retirement plans, and business interests—this section serves as a catchall for additional sources of income. These may range from lottery winnings or proceeds from the sale of property to royalty payments.

In addition, while you provided information about your vehicles in the previous section and described many of your valuables when you listed your secured places, here you can identify any other important items of personal property. Personal property includes all your possessions other than real estate—that is, other than land or anything attached to it. Among other items, personal property includes tools, jewelry, artwork, and household furnishings. You can use this section to pass along directions and wishes for specific items of property that you haven't listed elsewhere, and you can indicate whether you have named a specific beneficiary for the item in your will or another estate planning document.

You can also use your planner to store materials related to the property you list in this section. For example, you might include photos, notes on the history of items, contracts, or other documents. Or, you might include a copy of another person's will or other documents—such as an insurance policy or transfer-on-death vehicle title certificate—that name you as beneficiary. (Be aware, however, that if you die before your benefactor, the property probably won't pass to your estate but, instead, to that person's alternate beneficiary.)

Finally, this is also the place to describe where you file documents related to personal property, such as warranty agreements and maintenance guides.

Naming Beneficiaries for Your Property

While money divides up evenly, personal property does not. We've all heard disturbing stories about grieving families feuding over sentimental items. You can help prevent rivalries by clearly documenting your wishes for property distribution in your will, living trust, or other estate planning documents. It is important that you include all items of sentimental or financial value—and identify the beneficiaries for each—in your legally binding estate planning documents. You may wish to discuss your plans with your loved ones while you are still living, helping your heirs to appreciate both the gifts that you want to make, as well as the fairness of your plans.

In Your Planner

Turn to the Other Income and Personal Property section of your planner (Section 27). The following guidelines will help you complete the pages there.

Other Income

If you receive income from sources not documented elsewhere in your planner, describe those sources here. Other income may include proceeds from the sale of property, charitable gift annuities, lottery winnings, or royalty payments for creative work—such as art, a song, lyrics, poetry, or other writing—that you've sold while still employed in your day job.

- **Source and Contact Information.** Provide the name and any contact information for the source of the income.

  EXAMPLES:

  Ms. Laura Gomez, Payout Coordinator, California State Lottery Commission, 1111 Townsend Street, Sacramento, CA 95611, 916-555-5555

  Placer Poetry Publishers, 444 Main Street, Cheyenne, WY 88111, Contact: Michael DeFlore, 626-444-4444

- **Description.** Provide a brief description of the source of the income.

  EXAMPLES:

  Monthly payments on California Lotto winnings, August 2002 through July 2022

  Royalties on book of poetry, *Summer Solstice*, published by Placer in 2003

- **Location of Documents.** Describe the location of any related documents. (If possible, include them with your planner; see the note below.) If you do not have a document describing the income, you should briefly outline any terms, including the status of payments and expected future income.

  EXAMPLES:

  Documents filed in back of this section

  Contract in cabinet, drawer N-Q, file "Placer Poetry"

  Payments of $100 per month expected to continue only until the time of my death

Additional Notes

Include any additional information about the sources of income listed in this section, noting the location for any related materials.

EXAMPLES:

I've almost finished *Vernal Equinox* (PC file folder: vernaleq); contact Placer Poetry to see if they're interested in this next one.

I have four cases of my book *Summer Solstice* in my storage space at Personal Rents in Santa Fe. See Secured Places and Passwords (Section 23) for access information.

TIP

Don't forget your eStuff. Do you have digital assets that might be of value to your loved ones—books on your Nook, games on your Fire, or music on iTunes or your iPod? If you own rights to books, movies, games, music, or other digital items, you might want to take a little time to figure out how your loved ones could use then once you're gone. For example, according to Amazon, your Kindle library will be available forever—until someone closes your account. If you want to share your books with your loved ones, simply leave a note in your planner along with your Amazon account information.

Other Personal Property

Do you own personal property that you want to highlight and describe in your planner—such as municipal bonds or stock certificates stored at home? Or family heirlooms or valuable jewelry not listed in other sections? Maybe you own items that require special care, or certain items you want destroyed when you die. Consider including any items with rich history or great sentimental or financial value, or for which you have special instructions. Provide the following information for each item of property that you list:

- **Item and Description.** Write the name and a brief description of the item.
- **Location and Access Information.** Provide the location and access information, so that your survivors can find the property. If someone else has the item, provide any contact information you may have for that person or facility—such as the name, address, telephone number, and email address.
- **Special Instructions.** Describe any requests for disposition or care of the item, and note whether you have specified in your will or other estate planning documents who should receive the item when you die.

EXAMPLES:

Feel free to sell the entire collection, so that my heirs are not saddled with maintenance!

Bequest stated in living trust.

Remove from stairs before home sold. Thomas Moore, my great grandfather, crafted the beautiful post around 1890. Specific bequest in will.

Use only Beatrice Marble Cream to retain the color and shine!

- **Location of Documents.** Identify any documents related to the item and describe where they are filed. Documents may include purchase or appraisal records, related contracts, a history of the item, or a copy of a title document. If possible, file the related documents in your planner.

EXAMPLES:

Appraisal certificate in back of this section.

History of organ in yellow file folder, organ music rack.

Additional Notes

Include any additional information about the property listed in this section. Include the location for other related materials, such as individual care manuals or a map for locating a given item.

EXAMPLES:

My sister, Miss Beulah Land (555-222-2222, in San Antonio), has written a beautiful story about the newel post on the stairs. Whoever gets the post should ask her for a copy of the story.

Purchase Beatrice Marble Cream directly from manufacturer: www.bmcco.com or 444-765-5555.

Property I Expect to Receive From Others

If you expect to receive property from others, you can describe the source, the nature of the property, and any related documents here. Consider listing property you expect to receive from any of the following sources:

- a will or other estate planning document
- an insurance policy
- a transfer-on-death vehicle title
- a pay-on-death bank or brokerage account (such as a bank account trust, revocable trust account, or Totten trust), or
- any other promise to pay or transfer property, such as an annual cash gift.

- **Source and Contact Information.** Provide the name and any contact information for the source of the property.
- **Description.** Provide a brief description of the expected property.

EXAMPLES:

Antique micro-mosaic necklace (brass, multi)

25% of estate, if I survive her

1976 Cadillac Fleetwood

$14,000 annually, typically paid by check each December

- **Location of Documents.** Describe the location where any related documents are filed. If possible, include them with your planner. (If you do not have a document that describes the property bequest, you should briefly outline any terms, such as conditions on the bequest, expected timing, or expected duration of payments.)

EXAMPLES:

See copies of G.L. Fudim will and living trust, filed in this section.

Copy of E.E. Crabtree life insurance policy included here.

Copy of transfer-on-death vehicle title certificate included at back of section.

No documents: Cash gift of $14,000 each year, expected to continue until my father's death (or until my own, if I die first).

Additional Notes

Include any additional information you have about property you expect to receive from others.

Warranty Records and Product Guides

Indicate where you store warranty documents, product guides, or repair and maintenance information for your personal property. If you store these materials in different locations—for example, you keep some records at home and others at your vacation cabin—be sure to indicate the address with your description of the storage location.

Depending upon the nature and volume of these materials, you may want to file them in the planner itself.

EXAMPLES:

There are two huge files (both marked "Warranties") at the very back of the bottom, left-hand drawer of my desk.

Stored in top-right drawer near kitchen telephone in San Francisco, and bottom left file drawer in desk (in a file labeled "Product Guides & Records") in Capitola.

BINDER

Including personal property materials in your planner. If you have documents related to other income or items of personal property—such as appraisal certificates or purchase records—you can file them in your planner binder. Also include documents listing you as beneficiary of another's property or detailed directions for locating particular items. For personal property of special significance, you may want to include a document that sets out the history of special items—such as who acquired or made the item, who has owned the item, in which years, or on what occasions the item has been used. You may also wish to include photographs, using three-ring photo album pages inserted directly into your planner binder.

Keeping Your Information Up to Date

Be certain to update this section of your planner if you:

- acquire or lose a source of other income
- acquire or dispose of important personal property
- move property for which you've specified a location, or
- change your wishes for handling an item at your death.

CHAPTER 28

Other Information

Is that all there is?
If that's all there is, my friends, then let's keep dancing.

—JERRY LEIBER AND MIKE STOLLER, "IS THAT ALL THERE IS?"

While the planner is designed to be comprehensive, it's inevitable that the unique and complex nature of your life means that you have wishes, instructions, documents, or other materials that don't fit neatly into one of its clearly labeled sections. For example, you might have family medical history, your memoirs, or family genealogy that you would like to store, safely and securely, with your planner. If there is any remaining information that you wish to organize and include in your planner, this is the place to do it.

The Other Information section of your planner (Section 28) is simple and free-form. Use it as you wish, inserting additional pages as necessary.

Whatever information you include or file in this section of your planner, remember to review it occasionally to be sure that it is complete and accurate, and that it still reflects your wishes.

APPENDIX

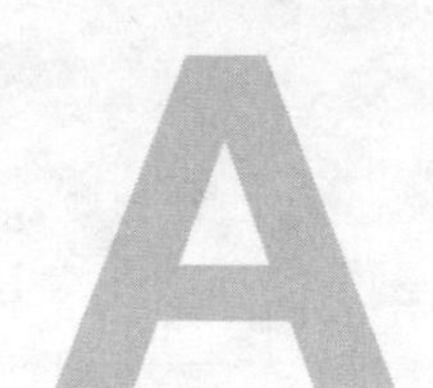

Using the eForms

Downloading the Files 238

Reviewing the Files 238

Editing RTFs 239

You can access an electronic version of this book's planner at: **www.nolo.com/back-of-book/GET.html** There you will find a button to download the planner forms. When you click the button, all of the *Get It Together* planner files will download to your computer. Here are some details about accessing and using those files.

> TIP
>
> **Note to Macintosh Users.** These forms were designed for use with Windows. They should also work on Macintosh computers; however Nolo cannot provide technical support for non-Windows users.

Downloading the Files

To download the files, go to the link shown above. Once there, you will see a green "Download Forms" button in the middle of the screen:

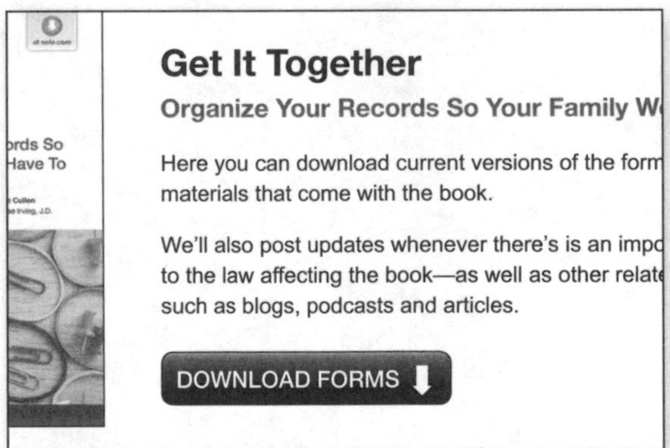

Click on the button and follow the instructions. This will save the files to your computer. Make a note about where they are saved.

> CAUTION
>
> **In accordance with U.S. copyright laws, the forms provided by this book are for your personal use only.**

> TIP
>
> **If a different page displays.** The most frequent problem with the download is due to an accumulation of "cookies" on your computer. If the page shown above does not display for you, try clearing the cache of cookies in your browser and try again.

Reviewing the Files

In the download, you will receive 30 files, including:

- one file that contains the cover page and table of contents for your personal planner (named **00_Planner**)
- 28 files that correspond with each section of your personal planner (named **01_Letter** to **28_Other**)
- one file containing a PDF of the complete planner (named **Planner**)

The files numbered **00** to **28** are RTFs (Rich Text Format). Use these files to create your planner sections on your computer. You will use a word processing program (like Microsoft *Word*) to type in your information, password-protect (optional), save, print, and later modify these files.

The **Planner** file is Adobe Portable Document Format (PDF). You can print pages or sections of this file, but you cannot type onto it or modify the layout. Printing pages of the PDF could be useful if, for example, you want to write your information by hand, then later sit down at your computer and type the information onto the RTF files.

Here is the one file provided as a PDF:

Planner Section Name	File Name
Planner (entire, including Cover Page and Table of Contents)	Planner.pdf

And here is a list of the 29 files provided as RTFs:

Planner Section Name	File Name
Cover Page and Table of Contents	00_Planner.rtf
1. Letter to Loved Ones	01_Letter.rtf
2. Instructions	02_Instructions.rtf
3. Biographical Information	03_Biography.rtf
4. Children	04_Children.rtf
5. Others Who Depend on Me	05_Dependents.rtf
6. Pets and Livestock	06_Pets.rtf
7. Employment	07_Employment.rtf
8. Business Interests	08_Business.rtf
9. Memberships and Communities	09_Memberships_Communities.rtf
10. Service Providers	10_Service.rtf
11. Health Care Directives	11_HealthCare.rtf
12. Durable Power of Attorney for Finances	12_Finances.rtf
13. Organ or Body Donation	13_OrganDonation.rtf
14. Burial or Cremation	14_Burial.rtf
15. Funeral and Memorial Services	15_Funeral.rtf
16. Obituary	16_Obituary.rtf
17. Will and Trust	17_Will.rtf
18. Insurance	18_Insurance.rtf
19. Bank and Brokerage Accounts	19_Accounts.rtf
20. Retirement Plans and Pensions	20_Pensions.rtf
21. Government Benefits	21_Benefits.rtf
22. Credit Cards and Debts	22_Debts.rtf
23. Secured Places and Passwords	23_Passwords.rtf
24. Taxes	24_Taxes.rtf
25. Real Estate	25_RealEstate.rtf
26. Vehicles	26_Vehicles.rtf
27. Other Income and Personal Property	27_OtherIncome.rtf
28. Other Information	28_Other.rtf

Editing RTFs

To complete a section of your planner:

1. **Open the downloaded file.** When you open a file, it will automatically open in the word processing software installed on your computer, such as Microsoft *Word*, Windows *WordPad*, or recent versions of *WordPerfect*.
2. **Complete the section.** Type your information into the tables provided. Skip from field to field using your Tab (or ⇄) key.
   - **Refer to instructions and examples.** As you work through a section, open your book to the corresponding chapter of the book so that you read step-by-step instructions and examples.
   - **Learn more.** If you want to learn more about a topic—for example, *Arranging Care for Pets, How Durable Powers of Attorney for Finances Work*, or *What Happens to Retirement Accounts When You Die*—take time to read the corresponding guide chapter.
   - **Customize.** You can modify the planner tables to suit your needs but, before you do, review the original pages to ensure you do not delete important direction or information. In most word processing programs, you can use "table" commands —such as "Insert Row(s)", "Delete Column(s)", or "Copy Table"—to modify the tables.
3. **Password-protect (optional).** For security, you may wish to password-protect each of your planner files. For step-by-step instructions, search your word processing software for "password-protect."
4. **Save the file and change its name.** Save the file to your computer or to portable media (like a flash drive), to store safely with your planner or in your safe deposit box. When you save your file, give it a new name. For example, you could add your name and date like this: 06 Pets Mary 150815. By changing

the name, you can easily identify the latest version of your file.

5. **Print.** Print your completed file.
6. **Compile and file.** Insert your printed file into your planner and add any related materials.

If a section does not apply to you—for example if you have no pets or livestock and do not need the pet section—add a notation "Does not apply to me" on the section's first page, then insert it into your planner.

Continue to complete sections until you have completed each of the planner's 28 sections and the cover page.

TIP

Your word processing software. Every word processing program uses different commands to open, format, save, and print documents, so refer to your software's help documents for assistance using your program. Nolo cannot provide technical support for questions about how to use your computer or your software.

APPENDIX

B

Lawyers and Other Experts

What Kind of Expert Do You Need?.....242

Finding an Expert.....243

Working With an Expert.....244

Making a Fee Agreement.....244

An expert is a man who has made all the mistakes that can be made, in a narrow field.

—NIELS BOHR (1885–1962)

While working on your planner, you may discover that you want advice or help with certain tasks—such as making estate planning choices, preparing legal documents, managing investments, or developing a plan for your retirement. If you want to seek expert help, this appendix offers some guidance.

What Kind of Expert Do You Need?

Most of the documents at the heart of your planner—your will, living trust, durable power of attorney for finances, health care directives—are legal documents. If you need help with them, you'll probably want to look for a good lawyer. But a lawyer may not be the best person to handle some of the questions or tasks that arise as you complete your planner. You may be better off seeking an accountant, financial planner, document preparer, or other expert. Here's a list of some different types of experts and how they can help:

- **Accountants.** For most tax or accounting tasks, you can get the help you need from a tax preparer or a Certified Public Accountant (CPA). If you just need help with your taxes, a good tax preparer can probably do the job. If your financial situation is fairly straightforward, your executor or successor trustee may also be able to turn to a tax preparer for help with your final tax returns. For more complex jobs, such as business accounting and planning, you'll want to look for a CPA. Depending upon where you live, you can expect to pay as much as $100 an hour for routine tax preparation, and from $150 to $350 an hour for more sophisticated accounting and planning.
- **Financial planners.** If you need help with investments, a small business, or retirement decisions, a financial planner may be the right choice. There are basically two categories of financial planners: those who are licensed and those who are not. A license is not required to serve as a personal financial adviser, and many competent advisers have solid backgrounds in financial services, accounting, or law—and the education to match. A licensed financial planner may be called a Certified Financial Planner (CFP), Chartered Financial Consultant (ChFC), or CPA (described above). Some planners also hold separate licenses to sell financial products or insurance. Depending on the adviser and the work done, you may pay an hourly or fixed rate, or a percentage of the assets involved. Hourly rates range from $100 to $400, with a national median of about $250.
- **Insurance agents.** Insurance agents can do a lot more than just sell you a policy. Many agents are also licensed financial advisers. They can help you understand your insurance needs, your risk level, and your investment options. Some agents specialize in personal insurance for individuals and families, while others specialize in business insurance. Many agents hold an additional license to sell financial products, such as

mutual funds, retirement funds, variable annuities, or securities.

- **Lawyers.** Lawyers can help you develop a comprehensive estate plan, prepare legal documents for you, or simply explain how the law applies to your particular situation. But lawyers, of course, are costly. Depending upon where you live, hourly fees will range from $150 to $450 or more for an experienced estate planning lawyer. If your situation is complex, however, a good estate planning specialist can be well worth the cost. And if your needs are simple—for example, you want a basic will but you'd rather have a lawyer help you than do it yourself—you may be able to find a good general practice lawyer who can handle limited tasks for a reasonable fee.
- **Document preparers (paralegals).** Even if you need "legal" help, you may not need a lawyer. People who operate document preparation services, also known as independent paralegals, are experts at typing up legal documents. They are not lawyers and do not give legal advice, but if you know what you want, a document preparer can help you prepare the legal paperwork at an affordable price. For example, if you're working with a self-help book or software and need assistance in expanding the document or removing optional parts in the document, a document preparer can probably help.

The advice below can help you find a good expert, no matter what type you need.

Finding an Expert

When looking for an expert, you want to find someone who has the information you need, but you'll also want someone with whom you can develop a good working relationship. You should feel comfortable asking questions and be confident that you understand the expert's answers. Here are some suggestions to help you find a good match.

Ask Your Family, Friends, and Acquaintances

When looking for an expert, especially one who specializes in estate planning, word of mouth is the best method.

- Ask a relative or friend who has good business and financial sense to recommend an expert.
- Check with people you know in a business, political, or social organization—especially those groups with members over age 40 who are also working through estate planning issues.

People you know can point you to local experts, and can give you opinions on an expert's competence, point of view, and personal style. There's no better way to find a professional that meets your needs.

Ask Another Expert

Another good approach is to ask for a recommendation from a professional you know and like personally, but who works in another field. For example, ask your neighbor, the public defender, to recommend a lawyer who specializes in estate planning or family businesses. Very likely the expert you know can refer you to a trustworthy specialist.

Ask Business Managers

Yet another possibility is to check with people you respect who own their own businesses or manage a business. Almost anyone running a business has relationships with a lawyer and an accountant—and chances are they have found professionals that they respect. Or, contact the Chamber of Commerce for your city or the local Rotary International club, and ask for referrals to experts that are reliable, longstanding members of the association. While the recommended professionals may not be estate planning experts, they can in turn refer you to experts who will meet your needs.

Finding a Good Document Preparer

If you think a document preparer is what you need, here are some tips to help you find a good one.

- **Choose an established or recommended service.** Few document preparers stay in business unless they provide honest and competent services. A recommendation from a friend, social service agency, court clerk, or lawyer is probably a good place to take your business.
- **Look for reasonable fees.** Document preparers typically charge between $50 and $150 to type up your documents, depending on where you live and the complexity of your forms.
- **Insist on a trained staff.** One indication of whether or not people are committed to providing good service is if they have undertaken skills training through independent paralegal associations and continuing education seminars.

CAUTION

Use legal referral services with caution. Legal referral services usually conduct very minimal screening of attorneys they list, which means that those listed may not be very experienced—or even necessarily competent. While it may be possible for you to find a skilled attorney through a referral service, you should still evaluate his or her credentials and experience for yourself.

RESOURCE

Try Nolo's Lawyer Directory. The Nolo Lawyer Directory provides detailed profiles of its attorneys. In their own words, the lawyers in the directory describe their qualifications, approach to the law, and fees so that you can get a good sense of their services before you call. To visit the Nolo Lawyer Directory, go to www.nolo.com/lawyers.

Working With an Expert

Before you talk to an expert, decide what kind of help you need. Do you want someone to review your documents to make sure they look right? Or do you want advice on a complete estate plan? If you don't clearly define—and tell the expert—what you need, you may find yourself agreeing to more than you really want.

Before you see the expert, write down your questions as specifically as you can. Then meet with the expert. If you don't get clear, concise answers, say thank you and try someone else. For example, many legal tasks—such as preparing a will, living trust, durable power of attorney for finances, or health care directives—are not overly complicated jobs. In most cases, a knowledgeable lawyer should be able to give you satisfactory answers on the spot.

If the expert acts wise but says little—except to ask that matters be placed in his or her hands, for a substantial fee—watch out. You're either dealing with someone who doesn't know the answer (and is not openly sharing that with you) or someone who feels that, as an expert, he or she does not need to treat you as an equal. Both of these traits are common, but you can find better. You'll achieve great satisfaction if you truly understand what the expert is doing and how it meets your needs, so move on and find someone who will include you in the process.

Making a Fee Agreement

Fees for financial or estate planning professionals can be steep—sometimes hundreds of dollars an hour. Yet price is not always related to quality. A fancy office and a

My Planner

These pages will serve as a guide in the event of my incapacity or death. Please begin by reading the first section, "Letter to Loved Ones," then turn to Section 2, "Instructions," for direction—what to do and when.

Name
Date

Table of Contents

1. Letter to Loved Ones 5
2. Instructions 7
3. Biographical Information 13
4. Children 23
5. Others Who Depend on Me 29
6. Pets and Livestock 33
7. Employment 37
8. Business Interests 41
9. Memberships and Communities 51
10. Service Providers 53
11. Health Care Directives 59
12. Durable Power of Attorney for Finances 61
13. Organ or Body Donation 63
14. Burial or Cremation 65
15. Funeral and Memorial Services 71
16. Obituary 77
17. Will and Trust 79
18. Insurance 83
19. Bank and Brokerage Accounts 93
20. Retirement Plans and Pensions 97
21. Government Benefits 101
22. Credit Cards and Debts 105
23. Secured Places and Passwords 111
24. Taxes 121
25. Real Estate 123
26. Vehicles 131
27. Other Income and Personal Property 135
28. Other Information 145

1

Letter to Loved Ones

To: ______________________________

If you're reading this, it is because I am incapacitated and no longer able to manage my own affairs, or because I have passed away. Use this planner knowing that I have prepared for this moment, wishing to help you through this difficult time.

My Instructions

After you've read this letter, turn to Section 2, Instructions. The instructions, and the rest of the information in this planner, will assist you with the tasks you face this week, and provide guidance as you wrap up my affairs over time.

Thoughts About My Death

Messages for My Loved Ones

My Last Words to You

Signature

2

Instructions

This section is the master guide to my planner. It is organized to help you through the first days, weeks, and months following my incapacity or death. The instructions that follow will remind you of important tasks and tell you where to look in my planner for the additional information you will need.

Most of the tasks listed here will apply whether I am incapacitated or have died, though how you handle an individual task may vary depending on the circumstances. If I am incapacitated, however, there are two important tasks you'll want to take care of immediately. These are listed just below.

If I Am Incapacitated

Review Health Care Directives Applicable: ☐ Yes ☐ No

☐ **Health Care Directives.** Turn to Section 11 for information about documents I have made to direct my health care.

Review Power of Attorney for Finances Applicable: ☐ Yes ☐ No

☐ **Durable Power of Attorney for Finances.** Turn to Section 12 for information about the document that names someone to manage my finances for me.

Days 1 and 2

These are some of the important tasks you will have to handle in the first 48 hours following my incapacity or death.

Care for Children Applicable: ☐ Yes ☐ No

☐ **Children.** Turn to Section 4 for details about the children who rely on me for care.

Care for Others Applicable: ☐ Yes ☐ No

☐ **Others Who Depend on Me.** Turn to Section 5 for details about other people who rely on me for care.

Care for Animals Applicable: ☐ Yes ☐ No

☐ **Pets and Livestock.** Turn to Section 6 for information about taking care of my animals, including my wishes for placing them with others.

Contact Employer Applicable: ☐ Yes ☐ No

☐ **Employment.** Notify my employer of my incapacity or death. See Section 7 for contact information and other details about my current employment and my employment history.

2 Instructions

Contact Business

Applicable: ☐ Yes ☐ No

☐ **Business Interests.** Notify any business partners or key employees of my incapacity or death. See Section 8 for contact information and details about my current and former business interests.

Make Final Arrangements

After my death, please review the next four items before making any final arrangements.

☐ **Arrange for the Death Certificate.** Those in charge of handling my estate will need certified copies of my death certificate to wrap up business with insurance companies, banks, the Social Security Administration, and others.

As you make arrangements for the disposition of my body, you will be asked to provide information for the death certificate. The Biographical Information section of my planner (Section 3) contains the information you will need. At this time, you should request multiple certified copies of the death certificate; you may need as many as ten.

If you are unable to request copies of my death certificate while making final arrangements, you can get them later. To find out where to send your request, you can do a simple search on the National Center for Health Statistics (NCHS) website. Go to www.cdc.gov/nchs, select "Need a birth, death or marriage certificate?" from the options on the right. Click on the state you're looking for, and the site will display specific directions for submitting your request.

☐ **Organ or Body Donation.** Turn to Section 13 for my wishes about donating my body, organs, or tissues—as well as information about any plans I have already made.

☐ **Burial or Cremation.** Turn to Section 14 for details about burial or cremation, including my wishes and information about any plans I have already made.

☐ **Funeral and Memorial Services.** Turn to Section 15 for details about my funeral, memorial, or related services, including my wishes and information about any plans I have already made.

Publish Obituary

☐ **Obituary.** Turn to Section 16 for details about publishing my obituary.

Contact Family and Friends

☐ Contact all friends and relatives who should know of my incapacity or death.

If you will hold a funeral or memorial service in the next few days, contact everyone who might attend. (See Section 15 for my wishes about whom to invite.) Others will learn of my passing only by reading the obituary, if published.

Except for those who need to know about my death right away, it will help to make any arrangements for services before you make phone calls—then you won't have to call everyone twice.

You can find names and contact information for family and friends in the following locations:

____

____

____

____

☐ **Protect the House.** My obituary or death notice may serve to alert thieves that the house is empty. If necessary, arrange for a neighbor, a familiar service provider (see Section 10), a church member, or the reception caterer to be at the house during services.

Review Appointment Calendar

☐ Review my calendar and cancel any scheduled appointments. You can find my calendar in the following locations:

Manage Mail and Newspaper

☐ Pick up my mail. See Section 23 for access information, if needed. Over time, file a Mail Forwarding order with USPS.

☐ Cancel my newspaper subscriptions, if any. See Section 22 for payment and account information.

Additional Notes

2

Instructions

Week 2

This section outlines the essential tasks you should handle in the two weeks following my incapacity or death.

Locate Will or Other Estate Planning Documents

- ☐ **Will and Trust.** After my death, see Section 17 for information about my will, trusts, or other estate planning documents that I have made.

Contact Organizations and Service Providers

Please notify financial institutions, brokers, government agencies, and others with whom I do business that I have become incapacitated or have died. The following sections will help you:

- ☐ **Insurance.** Turn to Section 18 for information about my insurance agents and policies. The information there will help you claim benefits, cancel, or continue coverage as appropriate.
- ☐ **Bank and Brokerage Accounts.** Turn to Section 19 for financial institution contact information and details about my bank and brokerage accounts.
- ☐ **Retirement Plans and Pensions.** Turn to Section 20 for information about my retirement and pension plan accounts, including contact information for the administrators.
- ☐ **Government Benefits.** Turn to Section 21 for details about my Social Security and other government benefits, including contact information for each agency.
- ☐ **Service Providers.** Turn to Section 10 for information about service providers, including medical, personal, and household care providers.
- ☐ **Other:** ______________________________
- ☐ **Other:** ______________________________
- ☐ **Other:** ______________________________
- ☐ **Other:** ______________________________

Review Current Bills and Accounts

- ☐ **Credit Cards and Debts.** Please review my current bills to be sure they are paid on time. Cancel and close accounts as necessary. See Section 22 for more information.
- ☐ **Secured Places and Passwords.** Turn to Section 23 for help with locked or password-protected products, services, and accounts.

Additional Notes

____

____

____

____

____

____

____

____

____

____

____

____

____

____

Working Through Grief

Whether my death was sudden or long in coming, you will experience loss after I'm gone. You may grieve for weeks, months, or even years. Grieving is uniquely personal; your grief may not mirror that of other family and friends.

During the grieving process it is normal to feel strong emotions, such as deep sadness, despair, or anger. You may even go through a time of depression.

You will heal more quickly and completely if you share your grief with supportive people—family members, friends, your faith community, therapists or physicians, or grief support groups. To find a local group (and helpful information) consult your health care providers or visit these organizations online:

- American Hospice Foundation (www.AmericanHospice.org/grief or 800-347-1413)
- Caring Connections (www.caringinfo.org or 800-685-8898)
- Legacy Connect (www.connect.legacy.com)

Month 1 and Beyond

Following is a list of tasks that you should initiate in the first month or two following my incapacity or death.

Take Inventory

- ☐ **Real Estate.** Turn to Section 25 for details about any real estate that I own or rent.
- ☐ **Vehicles.** Turn to Section 26 for information about all vehicles that I own.
- ☐ **Other Income and Personal Property.** Turn to Section 27 for information about important sources of income or items of personal property not described elsewhere in my planner.
- ☐ **Other Information.** See Section 28 for any other details that I feel you need to know.

Cancel Memberships and Driver's License

- ☐ **Memberships and Communities.** Over time, you will want to cancel my memberships with various organizations. See Section 9 for contact information.
- ☐ **Driver's License.** Notify the state motor vehicles department of my death and cancel my license. See Section 3 for my driver's license information. Also, please turn in my handicap placard, if I had one.

Prepare Tax Returns

- ☐ **Taxes.** Section 24 will help you gather the information you need to prepare my final tax returns. Keep returns and related records for seven years.

Additional Notes

____

____

____

____

____

____

Where to Get Help

As you work through the steps you must take to wrap up my affairs, you will find a number of sources for help. Where applicable, the various sections of my planner list lawyers, accountants, or others who can help with each task.

For general guidance, you may want to turn to *The Executor's Guide: Settling a Loved One's Estate or Trust*, by Mary Randolph (Nolo). It provides a detailed explanation of an executor's or successor trustee's duties.

3

Biographical Information

In this section, you will find important personal information about me and those closest to me. You may need these vital statistics for a number of tasks, such as preparing my death certificate, writing my obituary, filing tax returns, and distributing assets to my beneficiaries.

Residence Information

Name	
Address	
Telephone(s)	
Resident of City Since (year)	
Resident of State Since (year)	

Self and Parents

	Self	Mother	Father	Stepmother	Stepfather
First Name					
Middle Name					
Last Name					
Maiden Name					
Date of Birth					
Birthplace (City, State, County, Country)					
Location of Birth Certificate					
Location of Adoption Documents					
Social Security Number					
Location of Social Security Card					
Driver's License Number and State					
Military Service: Country and Branch					

Self and Parents (continued)

	Self	Mother	Father	Stepmother	Stepfather
Military Rank					
Military Induction Date					
Military Discharge Date					
Military Citations					
Location of Military Documents					
Date of First Marriage					
First Spouse's Name					
Location of Marriage Certificate					
Date of Divorce, Annulment, Legal Separation, or Death					
Location of Documents					
Date of Second Marriage					
Second Spouse's Name					
Location of Marriage Certificate					
Date of Divorce, Annulment, Legal Separation, or Death					
Location of Documents					
Date of Third Marriage					
Third Spouse's Name					
Location of Marriage Certificate					
Date of Divorce, Annulment, Legal Separation, or Death					
Location of Documents					
Date of Death					
Location of Death Certificate					
Address					
Telephone(s)					
Email					
Other					
Other					
Other					

Spouse or Partner

	Spouse #1	Spouse #2	Spouse #3		
First Name					
Middle Name					
Last Name					
Maiden Name					
Date of Birth					
Birthplace (City, State, County, Country)					
Location of Birth Certificate					
Location of Adoption Documents					
Social Security Number					
Location of Social Security Card					
Driver's License Number and State					
Military Service: Country and Branch					
Military Rank					
Military Induction Date					
Military Discharge Date					
Military Citations					
Location of Military Documents					
Date of First Marriage					
First Spouse's Name					
Location of Marriage Certificate					
Date of Divorce, Annulment, Legal Separation, or Death					
Location of Documents					
Date of Second Marriage					
Second Spouse's Name					
Location of Marriage Certificate					
Date of Divorce, Annulment, Legal Separation, or Death					

3

Biographical Information

Spouse or Partner, continued

	Spouse #1	Spouse #2	Spouse #3		
Location of Documents					
Date of Third Marriage					
Third Spouse's Name					
Location of Marriage Certificate					
Date of Divorce, Annulment, Legal Separation, or Death					
Location of Documents					
Date of Death					
Location of Death Certificate					
Address					
Telephone(s)					
Email					
Other					
Other					
Other					

Children

	Child #1	Child #2	Child #3	Child #4	Child #5
First Name					
Middle Name					
Last Name					
Maiden Name					
Date of Birth					
Birthplace (City, State, County, Country)					
Location of Birth Certificate					
Location of Adoption Documents					
Social Security Number					
Location of Social Security Card					
Driver's License Number and State					

Children, continued

	Child #1	Child #2	Child #3	Child #4	Child #5
Military Service: Country and Branch					
Military Rank					
Military Induction Date					
Military Discharge Date					
Military Citations					
Location of Military Documents					
Date of First Marriage					
First Spouse's Name					
Location of Marriage Certificate					
Date of Divorce, Annulment, Legal Separation, or Death					
Location of Documents					
Date of Second Marriage					
Second Spouse's Name					
Location of Marriage Certificate					
Date of Divorce, Annulment, Legal Separation, or Death					
Location of Documents					
Date of Third Marriage					
Third Spouse's Name					
Location of Marriage Certificate					
Date of Divorce, Annulment, Legal Separation, or Death					
Location of Documents					
Date of Death					
Location of Death Certificate					
Address					
Telephone(s)					
Email					

Children, continued

Other					
Other					
Other					

Siblings

	Sibling #1	Sibling #2	Sibling #3	Sibling #4	Sibling #5
First Name					
Middle Name					
Last Name					
Maiden Name					
Date of Birth					
Birthplace (City, State, County, Country)					
Location of Birth Certificate					
Location of Adoption Documents					
Social Security Number					
Location of Social Security Card					
Driver's License Number and State					
Military Service: Country and Branch					
Military Rank					
Military Induction Date					
Military Discharge Date					
Military Citations					
Location of Military Documents					
Date of First Marriage					
First Spouse's Name					
Location of Marriage Certificate					
Date of Divorce, Annulment, Legal Separation, or Death					

Siblings, continued

	Sibling #1	Sibling #2	Sibling #3	Sibling #4	Sibling #5
Location of Documents					
Date of Second Marriage					
Second Spouse's Name					
Location of Marriage Certificate					
Date of Divorce, Annulment, Legal Separation, or Death					
Location of Documents					
Date of Third Marriage					
Location of Marriage Certificate					
Third Spouse's Name					
Date of Divorce, Annulment, Legal Separation, or Death					
Location of Documents					
Date of Death					
Location of Death Certificate					
Address					
Telephone(s)					
Email					
Other					
Other					
Other					

Others

First Name					
Middle Name					
Last Name					
Maiden Name					

3

Biographical Information

Others, continued

Date of Birth					
Birthplace (City, State, County, Country)					
Location of Birth Certificate					
Location of Adoption Documents					
Social Security Number					
Location of Social Security Card					
Driver's License Number and State					
Military Service: Country and Branch					
Military Rank					
Military Induction Date					
Military Discharge Date					
Military Citations					
Location of Military Documents					
Date of First Marriage					
First Spouse's Name					
Location of Marriage Certificate					
Date of Divorce, Annulment, Legal Separation, or Death					
Location of Documents					
Date of Second Marriage					
Second Spouse's Name					
Location of Marriage Certificate					
Date of Divorce, Annulment, Legal Separation, or Death					
Location of Documents					
Date of Third Marriage					
Third Spouse's Name					
Location of Marriage Certificate					

Date of Divorce, Annulment, Legal Separation, or Death					
Location of Documents					
Date of Death					
Location of Death Certificate					
Address					
Telephone(s)					
Email					
Other					
Other					
Other					

Additional Notes

4

Children

This section lists all young children—whether my own or others—for whom I regularly provide care. For my own children, the "Guardians and Property Managers" section just below lists the people who should be their primary caretakers following my incapacity or death.

Guardians and Property Managers

I have named the following people to serve as caretakers for my children. I have also noted the documents in which the caretaker has been named—for example, my will, living trust, another trust, or a life insurance policy.

Caretaker	Child's Name	Child's Name	Child's Name	Child's Name
Personal Guardian				
Alternate				
Document				
Property Manager				
Alternate				
Document				

Caretaker	Child's Name	Child's Name	Child's Name	Child's Name
Personal Guardian				
Alternate				
Document				
Property Manager				
Alternate				
Document				

Information About Children

The children listed below rely on me for care and support. Please help to fill in for me until new caregivers assume their roles.

Child's Name and Contact Information	Date of Birth	Child's Relationship to Me	Type of Care

Additional Care Providers

Here, you'll find contact information for others who help with the children's care.

Child's Name	Care Provider or Family Member's Contact Information	Relationship to Child	Type of Care

4

Children

Additional Care Providers, continued

Child's Name	Care Provider or Family Member's Contact Information	Relationship to Child	Type of Care

Additional Care Providers, continued

Child's Name	Care Provider or Family Member's Contact Information	Relationship to Child	Type of Care

Additional Notes

4 Children

Others Who Depend on Me

This section provides basic information about adults who depend on me for care.

Information About People Who Depend on Me

The people listed below rely on me for care and support. Please help to fill in for me until new caregivers assume their roles.

Person's Name and Contact Information	Date of Birth	Person's Relationship to Me	Type of Care

Additional Care Providers

The following people also provide care for the individuals listed above.

Person's Name	Care Provider's Contact Information	Relationship to Person	Type of Care

5

Others Who Depend on Me

Person's Name	Care Provider's Contact Information	Relationship to Person	Type of Care

Additional Notes

6

Pets and Livestock

This section lists the animals I own and describes my wishes for their care and placement.

Animal Care

Pet Name, Chip ID, Species, and Coloring	Location	Food and Water	Other Care	Veterinarian's Contact Information

Animal Care, continued

Pet Name, Chip ID, Species, and Coloring	Location	Food and Water	Other Care	Veterinarian's Contact Information

Wishes for Placement

Pet Name, Chip ID, Species, and Coloring	Desired Placement	Individual or Organization and Contact Information

Pet Name, Chip ID, Species, and Coloring	Desired Placement	Individual or Organization and Contact Information

Additional Notes

7

Employment

In this section, you'll find information about my current and former employment, whether full time or part time, paid or volunteer. For every position I've listed, I've indicated whether or not benefits are available if I become incapacitated or die. (These benefits may be detailed elsewhere in this planner—for example, in the Insurance or Retirement Plans and Pensions sections—but I include them here so they will not be overlooked.)

Current Employment

Please contact my current employers if I become incapacitated or when I die. In addition to collecting any benefits due, if I have worked until the time of my incapacity or death, my agent or executor should ask my employer for any unpaid wages or commissions, expense reimbursements, or bonuses that are due to me or to my estate.

Employer's Contact Information	Current Benefits and Location of Documents	
	Position	
	Start Date	
	Ownership Interest	☐ Yes (_____%) ☐ No
Employer's Contact Information	**Current Benefits and Location of Documents**	
	Position	
	Start Date	
	Ownership Interest	☐ Yes (_____%) ☐ No
Employer's Contact Information	**Current Benefits and Location of Documents**	
	Position	
	Start Date	
	Ownership Interest	☐ Yes (_____%) ☐ No

Current Employment, continued

Employer's Contact Information	Current Benefits and Location of Documents	
	Position	
	Start Date	
	Ownership Interest	☐ Yes (_____%) ☐ No
Employer's Contact Information	**Current Benefits and Location of Documents**	
	Position	
	Start Date	
	Ownership Interest	☐ Yes (_____%) ☐ No
Employer's Contact Information	**Current Benefits and Location of Documents**	
	Position	
	Start Date	
	Ownership Interest	☐ Yes (_____%) ☐ No

Additional Notes

Previous Employment

Employer's Contact Information	Current Benefits and Location of Documents	
	Last Position	
	Start and End Dates	
	Ownership Interest	☐ Yes (______%) ☐ No
Employer's Contact Information	**Current Benefits and Location of Documents**	
	Last Position	
	Start and End Dates	
	Ownership Interest	☐ Yes (______%) ☐ No
Employer's Contact Information	**Current Benefits and Location of Documents**	
	Last Position	
	Start and End Dates	
	Ownership Interest	☐ Yes (______%) ☐ No
Employer's Contact Information	**Current Benefits and Location of Documents**	
	Last Position	
	Start and End Dates	
	Ownership Interest	☐ Yes (______%) ☐ No
Employer's Contact Information	**Current Benefits and Location of Documents**	
	Last Position	

	Start and End Dates	
	Ownership Interest	☐ Yes (_____%) ☐ No
Employer's Contact Information	**Current Benefits and Location of Documents**	
	Last Position	
	Start and End Dates	
	Ownership Interest	☐ Yes (_____%) ☐ No
Employer's Contact Information	**Current Benefits and Location of Documents**	
	Last Position	
	Start and End Dates	
	Ownership Interest	☐ Yes (_____%) ☐ No

Additional Notes

8

Business Interests

Following is an overview of my current and former business interests. It contains information to help you notify the right people (co-owners, employees, and so on) of my incapacity or death. Over time, this information will also help you manage or sell my business interests.

Current Business Interests

This section provides detailed information about businesses in which I have a current ownership interest.

Name and Location

Business Name and Type of Business	Main Office Address and Telephone	Subsidiaries or Branch Offices

Ownership

Business Owners	Contact Information	Job Title or Position	Ownership Percentage

8

Business Interests

Ownership, continued

Business Owners	Contact Information	Job Title or Position	Ownership Percentage

Ownership Documents	Location of Documents

Disposition

These instructions will help you manage or wind up my business affairs if I become incapacitated, or upon my death.

Disposition of Entire Business	☐ Continue	☐ Transfer	☐ Sell	☐ Liquidate
Disposition of My Interest		☐ Transfer	☐ Sell	☐ Liquidate

Contact Information for Key Individuals				
Attorney	Accountant			

Disposition Notes

Title and Location of Documents

Disposition, continued

Key Employees

This section lists employees who are essential to keeping the business running, or who have special agreements with the business.

Employee Name	Agreement	Location of Documents	Other Information

Business Taxes

Business tax records are located as follows:

Current-Year Records	
Prior-Year Records	

Significant Assets and Liabilities

This section lists important assets and liabilities, to help you manage, transfer, or sell the business.

Assets

Description of Asset	Location of Asset	Access Information	Contact Name and Information	Location of Documents

Assets, continued

Description of Asset	Location of Asset	Access Information	Contact Name and Information	Location of Documents

Liabilities

Description of Liability	Contact Name and Information	Location of Documents

Liabilities, continued

Description of Liability	Contact Name and Information	Location of Documents

Additional Notes

8

Business Interests

Prior Business Interests

My prior business interests are outlined below. My investments, rights, and responsibilities in these businesses have been fully resolved and terminated; no additional expenses will be incurred and no income realized. I have described these business interests for your reference, in case you have questions or receive any future claims.

Business Name and Type of Business	Main Office Address and Telephone	Ownership and Dissolution Documents	Location of Documents
Contact Information			

Business Name and Type of Business	Main Office Address and Telephone	Ownership and Dissolution Documents	Location of Documents
Contact Information			

8

Business Interests

Business Name and Type of Business	Main Office Address and Telephone	Ownership and Dissolution Documents	Location of Documents
Contact Information			

Additional Notes

9

Memberships and Communities

Following is a list of clubs, groups, programs, and organizations to which I belong. You may need this information to notify others of my incapacity or death, complete my obituary, cancel memberships, or transfer membership benefits.

Organization Name and Contact Information	Account Name, Password, Membership Number, or Position Held	Additional Notes

Organization Name and Contact Information	Account Name, Password, Membership Number, or Position Held	Additional Notes

10

Service Providers

My current service providers are listed below. This information may help you manage bills and expenses or provide ongoing care for me, my home, or my other property. Over time, you should cancel or modify these service arrangements, as necessary.

Health Care Providers

Name and Contact Information	Type of Care and Location

Health Care Providers, continued

Name and Contact Information	Type of Care and Location

Health Care Providers, continued

Name and Contact Information	Type of Care and Location

Other Service Providers

Name and Contact Information	Type of Service and Location

Other Service Providers, continued

Name and Contact Information	Type of Service and Location

10

Service Providers

Other Service Providers, continued

Name and Contact Information	Type of Service and Location

Additional Notes

10

Service Providers

11

Health Care Directives

In this section, you'll find information about documents I have made to direct my health care if I am incapacitated and unable to speak for myself.

Health Care Agent

In my health care documents, I have named the person listed below to be my health care agent. My agent will supervise my care if I am incapacitated. If he or she is unable to serve, I have named alternates to serve in the order listed.

Health Care Agent	
Alternate 1	
Alternate 2	
Alternate 3	

Health Care Documents

Following is basic information about my health care documents.

If an attorney or other professional helped me prepare a document listed here, I have included contact information for him or her. You can consult the listed professional if you have questions about the document or need help carrying out its terms.

Document Title	
Date Prepared	
Effective Date	☐ Immediately ☐ Upon my incapacity ☐ Other:
Professional Help	An attorney or other professional helped me prepare this document: ☐ Yes ☐ No
Professional's Name, Title, and Contact Information	
Location of Original Document	
Locations of Copies of This Document	
Additional Notes	

Document Title	
Date Prepared	
Effective Date	☐ Immediately ☐ Upon my incapacity ☐ Other:
Professional Help	An attorney or other professional helped me prepare this document: ☐ Yes ☐ No
Professional's Name, Title, and Contact Information	
Location of Original Document	
Locations of Copies of This Document	
Additional Notes	

Document Title	
Date Prepared	
Effective Date	☐ Immediately ☐ Upon my incapacity ☐ Other:
Professional Help	An attorney or other professional helped me prepare this document: ☐ Yes ☐ No
Professional's Name, Title, and Contact Information	
Location of Original Document	
Locations of Copies of This Document	
Additional Notes	

Durable Power of Attorney for Finances

This section contains information about my durable power of attorney for finances.

I have also listed any nondurable powers of attorney for finances I have made. Nondurable powers of attorney are no longer valid if I become incapacitated. Please destroy them.

If an attorney or other professional helped me prepare a document listed here, I have included contact information for him or her. You can consult the listed professional if you have questions about the document or need help carrying out its terms.

Durable Power of Attorney for Finances

The following document is durable, which means it remains effective after I am incapacitated and unable to manage my own affairs. All powers granted under the document terminate upon my death. For information about who has authority to handle my affairs after death, see Section 17, Will and Trust.

Document Title	
Date Prepared	
Agent's Name	
Alternate Agents' Names	
Effective Date	☐ Immediately ☐ Upon my incapacity ☐ Other:
Professional Help	An attorney or other professional helped me prepare this document: ☐ Yes ☐ No
Professional's Name, Title, and Contact Information	
Location of Original Document	
Locations of Copies of This Document	
Additional Notes	

Other Financial Power of Attorney

The following documents are not durable, which means that they are no longer valid if I become incapacitated. If possible, please locate and destroy all copies of these documents to prevent anyone from mistakenly taking action under them.

Document Title	
Date Prepared	
Agent's Name	
Alternate Agents' Names	
Effective Date	☐ Immediately ☐ Other:
Termination Date	☐ Upon my incapacity or death ☐ Other:
Professional Help	An attorney or other professional helped me prepare this document: ☐ Yes ☐ No
Professional's Name, Title, and Contact Information	
Location of Original Document	
Locations of Copies of This Document	
Additional Notes	

Document Title	
Date Prepared	
Agent's Name	
Alternate Agents' Names	
Effective Date	☐ Immediately ☐ Other:
Termination Date	☐ Upon my incapacity or death ☐ Other:
Professional Help	An attorney or other professional helped me prepare this document: ☐ Yes ☐ No
Professional's Name, Title, and Contact Information	
Location of Original Document	
Locations of Copies of This Document	
Additional Notes	

13

Organ or Body Donation

In this section, I have outlined my wishes and any arrangements I have made for donation of my remains. If I have chosen to donate my body, organs, or tissues, I have also selected either burial or cremation (outlined in the next section) to follow the donation or to be carried out in the event that the donation is not accepted. Please review this section along with Sections 14, 15, and 16 prior to making my final arrangements.

After my death, I want to donate my body, organs, or tissues: ☐ Yes ☐ No

If "No," skip the rest of this section and turn to the next section.

Wishes for Donation

I would like to donate:	☐ My body
	☐ Any needed organs or tissues
	☐ Only the following organs or tissues:

Arrangements for Donation

Receiving Organization's Name, Address, and Telephone Number			
Location of Documents			
Additional Notes			

14

Burial or Cremation

In this section, I have outlined my wishes and any arrangements I have made for burial or cremation of my remains. Please review this section along with Sections 13, 15, and 16 prior to making my final arrangements.

Disposition of Remains

I have selected either burial or cremation, and have provided details about my wishes.

☐ **Burial**			
	Check One: ☐ Immediate ☐ After services	Check One: ☐ Embalm ☐ Do not embalm	Check One: ☐ In-ground ☐ Aboveground
Burial Organization Contact Information			
Burial Location and Contact Information			
Location of Documents			
Additional Notes			

☐ Cremation		
Check One: ☐ Immediate ☐ After services	**Check One:** ☐ Embalm ☐ Do not embalm	**Check One or All That Apply:** ☐ Niche in columbarium ☐ Scattered ☐ In-ground ☐ To individual
Cremation Organization Contact Information		
Final Location and Contact Information		
Location of Documents		
Additional Notes		

Casket or Urn

I would like a casket, urn, or other container to hold my remains: ☐ Yes ☐ No

Item	☐ Casket	☐ Urn	☐ Other
Material	☐ Wood Type: ______	☐ Metal Type: ______	☐ Other Type: ______
Model or Design			
Exterior Finish			
Interior Finish			
Cost Range	☐ Economical Approx. $______	☐ Moderate Approx. $______	☐ Luxury Approx. $______
Additional Notes			

Casket or Urn, continued

Item	☐ Casket	☐ Urn	☐ Other
Material	☐ Wood Type: ________	☐ Metal Type: ________	☐ Other Type: ________
Model or Design			
Exterior Finish			
Interior Finish			
Cost Range	☐ Economical Approx. $________	☐ Moderate Approx. $________	☐ Luxury Approx. $________
Additional Notes			

Item	☐ Casket	☐ Urn	☐ Other
Material	☐ Wood Type: ________	☐ Metal Type: ________	☐ Other Type: ________
Model or Design			
Exterior Finish			
Interior Finish			
Cost Range	☐ Economical Approx. $________	☐ Moderate Approx. $________	☐ Luxury Approx. $________
Additional Notes			

Headstone, Monument, or Burial Marker

I would like a headstone or marker: ☐ Yes ☐ No

Description	
Material	
Design	
Finish	
Additional Notes	

Epitaph

I would like an epitaph or inscription: ☐ Yes ☐ No

Item	
Inscription	
Additional Notes	

Item	
Inscription	
Additional Notes	

Item	
Inscription	
Additional Notes	

Burial or Cremation Apparel

I wish to specify burial or cremation apparel: ☐ Yes ☐ No

For items marked "Yes," please ensure that the clothing or article is removed and given to my executor prior to burial or cremation.

Clothing, Accessory, or Other Item	Location	Remove Before Interment or Cremation
		☐ Yes ☐ No
		☐ Yes ☐ No
		☐ Yes ☐ No
		☐ Yes ☐ No
		☐ Yes ☐ No
		☐ Yes ☐ No
		☐ Yes ☐ No
		☐ Yes ☐ No
		☐ Yes ☐ No
		☐ Yes ☐ No
		☐ Yes ☐ No
Additional Notes		

15

Funeral and Memorial Services

In this section, I have outlined my wishes and any arrangements I have made for services or ceremonies after my death. Please review this section along with Sections 13, 14, and 16 prior to making my final arrangements.

Viewing, Visitation, or Wake

I would like a viewing, visitation, or wake: ☐ Yes ☐ No

Type of Service		
Location and Contact Information		
Existing Arrangements and Location of Documents		
Body Present ☐ Yes ☐ No	**Casket** ☐ Yes ☐ No	**Casket** ☐ Open ☐ Closed
Invitees ☐ Public ☐ Private	**Timing and Days/Hours**	
Special Requests		
Additional Notes		

Viewing, Visitation, or Wake, continued

Type of Service		
Location and Contact Information		
Existing Arrangements and Location of Documents		
Body Present ☐ Yes ☐ No	**Casket** ☐ Yes ☐ No	**Casket** ☐ Open ☐ Closed
Invitees ☐ Public ☐ Private	**Timing and Days/Hours**	
Special Requests		
Additional Notes		

Funeral or Memorial Service

I would like a funeral or memorial: ☐ Yes ☐ No

Location and Contact Information	
Existing Arrangements and Location of Documents	

Body and Casket Present	**Casket**	**Other Items**
☐ Yes ☐ No	☐ Open ☐ Closed	☐ Photo—Location: ☐ Other: ______________
Flowers	**Invitees** ☐ Public ☐ Private	**Timing and Days/Hours**

Type of Service	Service Contact	Facilitator
☐ Religious	Name	Name
☐ Military		
☐ Other	Contact Information	Contact Information

Eulogy

Name	Name	Name
Contact Information	**Contact Information**	**Contact Information**

Music Selections and Musicians

Readings

Pallbearers

Name #1	Name #2	Name #3
Contact Information	**Contact Information**	**Contact Information**
Name #4	**Name #5**	**Name #6**
Contact Information	**Contact Information**	**Contact Information**

Pallbearers, continued

Name #7	Name #8	Name-Alternate
Contact Information	**Contact Information**	**Contact Information**
Name-Alternate	**Name-Alternate**	**Name-Alternate**
Contact Information	**Contact Information**	**Contact Information**

Graveside Ceremony	Transportation to Service
☐ Graveside only ☐ Following funeral ☐ None	

Additional Notes	

Reception or Celebration of Life

I would like a reception or celebration of life: ☐ Yes ☐ No

Location and Contact Information		
Existing Arrangements and Location of Documents		
Invitees ☐ Public ☐ Private	**Food and Drink**	
Additional Notes		

16

Obituary

Please publish my obituary. ☐ Yes ☐ No

I have already drafted an obituary: ☐ Yes (Location: ______________________) ☐ No

If I have not drafted an obituary, please prepare one using the information and instructions below.

Obituary Overview

Obituary Length	☐ Brief	☐ Moderate	☐ Article Length
Photograph	☐ Yes (Location: ______________________) ☐ No		
Publications			

Obituary Details

Date and Place of Birth	See Biographical Information, Section 3
Military Service	See Biographical Information, Section 3
Spouse, Children, Grand-children, Parents, Siblings	See Biographical Information, Section 3
Employment	See Employment, Section 7
Memberships and Communities	See Memberships and Communities, Section 9
Education	
Awards and Achievements	
Interests and Hobbies	
Values	
Public or Private	See Funeral and Memorial Services, Section 15, for my wishes for *public* or *private* ceremonies—(1) viewing, visitation, or wake; (2) funeral or memorial service; and (3) reception or celebration of life.
Flowers	☐ Yes. Send to:
	☐ No. "No flowers, please."
	☐ No. "In lieu of flowers, please send donations to [the organizations listed below]."

Obituary Details, continued

Donations or Remembrances (Organization and Contact Information)	
Other	

Additional Notes

17

Will and Trust

In this section, you will find important information about my will. If I have made other estate planning documents, such as a living trust, other trusts, or a marital property agreement, you will find those listed here as well.

If an attorney or other professional (such as a tax expert) helped me prepare a document listed here, I have included contact information for him or her. You can consult the listed professional if you have questions about the document or need help carrying out its terms.

Document Title	
Date Prepared	
Professional Help	An attorney or other professional helped me prepare this document: ☐ Yes ☐ No
Professional's Name, Title, and Contact Information	
Location of Original Document	
Locations of Copies of This Document	
Executor or Successor Trustee	
Alternate 1	
Alternate 2	
Alternate 3	
Additional Notes	

Will and Trust, continued

Document Title	
Date Prepared	
Professional Help	An attorney or other professional helped me prepare this document: ☐ Yes ☐ No
Professional's Name, Title, and Contact Information	
Location of Original Document	
Locations of Copies of This Document	
Executor or Successor Trustee	
Alternate 1	
Alternate 2	
Alternate 3	
Additional Notes	

Document Title	
Date Prepared	
Professional Help	An attorney or other professional helped me prepare this document: ☐ Yes ☐ No
Professional's Name, Title, and Contact Information	
Location of Original Document	
Locations of Copies of This Document	
Executor or Successor Trustee	
Alternate 1	
Alternate 2	
Alternate 3	
Additional Notes	

Document Title	
Date Prepared	
Professional Help	An attorney or other professional helped me prepare this document: ☐ Yes ☐ No
Professional's Name, Title, and Contact Information	
Location of Original Document	
Locations of Copies of This Document	
Executor or Successor Trustee	
Alternate 1	
Alternate 2	
Alternate 3	
Additional Notes	

Document Title	
Date Prepared	
Professional Help	An attorney or other professional helped me prepare this document: ☐ Yes ☐ No
Professional's Name, Title, and Contact Information	
Location of Original Document	
Locations of Copies of This Document	
Executor or Successor Trustee	
Alternate 1	
Alternate 2	
Alternate 3	
Additional Notes	

Will and Trust, continued

Document Title	
Date Prepared	
Professional Help	An attorney or other professional helped me prepare this document: ☐ Yes ☐ No
Professional's Name, Title, and Contact Information	
Location of Original Document	
Locations of Copies of This Document	
Executor or Successor Trustee	
Alternate 1	
Alternate 2	
Alternate 3	
Additional Notes	

Document Title	
Date Prepared	
Professional Help	An attorney or other professional helped me prepare this document: ☐ Yes ☐ No
Professional's Name, Title, and Contact Information	
Location of Original Document	
Locations of Copies of This Document	
Executor or Successor Trustee	
Alternate 1	
Alternate 2	
Alternate 3	
Additional Notes	

18

Insurance

This section lists all my insurance policies. It covers policies that I own and those owned by others that cover my life or my property.

My agent or executor should review each listed policy and contact the insurance company to:

- claim any benefits due—for example, medical, workers' compensation, life, or accidental death
- cancel policies that are no longer necessary—such as medical, dental, or vision insurance, after my death, and
- modify policies—for instance, modifying my home or vehicle insurance policies after my death but before transferring the property to beneficiaries.

Type of Policy and Policy Number	Insurance Company Name and Contact Information	Policy Owner	Description of Coverage and Status	Location of Policy
Medical				
No.				
Medical				
No.				
Medical				
No.				

Insurance Policies, continued

Type of Policy and Policy Number	Insurance Company Name and Contact Information	Policy Owner	Description of Coverage and Status	Location of Policy
Medical				
No.				
Dental				
No.				
Dental				
No.				
Vision				
No.				
Vision				
No.				

Insurance Policies, continued

Type of Policy and Policy Number	Insurance Company Name and Contact Information	Policy Owner	Description of Coverage and Status	Location of Policy
Home and Contents, Renters'				
No.				
Home and Contents, Renters'				
No.				
Vehicle				
No.				
Vehicle				
No.				
Vehicle				
No.				

18

Insurance

Insurance Policies, continued

Type of Policy and Policy Number	Insurance Company Name and Contact Information	Policy Owner	Description of Coverage and Status	Location of Policy
Vehicle				
No.				
Vehicle				
No.				
Umbrella Liability				
No.				
Personal Liability				
No.				
Personal Liability				
No.				

Type of Policy and Policy Number	Insurance Company Name and Contact Information	Policy Owner	Description of Coverage and Status	Location of Policy
Malpractice				
No.				
Malpractice				
No.				
Errors and Omissions				
No.				
Errors and Omissions				
No.				
Disability				
No.				

Insurance Policies, continued

Type of Policy and Policy Number	Insurance Company Name and Contact Information	Policy Owner	Description of Coverage and Status	Location of Policy
Disability				
No.				
Disability				
No.				
Disability				
No.				
Life				
No.				
Life				
No.				

18

Insurance

Type of Policy and Policy Number	Insurance Company Name and Contact Information	Policy Owner	Description of Coverage and Status	Location of Policy
Life				
No.				
Life				
No.				
Accidental Death				
No.				
Accidental Death				
No.				
Long-Term Care				
No.				

Insurance Policies, continued

Type of Policy and Policy Number	Insurance Company Name and Contact Information	Policy Owner	Description of Coverage and Status	Location of Policy
Long-Term Care				
No.				
Other				
No.				
Other				
No.				
Other				
No.				
Other				
No.				

Type of Policy and Policy Number	Insurance Company Name and Contact Information	Policy Owner	Description of Coverage and Status	Location of Policy
Other				
No.				
Other				
No.				
Other				
No.				
Other				
No.				

Additional Notes

19

Bank and Brokerage Accounts

Following is a complete list of my bank and brokerage accounts. See my estate planning documents—that is, my durable power of attorney for finances, will, and/or living trust—for complete information about managing or distributing the funds in these accounts. Contact each financial institution to arrange account access according to the powers granted in my estate planning documents.

If I have named a pay- or transfer-on-death beneficiary for an account, I have included the beneficiary's name with the account information, below. Upon my death, the beneficiary can go to the financial institution with a certified copy of the death certificate and collect the assets, without probate proceedings.

At the end of the section, you will also find important contact information in case checks are lost or stolen.

Financial Institution Contact Information	Account Number, Description of Assets, and Pay- or Transfer-on-Death Beneficiary	Debit Card and Online Access	Location of Checkbook, Check Stock, and Statements

Bank and Brokerage Accounts, continued

Financial Institution Contact Information	Account Number, Description of Assets, and Pay- or Transfer-on-Death Beneficiary	Debit Card and Online Access	Location of Checkbook, Check Stock, and Statements

Financial Institution Contact Information	Account Number, Description of Assets, and Pay- or Transfer-on-Death Beneficiary	Debit Card and Online Access	Location of Checkbook, Check Stock, and Statements

Additional Notes

If Checks Are Lost or Stolen

If checks are lost, stolen, or misused, you should immediately contact the bank or brokerage for the account. Then file a police report.

If checks are unexpectedly denied by a merchant, ask the merchant for contact information for the check verification service being used. Follow up with the service to learn why the check was denied and resolve any errors or fraud.

To help you quickly resolve problems, here is consumer contact information for commonly used check verification services:

Chex Systems, Inc.
800-428-9623—for consumer assistance
www.consumerdebit.com

CrossCheck, Inc.
800-843-0760—for customer service
www.cross-check.com

First Data TeleCheck
800-366-2425—for declined checks
800-710-9898—for stolen checks or fraud
www.firstdata.com/telecheck

20

Retirement Plans and Pensions

This section describes my retirement plans and pension benefits. Notify the managing company or organization of my incapacity or death. Then evaluate each plan for amounts due to my estate or survivors.

When you are ready to distribute the funds to my beneficiaries, please share with them the following information. It is important that my beneficiaries understand how to handle an inherited retirement plan. If a plan isn't handled correctly, the law may require its funds to be withdrawn sooner, with income tax paid earlier, and this would significantly reduce the plan's value to each beneficiary. It would be wise for all of my beneficiaries—which could include my spouse, other family or friends, organizations, or (rarely) a trust—to get good advice about how to deal with inheriting these types of plans.

- **Spouse.** A beneficiary spouse is entitled to rights and tax breaks that other beneficiaries are not. For example, a spouse can roll the inherited amount into a traditional IRA or qualified employer plan, can postpone distributions to age 70½, or can choose to be treated as the plan beneficiary (not owner) for tax treatment of withdrawals.
- **Nonspouse individuals.** Each nonspouse beneficiary should set up a separate account that is titled with my name, date of death, and the beneficiary's name. As an example:

  Mary Melone (deceased May 31, 2014) IRA for the benefit of Eliza Heron

The beneficiary should request a trustee-to-trustee transfer directly to the new account.

Note that a beneficiary younger than I was can extend the minimum distribution schedule according to their life expectancy, providing that he or she starts taking "required minimum distributions" in the year following my death.

Employer Retirement and Pension Plans

Company Contact Information	Description, Status of Plan, and Beneficiary	Account Number	Location of Statements

Employer Retirement and Pension Plans, continued

Company Contact Information	Description, Status of Plan, and Beneficiary	Account Number	Location of Statements

Additional Notes

Individual Retirement Accounts and Plans

Financial Institution Contact Information	Description, Status of Plan, and Beneficiary	Account Number	Location of Statements

Financial Institution Contact Information	Description, Status of Plan, and Beneficiary	Account Number	Location of Statements

20

Retirement Plans and Pensions

Additional Notes

21

Government Benefits

In this section, you'll find information about any federal or state government benefits that I either currently collect or expect in the future. These include any benefits for my family members and survivors.

Social Security Benefits

I have outlined my Social Security benefits below. Upon my incapacity or death, notify the Social Security Administration at 800-772-1213 or make an appointment with the local office. You can locate the local office by calling the SSA main number or checking the government listings in the phone book.

Review the status of my benefits and ask the SSA representative whether additional benefits are available to me or to my family. A one-time death benefit is normally available for qualifying survivors.

Information, publications, and forms are available at the Social Security Administration website, www.ssa.gov.

Program Name	Account Name and SSN	Account Access, Status, and Payment	Location of Documents
Retirement			
Disability			
Supplemental Security Income (SSI)			

Program Name	Account Name and SSN	Account Access, Status, and Payment	Location of Documents
Family			
Survivor			

Other Government Benefits

Following is a list of any other government benefits that I currently receive or expect in the future. For each program, notify the program administrator of my incapacity or death, review the status of my benefits, and discuss whether additional benefits are available to my family or to me.

Program Name and Contact Information	Program Description	Account Name and Identification	Account Access, Status, and Payment	Location of Documents

Other Government Benefits, continued

Program Name and Contact Information	Program Description	Account Name and Identification	Account Access, Status, and Payment	Location of Documents

21

Government Benefits

Additional Notes

22

Credit Cards and Debts

This section contains information about my bills, credit cards, and other debts. At the end of the section, you will also find important contact information in case a credit card is lost or stolen.

Bill Storage and Payment

I store paper bills in the following location (until I pay them):

Location of Pending Bills	

The table below provides information about how I receive and pay each of my bills. For example, I might receive a bill through the mail or electronically, and I might pay a bill by check or money order, online, automatically by preauthorized charge to my credit card, or through an automatic debit to my bank account. This chart also tells you where I've stored records of paid bills.

For additional information about banking, see Section 19 of my planner. For more about online accounts and email, see Section 23.

Payee	Account Number	Notice	Frequency and Amount	Method of Payment	Record of Payment

Automatic Payment of Bills, continued

Payee	Account Number	Notice	Frequency and Amount	Method of Payment	Record of Payment

Additional Notes

Credit Cards

Following is a list of all my credit cards, including customer service contact information. Note that my debit or ATM cards are listed in Section 19, along with the associated accounts.

Issuer	Account Number and Access	Customer Service Telephone

Additional Notes

Debts I Owe to Others

In addition to the bills and credit cards listed above, I owe the following debts:

Creditor Name and Contact Information	Amount	Terms of Debt and Status of Payment	Location of Documents

Additional Notes

Debts Others Owe to Me

Payment is due to me on the following debts:

Name and Contact Information	Amount	Terms of Debt and Status of Payment	Location of Documents

Debts Others Owe to Me, continued

Name and Contact Information	Amount	Terms of Debt and Status of Payment	Location of Documents

Additional Notes

If a Credit Card Is Lost or Stolen

In the event that a credit card is lost or stolen, immediately contact the issuing company, listed above.

In addition, to minimize the threat of identity theft and fraud, contact the national credit reporting organizations, the FTC, and the Social Security Administration. Also file a police report with the local police department.

Equifax Fraud Alert
888-766-0008
www.equifax.com
See link, "Request a fraud alert"

Experian Fraud Alert
888-397-3742
www.experian.com
See link, "Fraud Alert"

TransUnion Fraud Alert
800-680-7289
www.transunion.com
See tab, "Credit Disputes, Alerts & Freezes"

Federal Trade Commission
Complaint Assistant
202-326-3300
www.ftccomplaintassistant.gov

Social Security Fraud Hotline
Office of the Inspector General
800-269-0271
http://oig.ssa.gov

23

Secured Places and Passwords

This section provides the information you will need to access property that I manage or store in secured places—including online accounts with passwords, physical items secured with combination locks, access codes, or keys, safe deposit boxes, and secret locations.

Products, Services, and Passwords

Product or Service	Account Name, User Name, or Account Number	Password, Combination, or PIN	Location of Key

Common Passwords

Here are some of my common passwords:			

Additional Notes

Safe Deposit Boxes

If I am incapacitated. If I am incapacitated and you co-own a safe deposit box with me, your access rights are unaffected. If you do not already have access, however, you will need to meet special requirements before the financial institution will open a safe deposit box for you.

- If you are my agent for finances under a durable power of attorney, you will need to present the power of attorney document. If the document is a "springing" power of attorney, you will also need to present doctors' statements to verify that I am incapacitated.
- If you do not meet these requirements, you will need to obtain a court order to access a safe deposit box.

Upon my death. You will need to meet these special requirements before the financial institution will open a safe deposit box for you.

- If you are a co-owner on the box, your access will continue unimpeded unless the box is temporarily sealed (see below).
- If you are my executor or successor trustee, you will need to present a certified copy of my death certificate and a copy of the will or trust that names you to the job. (There may be a few weeks' delay, if the box is temporarily sealed. Again, see below.)
- If you meet none of these requirements, you will need to obtain a court order to access the safe deposit box.

Note that in some states, safe deposit boxes are sealed for a few weeks following the death of the owner so the state taxing authority can review the contents. During this time, you will not be able to obtain access to the box without a court order.

Here is a list of my safe deposit boxes:

Safe Deposit Boxes, continued

Bank Name and Contact Information	People With Authorized Access	Box Number and Location of Keys	Description of Contents

Additional Notes

Other Keys

Additional keys are located as follows:

Purpose	Location

Other Assets, Other Locations

These items of personal property are on loan to others, hidden away, stored elsewhere, or known only to me—and I want you to be able to locate them after my death. I have also listed any personal property I have that is on loan to me from someone else. Please return these items to their owners.

Item and Description	Location of Asset	Location of Documents

Other Assets, Other Locations, continued

Item and Description	Location of Asset	Location of Documents

Other Assets, Other Locations, continued

Item and Description	Location of Asset	Location of Documents

Other Assets, Other Locations, continued

Item and Description	Location of Asset	Location of Documents

23

Secured Places and Passwords

Additional Notes

24

Taxes

The following information will help you prepare any tax returns due while I am incapacitated or after my death.

Tax Professionals

The following attorneys, accountants, or other professionals have helped me with my taxes in the past and are recommended to you for future work. Turn to them if you need assistance with my final tax returns.

Name of Person or Firm	Contact Information	Notes

Location of Tax Records

All receipts and documents related to income tax returns—both current-year records as well as prior-year returns—are located as described below.

Location of Current-Year Records	
Location of Prior-Year Records	

Additional Notes

25

Real Estate

Following is a list of all the real estate I own or rent, either solely or with others. This information will help you to manage the property in the short term and to sell or otherwise transfer the property when that becomes necessary.

Property I Own

Property Address	Weeks/ Year Occupancy	Mortgage Company Contact Information	Current Occupants and Contact Information	Location of Documents

Property I Own, continued

Property Address	Weeks/ Year Occupancy	Mortgage Company Contact Information	Current Occupants and Contact Information	Location of Documents

25

Real Estate

Instructions for Care of Property I Own

Following are special instructions to help you care for the property listed above. If I hire someone to help with routine maintenance tasks, you can find that information in Section 10, Service Providers.

Property Address	Property Care

Instructions for Care of Property I Own, continued

Property Address	Property Care

25

Real Estate

Additional Notes

Property I Rent or Lease

Property Address	Weeks/Year Occupancy	Landlord's Contact Information	Term of Rental or Lease	Location of Documents

Instructions for Care of Leased or Rented Property

Following are special instructions to help you care for the property listed above. If I hire someone to help with routine maintenance tasks, you can find that information in Section 10, Service Providers.

Property Address	Property Care

Instructions for Care of Leased or Rented Property, continued

Property Address	Property Care

Additional Notes

26

Vehicles

Here is a summary of all vehicles in which I hold an ownership or lease interest. This information will help you to manage the interest in the short term and to terminate, transfer, or sell the vehicle over time.

If I have named a transfer-on-death beneficiary for a vehicle I own, I have included the beneficiary's name with the vehicle information, below. Upon my death, the beneficiary can go to the state motor vehicles department with a certified copy of the death certificate and transfer the vehicle title, without probate proceedings.

Vehicles I Own

Vehicle Type (Make, Model, Year, and Vehicle ID Number)	Creditor Contact Information	Garage or Storage Location	Transfer-on-Death Beneficiary	Location of Documents

Vehicles I Own, continued

Vehicle Type (Make, Model, Year, and Vehicle ID Number)	Creditor Contact Information	Garage or Storage Location	Transfer-on-Death Beneficiary	Location of Documents

Additional Notes

Vehicles I Lease

Vehicle Type (Make, Model, Year, and Vehicle ID Number)	Leaseholder Contact Information	Garage or Storage Location	Location of Documents

Vehicle Type (Make, Model, Year, and Vehicle ID Number)	**Leaseholder Contact Information**	**Garage or Storage Location**	**Location of Documents**

Additional Notes

27

Other Income and Personal Property

This section describes sources of income and important items of personal property that aren't listed in other sections of my planner, and it tells you where to find warranty records and maintenance guides for items of personal property. It also details any property that I expect to receive in the future.

Other Income

Following is a list of income sources not described elsewhere in my planner:

Source and Contact Information	Description	Location of Documents

Other Income, continued

Source and Contact Information	Description	Location of Documents

Other Income, continued

Source and Contact Information	Description	Location of Documents

Additional Notes

Other Personal Property

The following items of property are particularly valuable to me. For certain items, I have included instructions for special handling and/or noted whether I have named a beneficiary in my will or other estate planning document.

Item and Description	Location and Access Information	Special Instructions	Location of Documents

Other Personal Property, continued

Item and Description	Location and Access Information	Special Instructions	Location of Documents

Additional Notes

Property I Expect to Receive From Others

Following is a list of property that I expect to receive in the future. However, if I am named to receive property under a will, trust, or other estate planning document, and I die before I receive it, the property probably won't pass to my estate. Instead, it will most likely go to the benefactor's alternate beneficiary.

Source and Contact Information	Description	Location of Documents

Property I Expect to Receive From Others, continued

Source and Contact Information	Description	Location of Documents

27

Other Income & Personal Property

Property I Expect to Receive From Others, continued

Source and Contact Information	Description	Location of Documents

Additional Notes

Warranty Records and Product Guides

Warranty information, product guides, and repair records for my personal property are located as follows:

28

Other Information

This section includes any information and materials that didn't fit neatly into other sections of my planner.

Index

A

AARP on pensions, 182
AARP Retirement Survival Guide (Jason), 181
AB trusts for tax savings, 147, 211
accidental death insurance, 161
accountants, 242, 243–45
adoption records, 33
advance directives. *See* Health Care Directives section
affidavit for claiming property, 151
agents
- agent for finances, 97–99
- executors, 150, 210, 211
- overview, 98
- successor trustees, 98–99, 146, 148–50, 210
- *See also* durable power of attorney for finances; health care agent

Airfare Watchdog, 74
alternates
- agent for finances, 97, 99
- agent for health care, 85, 90
- beneficiaries, 180
- co-owner of safe deposit box, 203, 206
- executor or successor trustee, 148, 150
- pallbearers, 128
- personal guardian for children, 43
- property manager for children's property, 44

alternatives to writing a letter, 21, 23–24
Alzheimer's Disease and health care directives, 87
American Red Cross and frequent flyer miles, 73
Anatomy Gifts Registry, 106
annulment certificate, 33–34
appointment calendar review, instructions for, 28
assets, 67, 95, 144, 206–7. *See also* durable power of attorney for finances
Association of Personal Historians, 23, 39
Association of Real Estate License Law Officials, 220
attorney-in-fact, 96
attorneys. *See* lawyers

B

Bank and Brokerage Accounts section, 171–75
- accessibility of accounts, 172–73
- overview, 172
- planner pages, 174–75
- probate avoidance, 173–74
- resources, 174
- updating your planner, 175
- *See also* securities

banks
- as executor, 149
- as financial agent, 99
- joint accounts, 173
- joint tenancy ownership, 152
- pay-on-death accounts, 145, 151, 173, 232
- *See also* securities

baptismal records, 33
beneficiaries
- of brokerage accounts, 174
- of eStuff, 231
- of life insurance, 159, 162, 163
- of personal property, 230
- of retirement accounts, 179
- in trusts, 146
- of vehicles, 145, 152, 173–74, 226, 227
- in wills, 145

benefits
- employment-related, 58, 59
- and long-term care insurance, 167–68
- membership-related, 72–74
- *See also* Government Benefits section

binder for your planner
- bank and brokerage account materials, 175
- biographical information, 39
- burial or cremation materials, 123
- business documents, 68
- children's records, 45
- credit card and debt materials, 200
- dependents other than children, 49
- employment records, 59
- funeral or memorial service materials, 134
- government benefits documents, 191
- health care documents, 90
- instructions, 29
- insurance documents, 170
- membership information, 75
- obituary materials, 139
- organ or body donation arrangements, 107
- overview, 13–15, 24
- personal property documents, 233
- pet or livestock records, 54
- powers of attorney, 101
- real estate documents, 222–23
- retirement and pension documents, 183
- secured materials access, 207
- service provider materials, 80
- tax materials, 214
- vehicle documents, 228
- will, trust, and related documents, 155
- *See also* planner

biographical information
- of children, 32–33, 45
- of people you provide care for, 48, 49

Biographical Information section, 31–39
- adoption records, 33
- baptismal records, 33
- birth certificates, 32–33
- citizenship documents, 36
- death certificates, 37
- divorce, annulment, or legal separation documents, 33–34
- marriage certificates, 33
- military records, 34–36
- overview, 32
- planner pages, 37–39
- Social Security cards or records, 36
- updating your planner, 39

birth certificates, ordering, 32–33

Bogleheads' Guide to Retirement Planning (Larimore, et al.), 181

brokerage accounts, 152, 173–74. *See also* Bank and Brokerage Accounts section

budgets, 195, 197–98

burial or cremation
- and agent for health care, 88
- open or closed casket, 128
- prepayment plans, 118
- and whole body donation, 105

Burial or Cremation section, 109–23
- apparel, 117, 122–23
- burial, 111–12, 115–16, 117, 118, 119–20
- casket or urn, 115–16, 120–21
- cremation, 112–14, 116, 117, 119, 120
- embalming, 112, 113, 114
- epitaph, 117, 122
- headstone, monument, or burial marker, 116, 121–22
- overview, 110–11, 115
- planner pages, 119–23
- resources, 117–18
- updating your planner, 123
- veterans' benefits, 114
- *See also* Funeral and Memorial Services section

Business Interests section, 61–68
- estate planning for small business owners, 62–63
- overview, 62
- planner pages, 64–68
- pointing to, in Instructions, 27
- resources, 64
- updating your planner, 68

Business Owner's Tookit, 64

C

caretakers
- for children of deceased, 42–45, 163
- for pets and livestock, 52
- planning ahead for death of loved one, 4–5

casket or urn, 115–16, 120–21, 128

Catholic annulment documents, 34

Celebrating a Life (Moore), 130

celebration of life, 126–27, 129

Celebrations of Life, 23

Certified Public Accountants (CPAs), 242, 243–45

certified vs. informational copies, 33

charitable memberships, 72

charitable trusts, 211

children
- biographical information, 32–33, 45
- court appointment of personal guardian, 42, 44
- life insurance benefits for, 162, 163
- parental estate planning documents, 143
- personal guardian for, 42–43, 44–45
- property manager for, 43–45, 143, 163

Children section, 41–46
- biographical information, 45
- overview, 42
- personal guardian for, 42–43, 44–45
- planner pages, 44–45
- pointing to, in Instructions, 27
- property manager for, 43–45
- resources, 44
- updating your planner, 46

citizenship documents, 36

civic memberships, 70

ClarkHoward.com, 168, 197

Clark Howard's Living Large in Lean Times (Howard, Meltzer, and Thimou), 197–98

Clinician's Orders for Life Sustaining Treatment (COLST), 87

comfort care and health care directives, 86–87

common law states, 218, 223

communities. *See* Memberships and Communities

community property states
- community property with right of survivorship, 145, 153, 217–18
- and domestic partners, 218
- and life insurance policies, 163
- and marital property agreements, 148, 154, 220
- and real estate, 217, 218, 219–20, 223
- and retirement plans, 179

computers, protecting information on, 196

consumer memberships, 72

Consumer Reports, 169

co-owner of safe deposit box, 203, 206

corporations, transferring ownership, 63

couples. *See* married couples; unmarried couples

court appointment of personal guardian for children, 42, 44

CPAs (Certified Public Accountants), 242, 243–45

credit bureaus, 197

Credit Cards and Debts section, 193–200
- evaluating and reducing debt, 194–95, 197
- overview, 194
- planner pages, 198–99
- pointing to, in Instructions, 28
- resources, 197–98
- updating your planner, 200

cremation, 112–14, 116, 117, 119, 120. *See also* Burial or Cremation section

cremation.com, 119

Cremation Society, 118, 119

Crossings: Caring for Our Own Death, 130

D

DaveRamsey.com, 197

death
- beliefs about, 21–22
- burial or cremation prepayment plans, 118
- planning ahead for, 4–6
- post-death process of loved ones, 1, 162, 163
- response to, 26

sealing of safe deposit boxes at time of, 203–4, 205–6
thoughts about your own, 21–22
death certificates, 37
debts, 197–200. *See also* Credit Cards and Debts section
dementia and health care directives, 87
dependents other than children, 27, 47–49
digital assets, 95, 144
digital vs. paper files, 12, 13–14
directive to physicians. *See* Health Care Directives section
disability benefits from Medicare program, 187
disability insurance, 158
disposition plan for a small business, 65–66
divorce
and agent for finances, 98, 101
documentation, 33–34, 38
and health care documents, 84
DNR (Do Not Resuscitate) orders, 87, 91
document preparers, 243, 244
domestic partners, 218. *See also* married couples
Donate Life America, 107
donations in lieu of flowers, 139
donor cards, 106
donors. *See* organ or body donation
Do Not Resuscitate (DNR) orders, 87, 91
driver's license, 29, 38, 106
Dropbox.com, 71
durable power of attorney for finances, 93–101
agent for finances, 97–99
and agent for health care, 85
effective date and end date, 96–97
overview, 94–96, 143–44, 172
planner pages, 100–101
pointing to, in Instructions, 26, 27
recording, 96
resources, 99–100
and safe deposit box, 203
updating your planner, 101
durable power of attorney for health care, 82, 84, 88–89, 94. *See also* health care agent

E

educational memberships, 70–71
Effective Succession Planning (Rothwell), 64
eForms, about, 237–40
eHarmony, 71
8 Ways to Avoid Probate (Randolph), 154, 174
elderly, 4–5, 143
embalming, 112, 113, 114
employees of a small business, 66–67
Employment section, 27, 57–59
employment taxes, 186
epitaph, 117, 122
estate planning documents, 142–44, 156. *See also* trusts; wills
estate planning for small business owners, 62–63
estate taxes
federal, 147, 164, 211
state, 212
eStuff, beneficiaries for, 231
ethical wills, 23, 145–46
executors, 150, 210, 211
Executor's Guide, The (Randolph), 212

F

Facebook, 71, 74
facilitator for funeral service, 128
family
and agent for finances, 97
collaboration with your parents, 5
including in Biographical Information section, 37–39
instructions for contacting, 28
as retirement plan beneficiary, 180
Social Security benefits, 187–88
Family Business Succession (Couvie and Pendergast), 64
family heirlooms, 231–31
family income insurance coverage, 161
FCA (Funeral Consumers Alliance), 118, 128
federal estate tax, 147, 164, 211
fee agreements with experts, 244–45
Final Passages, 130
Final Rights (Slocum and Carlson), 118
finances. *See* Credit Cards and Debts section; durable power of attorney for finances
financial planners, 242, 243–45
"first to die" life insurance, 161
fraternal memberships, 71
FrequentFlier.com, 74
frequent flyer miles, 72–74
friends
including in Biographical Information section, 37–39
instructions for contacting, 28
as life insurance beneficiaries, 162, 163
as retirement plan beneficiary, 180
funeral and memorial services
family-directed services, 128
home funerals, 113, 118, 130
and whole body donation, 105
Funeral and Memorial Services section, 125–34
funerals, 127–29, 131–33
graveside ceremonies, 128, 129
memorial services, 126–27, 129, 131–33
overview, 126
planner pages, 130–34
pointing to, in Instructions, 27–28
reception or celebration of life, 129
resources, 130
updating your planner, 134
viewing, visitation, or wake, 126–27, 130–31
See also Burial or Cremation section
Funeral Consumers Alliance (FCA), 118, 128

G

gifts for probate avoidance, 151, 152, 211
Good Goodbye, A (Rubin), 130
Google, 71
Government Benefits section, 185–91
overview, 186
pointing to, in Instructions, 28
programs other than Social Security, 189, 190–91

resources, 188–89
Social Security, 186–88
updating your planner, 189–91
graveside ceremonies, 128, 129

H

handwritten wills, 146
headstone, monument, or burial marker, 116–17, 121–22
healing memberships, 71
health care agent
and agent for finances, 98–99
authority of, 84, 89
choosing your, 84–86
communicating with, 17, 20
and durable power of attorney for health care, 82, 84, 88–89
and mental health treatment, 87–88
and organ or body donation, 106
planner page on, 90
See also Health Care Directives section
health care directives, 106, 143
Health Care Directives section, 81–91
durable power of attorney for health care, 84, 88–89, 94
duty of medical personnel to honor your directives, 89
health care declaration, 86–88
overview, 82–84
planner pages, 89–91
pointing to, in Instructions, 26, 27
resources for forms, 89
updating your planner, 91
See also health care agent
health care providers, 78, 89
heirlooms, 231–31
Hero Miles and frequent flyer miles, 73
holographic wills, 146
home care coverage, 166
Home Funeral Directory, 118
home funerals, 113, 118, 130
How to Get Out of Debt, Stay Out of Debt, and Live Prosperously (Mundis), 197
How to Retire Happy, Wild and Free (Zelinski), 181

I

ICE (In Case of Emergency) entries in cell phone, 89
identity theft avoidance, 196
identity theft reports, 198
identity thieves and obituaries, 137, 139
illness and planning for death, 4
incapacity, defining, 83–84
In Case of Emergency (ICE) entries in cell phone, 89
income and expenses review, 195
income not previously addressed, 230, 231
income taxes, 179, 210, 213–14, 221, 222
Individual Retirement Accounts (IRAs), 181
Individual Retirement Arrangements (IRS), 181
inflation protection for long-term care insurance, 167
informational vs. certified copies, 33
inheritance rights, 148, 218
inheritance taxes, state, 173, 212
Instructions section, 25–29
overview, 26–27
planner pages, 27–29
pointing to, in Letter to Loved Ones, 21
updating your planner, 29
insurance agents, 242–45
Insurance section, 157–70
life insurance, 159–64, 168
long-term care insurance, 162, 164–69
need for insurance, 158–59
overview, 158, 168
planner pages, 169–70
pointing to, in Instructions, 28
resources, 168–69
updating your planner, 170
InsWeb, 168
Internet Cremation Society, 118, 119
inventory and instructions, 28–29
IRAs (Individual Retirement Accounts), 181
IRAs, 401(k)s, & Other Retirement Plans (Slesnick and Suttle), 181
irrevocable trust as retirement account beneficiary, 180–81

J

joint accounts, 173. *See also* property ownership
joint ownership for probate avoidance, 152–53
joint tenancy ownership, 145
joint tenancy with right of survivorship, 152–53, 217
Just a Note to Say (Isaacs), 23

L

last words, in Letter to Loved Ones, 22
lawyers, about, 243, 244–45
lawyers, consulting with
for durable power of attorney for finances, 99–100
for estate planning, 147, 148, 153–54, 211
for irrevocable trusts, 181
leasing real estate, 222
leasing vehicles, 228
Legal Guide for Lesbian & Gay Couples (Clifford, et. al), 220
Letter to Loved Ones section, 19–24
addressing your letter, 20–21
alternatives to, 21, 23–24
on beliefs about death, 21–22
on Instructions section, 21
messages and last words, 22–23
overview, 20
planner pages, 23–24
resources, 23
signature, 23
updating your planner, 24
liabilities of a small business, 67
life insurance and children as beneficiary, 43
Life Insurance section, 159–64
and after-death expenses, 162
beneficiaries, 43, 163
evaluating your need for, 161–62
hybrid policy with long-term care, 162
as method for giving money to others, 162
permanent insurance, 159–61
planner pages, 169–70
resources, 168
for surviving spouse or children, 162

term insurance, 159
transferring ownership of policy, 164
life insurance trusts, 211
limited liability companies, transferring ownership, 63
LinkedIn, 71
livestock. *See* Pets and Livestock section
Living Together (Ihara, et. al), 220
living trusts
and bank and brokerage accounts, 173
choosing your successor trustee, 98–99, 149–50
as life insurance beneficiary, 163
naming a child's property manager, 143
overview, 146–47
for probate avoidance, 151
as retirement account beneficiary, 180
living will. *See* Health Care Directives section
Long-Term Care (Matthews), 169
LongTermCare.gov, 169
long-term care (LTC) insurance
conditions and exclusions, 167–68
costs of, 165
hybrid policy with life insurance, 162
need for, 164–65
overview, 164
planner pages, 169–70
policy types, 165–66
resources, 168–69

M

Make-A-Wish Foundation and frequent flyer miles, 73
Managing Retirement Wealth (Jason), 181
marital deduction for federal estate taxes, 211
marital property agreements, 148, 154, 220
marriage certificates, 33
married couples
and agent for finances, 98
common law states, 218, 223
estate tax advantages, 211
and guardian for children, 42, 43
and health care agent designation, 84
and health care documents, 83, 84
inheritance rights, 148, 218
marital property agreements, 148, 154, 220
and property manager for children, 43
and real estate ownership, 218–20
and retirement plan beneficiary requirements, 179–80
separate planners for, 11
shared living trusts, 146
spouse and children life insurance, 161
survivors benefits from Social Security, 188
and tenancy by the entirety ownership, 153
See also community property states
Match.com, 71
MedCure, Inc., 106
Medicaid, 169
medical directives. *See* Health Care Directives section
Medic Alert jewelry, 87
Medical Orders for Scope of Treatment (MOST), 87
Medicare, 169
Medicare- or Medicaid-certified care facilities, 166
Memberships and Communities section, 69–75
benefits for survivors, 72
frequent flyer miles, 72–74
overview, 70
planner pages, 74–75
pointing to, in Instructions, 29
resources, 74
types of, 70–72
updating your planner, 75
memberships and funeral service, 127–28
memoir writing classes, 39
memorial services, 126–27, 129, 131–33. *See also* Funeral and Memorial Services section
mental health, 87–88, 168
messages for your loved ones, 22
military personnel
funeral for, 127, 132
planning ahead for death, 5
Presidential Memorial Certificate for veterans, 133
veterans' benefits for burial or cremation, 114, 133
military records, 34–36
mortuary services
arrangements for, 130–31
and casket prices, 115
and casket transportation to the cemetery, 129
cost of, 111, 112
cremation, 119
independent plans vs., 117–18, 130
renting a casket from, 112
See also Funeral and Memorial Services section
MOST (Medical Orders for Scope of Treatment), 87
Motley Fool website, 197
MySpace, 71

N

National Archives & Records Administration (NARA), 34–36
National Association of Financial and Estate Planning, 144
National Center for Health Statistics (NCHS), 32–33
National Foster Care & Adoption Directory, 33
National Resource Center on Psychiatric Advance Directives, 88
N/A, using in planner, 12
New Life Insurance Investment Advisor (Baldwin), 168
Nolo estate planning resources, 154
nondurable power of attorney, 94, 101
nursing homes, 166

O

Obituary section, 135–39
identity thieves and obituaries, 137, 139
overview, 136–37
planner pages, 137–39
pointing to, in Instructions, 28

resources, 137
updating your planner, 139
online communities, 71
online storage services, 14
oral wills, 146
organizations as beneficiaries, 180
Organ or Body Donation section, 103–7
and burial or cremation, 104–5, 110
driver's license as donor card, 106
overview, 104–6
planner pages, 107
resources, 106–7
updating your planner, 107
Other Income and Personal Property section, 229–33
overview, 230
planner pages, 230–33
pointing to, in Instructions, 28–29
updating your planner, 233
Other Information section, 28–29, 235–36
Others Who Depend on Me section, 27, 47–49
ownership. *See* property ownership

P

pallbearers, 128
palliative care and health care directives, 86–87
paper vs. digital files, 12, 13–14
paralegals, 243, 244
parents, 5. *See also* family
partnerships, transferring ownership, 63
Party of Your Life, The (Dillman), 130
passwords
and identity theft, 196
password managers, 202
storing, 204–5
See also Secured Places and Passwords section
patient advocate designation. *See* health care agent
pay-on-death (POD) bank accounts, 145, 151, 173, 232
Pension and Annuity Income (IRS), 182
Pension Rights Center, 182
pensions, resources, 182
permanent life insurance, 159–61
personal guardian for your children, 42–43, 44–45
personal liability insurance, 158
Personal Notes (Lamb), 23
personal property, 230, 231–33
Pets and Livestock section, 27, 51–55
Physician's Orders for Life Sustaining Treatment (POLST), 87
Picasa, 71
placement of pets and livestock, 54
planner
complex topics, 16
essential topics, 16
final topics, 16
and Instructions section, 27–29
overview, 6, 10–11, 17
simple topics, 15
steps for completing, 11–17
urgent topics, 13
See also binder for your planner
Plan Your Estate (Clifford), 154, 212, 220
POLST (Physician's Orders for Life Sustaining Treatment), 87
post-death expenses, 162, 163
power of attorney documents, 85, 96, 98–99. *See also* durable power of attorney for finances; durable power of attorney for health care
preexisting conditions and LTC policies, 167
prenuptial agreements, 148
Prenuptial Agreements (Stoner and Irving), 154, 220
probate avoidance
for bank and brokerage accounts, 173–74
overview, 150–53
pay-on-death accounts, 145, 151, 173, 232
for retirement accounts, 179
for vehicles, 145, 152, 173–74, 226–27
See also trusts
probate, benefits of, 147
product guides and warranty records, 233
professional memberships, 70
property manager for your children, 43–45, 143, 163
property ownership
common law states, 218, 223
community property with right of survivorship, 145, 153, 217–18
joint ownership for probate avoidance, 152–53
joint tenancy, 145
joint tenancy with right of survivorship, 152–53, 217
personal property, 230, 231–33
tenancy by the entirety, 145, 153, 217
tenancy in common, 216–17
and wills, 145
See also community property states
psychiatric advance directive, 87–88
publication of obituaries, 136, 137

Q

QTIP trusts for tax savings, 147, 211
Questions and Answers on Life Insurance (Steuer), 168
Quicken WillMaker Plus, 99, 154
QuickQuote, 168

R

real estate
and joint tenancy ownership, 152
protecting vacant, 28
rented or leased, 222
residence information in Biographical Information section, 37
transfer-on-death deeds for, 145, 152
Real Estate section, 215–23
overview, 216
planner pages, 220–23
pointing to, in Instructions, 28–29
resources, 220
rules for married couples, 218–20
shared ownership, 216–18
sole ownership, 216, 221–22, 227–28
updating your planner, 223

recording a power of attorney for finances, 96
record keeping
digital vs. paper files, 12, 13–14
divorce documents, 33–34, 38
income from unusual sources, 231
income tax records, 213–14
informational vs. certified copies, 33
and location of documents, 207
overview, 6
real estate, 220
tax records, 213
See also binder for your planner
recreational memberships, 72
religious memberships, 71
religious views on organ and body donation, 105
remembrances in lieu of flowers, 139
renewal provision of life insurance, 161
renting real estate, 222
rescue programs for pets, 53
residence information, 37
residential care coverage, 166
retirement plans and pensions
beneficiary for, 145
for probate avoidance, 151–52
retirement benefits from Social Security, 187
See also Government Benefits section
Retirement Plans and Pensions section, 177–83
at death of owner, 178–81
overview, 178
planner pages, 182–83
planning for your retirement, 178
pointing to, in Instructions, 28
probate and taxes, 179
resources, 181–82
updating your planner, 183
Retirement Plans for Small Business (IRS), 181
revocable living trusts. *See* living trusts
revocations
power of attorney, 84, 96–97, 98, 101
transfer-on-death deed, 146, 217
trusts, 146
wills and codicils, 156
Roman Catholic annulment documents, 34

S

safe deposit boxes, 203–4, 205–6
SBA (U.S. Small Business Administration), 64
schedule
for completing your planner, 12
for working with parents, 5
Science Care, Inc., 106
SCORE (Service Corps of Retired Executives), 64
2nd Chance 4 Pets, 53
secured places and passwords, 201–7
avoiding identity theft, 196
overview, 202, 206–7
password managers, 202
planner pages, 204–7
pointing to, in Instructions, 28
safe deposit boxes, 203–4, 205–6
updating your planner, 207
securities
brokerage accounts, 152, 173–74
and joint tenancy ownership, 152
stocks on hand and U.S. savings bonds, 174
transfer-on-death registration of, 145, 152, 173–74
See also Bank and Brokerage Accounts section
Select Quote Life, 168
seniors, 4–5, 143
separation document, 33–34
Service Corps of Retired Executives (SCORE), 64
service memberships, 71
service providers
common types of services, 79
contact information, 28
for real estate, 221
in your planner, 204–5, 221, 222
See also mortuary services
Service Providers section, 28, 77–80
Shutterfly, 71
signature
on durable power of attorney for finances, 95–96
on health care directives, 83, 84
on Letter to Loved Ones, 23
on wills, 144
single-premium life insurance, 160
small estate simplified probate procedures, 151
social memberships, 71–72
Social Security Administration, 36, 188
Social Security benefits, 186–88, 189–90
Social Security cards or records, 36, 188, 196
sole ownership of property, 216, 221–22, 227–28
sole proprietorships, transferring ownership, 63
SPCA (Society for the Prevention of Cruelty to Animals), 53
special needs trusts, 147–48
Special Needs Trusts (Elias and Urbatsch), 154
Special Olympics and frequent flyer miles, 73
spendthrift trusts, 147
spiritual memberships, 71
springing power of attorney, 96
state inheritance taxes, 173
state laws
on agent for health care, 84, 85, 88
on burial, cremation, and funerals, 118
common law states, 218, 223
on estate and inheritance taxes, 212
on health care directives, 89
on joint tenancy, 153
on power of attorney signatures, 95–96
on recording a power of attorney for finances, 96
on safe deposit access for family members, 203–4, 205–6
on small estate qualifications, 151
See also community property states
stocks on hand and U.S. savings bonds, 174
stories, preserving your, 39
succession plan for a small business, 63
successor trustees, 98–99, 146, 148–50, 210

survivors and your Letter to Loved Ones, 20–21
survivors benefits from Social Security, 188
Survivors, Executors, and Administrators (IRS), 212
survivorship life insurance, 160–61

T

taxes
- on contents of a safe deposit box, 203, 204
- federal estate tax, 147, 164, 211
- FICA taxes, 186
- on gifts, 151, 152
- income taxes, 179, 210, 213–14, 221, 222
- overview, 210
- resources, 182
- and retirement accounts, 179
- and small businesses, 67
- state inheritance taxes, 173, 212
- and trusts, 147, 211

Taxes section, 209–14
- federal estate tax, 211
- overview, 210
- planner pages, 212–14
- pointing to, in Instructions, 29
- resources, 212
- state estate taxes, 212
- updating your planner, 214

Tax Guide for Seniors (IRS), 182
tax professionals, 212–13, 242, 243–45
tax records, 213
tenancy by the entirety, 145, 153, 217
tenancy in common, 216–17
term life insurance, 159
time
- and phases of Instructions, 26, 27–28
- running out of, 13

Total Money Makeover, The (Ramsey), 197
Totten trusts (POD bank accounts), 145, 151, 173, 232
transfer-on-death deeds for real estate, 145, 152
transfer-on-death registration
- for securities, 145, 152, 173–74
- for vehicles, 145, 152, 173–74, 226, 227

transferring ownership of a business, 63
TransWeb, 105
traveling, planning for death prior to, 5
trusts
- AB trusts for tax savings, 147, 211
- complex trusts, 147–48
- irrevocable life insurance trust, 164
- irrevocable trust as retirement account beneficiary, 180–81
- overview, 146
- for pets, 52
- successor trustee for, 148–50
- for tax avoidance, 147, 211
- Totten trusts (POD bank accounts), 145, 151, 173, 232
- updating, 156
- and wills, 143, 148
- *See also* living trusts; Will and Trust section

Twitter, 71

U

universal life insurance, 160
unmarried couples
- and agent for finances, 97
- estate planning documents, 142–43
- and health care documents, 83
- naming a guardian for children, 42, 43
- and property manager for children, 43
- separate planners for, 11

urn or casket, 115–16, 120–21, 128
U.S. savings bonds, 174
U.S. Small Business Administration (SBA), 64

V

variable and variable universal life insurance, 160
vehicles, probate avoidance for, 145, 152, 173–74, 226–27
Vehicles section, 28–29, 225–28
Veterans Affairs Department, 118, 133
veterans' benefits for burial or cremation, 114, 133
veterinary school programs for pets, 53
viewing, visitation, or wake, 126–27, 130–31
vital statistics. *See* Biographical Information section

W

waiver of premium for life insurance, 161
wake, visitation, or viewing, 126–27, 130–31
warranty records and product guides, 233
WebFlyer, 74
whole body donation, 105, 106
whole life insurance, 160
Will and Trust section, 141–56
- estate planning documents, 142–44, 156
- overview, 142
- planner pages, 154–56
- pointing to, in Instructions, 28
- probate avoidance, 150–53
- resources, 153–54
- updating your planner, 156
- *See also* trusts; wills

WillMaker Plus, 99, 154
wills
- ethical wills, 23, 145–46
- executor for, 148–50
- executors, 150, 210, 211
- holographic, 146
- naming a child's property manager, 143
- naming a guardian for children, 42–43
- overview, 144–46
- and trusts, 143, 148
- updating, 156
- *See also* Will and Trust section

withdrawal provision of life insurance, 161

Y

Yahoo!, 71
young adults, planning ahead for death, 5
YouTube, 71 

The *Get It Together* Binder

The *Get It Together* binder is a great place to store your planner and all your related materials—birth certificate, title to your car, insurance policies, health care directives, will, and more. With a binder, it's easy for you to organize and get to your records. And when the time comes, the binder is a portable reference for your family.

The three-inch *Get It Together* binder comes with Mylar-reinforced white tab dividers, already set up for the 28 sections of your planner. "PLANNER" is printed down the spine, making it easy for you (and others, eventually) to identify it.

- The price of the Binder & Tab Set is $26.50. We pay the sales tax, and shipping is free! You may order online or by mail:

  Online orders. You can conveniently order online at www.GetItTogetherBook.com.

  U.S. mail orders. You can order by mail by sending the completed Order Form (below), with your check or money order payable to *Get It Together,* to:

  Get It Together
  P.O. Box 4355
  Walnut Creek, CA 94596

- With questions or for more information—about the book, regarding quantity discounts, to buy the binder together with the book, or to purchase an inscribed book—please see www.GetItTogetherBook.com.
- Offer available only in the United States.

Order Form

Name		And in case we have questions about your order ...	
Address		**Telephone**	
City, State, Zip		**Email**	
Product Ordered	**Quantity**	**Unit Price**	**Total Price**
			$
Total			**$**